havana
in my heart

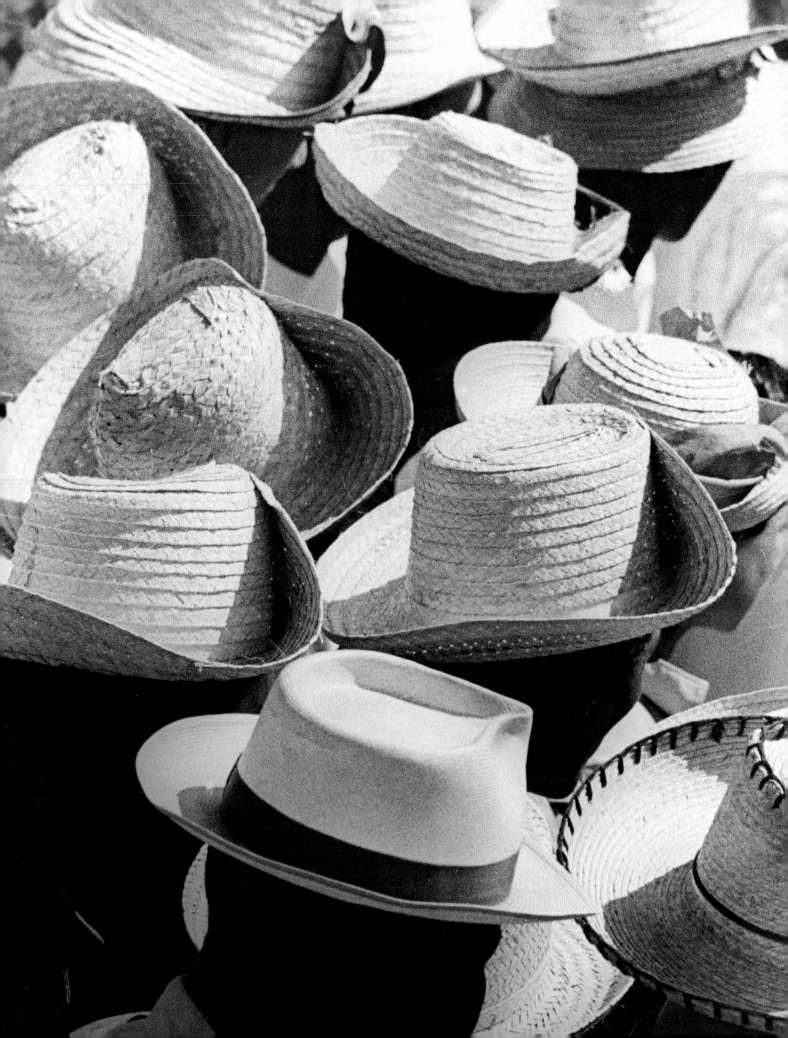

havana
in my heart

a celebration of Cuban photography

gareth jenkins

MQP

MQ Publications Ltd

For my parents

Published by MQ Publications Limited
12 The Ivories, 6–8 Northampton Street, London N1 2HY
Tel: 020 7359 2244
Fax: 020 7359 1616
email: mail@mqpublications.com

Copyright © MQ Publications Limited 2002
Text copyright © Gareth Jenkins 2002
DESIGN: Balley Design Associates

ISBN: 1 84072 200 2

1 3 5 7 9 0 8 6 4 2

Printed and bound in China

Acknowledgments

Many people have contributed their experience and insights to make this book possible. I wish particularly to thank Zaro Weil and Ljiljana
Ortolja-Baird at MQ Publications for their encouragement and for transforming the raw material they received into this beautiful book.

In Cuba I was given support and inspiration by many people and institutions. Casa de las Américas, the Fototeca Nacional de Cuba, the
Biblioteca Nacional de Cuba, Bohemia magazine, and Prensa Latina all embraced this project wholeheartedly, as did the photographic rights
agency ADAVIS. Hilda Barrio (researcher), Guillermo Bello (photographer), Marilyn Sampera (art specialist), and Jorge Dalton (filmmaker and
writer) all helped shape the conception of the book.

The picture research was undertaken with great tenacity by Hilda Barrio, who also provided the background to many of the photographs.

contents

What would become of me if you did not exist, my city of Havana.
If you did not exist, my city of dreams built of light and spray,
what would become of me without your gateways,
your columns, your kisses, your windows.
When I travelled the world you went with me, you were a song in
my throat.

FAYAD JAMIS, from "I OPENED THE IRON GATE"

Dilapidated, struggling, yet magnificent and brimming with life, Havana continues to cast its spell. It is a city of infectious energy that was a thriving commercial center when New York still went unnoticed, a city that has absorbed many different cultures and witnessed prolonged political and social upheaval.

This portrait of Havana takes the 1950s as its starting point, with a backward glance to the beginning of the century. It begins, therefore, with the years when the mob was building casinos, hotels, and night clubs, the years when Havana became a playground for the rich and the famous. Visitors delighted in the musical rhythms and dances they encountered, which had already been discovered by Tin Pan Alley and Hollywood.

But *habaneros*, the residents of Havana, have always been alert to the latest trends and long ago gained a reputation for being quick-witted and inventive. More than 150 years ago Cuba was the fourth country in the world to introduce steam locomotives. Its first cinema was opened in Havana's old Payret theater in 1897, one year after the Lumière brothers showed their first films in Paris. The motor car was introduced early to Cuba and quickly caught on, to the extent that 70 years ago Havana had more cars per capita than New York. Even so, Havana retained a unique charm derived from the mingling of different cultures in the sensual exuberance of the Caribbean, tempered by an awareness of the latest fashions from America and Europe.

Contemporary Havana is shaped, physically and emotionally, by the Malecón, the long sea wall that curves around the city from the harbor in the east to the Almendares river in the west, a mouth opening in a great smile to the ocean. It is one of the longest sea front drives in the world, extending for more than seven miles. Habaneros love their Malecón and hang out there for hours at a time, chatting, caressing, and staring out to sea.

The Malecón was built more for reasons of public health and aesthetics than to aid the flow of traffic, but it had the effect of opening up the development of the city along its western shore. It was completed by 1950, by which time the Cuban middle classes, who started moving out of the older parts of the city in the late 19th century, had constructed new districts with evocative names such as Vedado, Miramar, Kohly, Marianao, Cubanacán, and Siboney.

Soon after, the expansion of the city was brought to an abrupt halt by the Revolution of 1959, led by Fidel Castro. A large section of the middle classes, mostly concentrated in Havana, felt they no longer had a place in this new Cuba and left the country. Early on the new government decided that Havana had monopolized enough of the nation's resources, and sought to redress the balance by concentrating new construction throughout the rest of the island, many parts of which were mired in poverty. The decay of the city gathered pace in these years.

The first steps were taken to restore Old Havana in the 1970s, but although a plan was put in place in 1981, progress was slow. When the Soviet Union disappeared 10 years later, Cuba was forced to turn once again to tourism and foreign investment to bring money into the country. This gave a new impetus to restoration work in Old Havana, new hotels and restaurants opened, and other parts of the city began to recover their lost pride.

Cuba's recent opening to tourism, the fashion for cigars, and a revived interest in Cuban dance music have conspired to draw foreign photographers to Havana. They have produced images that have created new clichés of Havana life, the tourist's Havana: young women squeezed into lycra, older women smoking cigars, battered

American cars from the 1950s, the exuberant rites of the Santería religion, the tattered splendor of Old Havana's streets.

This tourist Havana is, of course, real, but it is a selective vision of the city's abundance. There are many other Havanas, worlds in which the complex emotional life of the city is lived among the relics and totems of a rich cultural heritage.

Havana is a forest of columns, Doric, Corinthian, Ionic, and other styles besides. They support galleries of colonnades that offer protection from sun and rain. Over the years a baroque style came to dominate the city, the result of the mingling of different immigrant groups with their contrasting aesthetics.

The development of the Cuban cultural identity mirrored this eclectic architectural process, remaining open to assimilate new influences. Spanish immigrants from Galicia and the Canary Islands, Africans from the Congo, and Chinese, as well as other smaller immigrant groups all contributed their own cultural elements. Perhaps this eclecticism explains why more angular modern buildings have integrated so well into the Havana landscape.

The photographs in this book were all taken by Cuban photographers. A few of them date back to the early years of the last century, when Havana was expanding beyond the carapace of the original walled city. But most of the photographs are by photographers who have worked in Havana over the past 50 years. These include photographers who have become known internationally—for instance Osvaldo Salas, Constantino Arias, Raúl Corrales, and Alberto Korda. All their work is in black and white, a reminder of the isolation imposed on Cuba by the U.S. embargo, which made color film and processing facilities virtually unavailable for 40 years. As Alberto Korda put it, "For me, Cuban photography is black-and-white realism, and not because of Soviet connections. Cubans' dislike of color is generally for practical reasons. We have no real laboratory here, no cibachrome facilities . . . it's so bad. We are isolated and forced to look at our culture, in color anyway, through the eyes of our foreign cousins."

below: **TITO ALVAREZ,** *Street photographer,* 1976

Street photographers sprang up in the area around Central Park around 1930, at the time the building of the Capitolio was finished. Their cameras became known as "Creole polaroids."

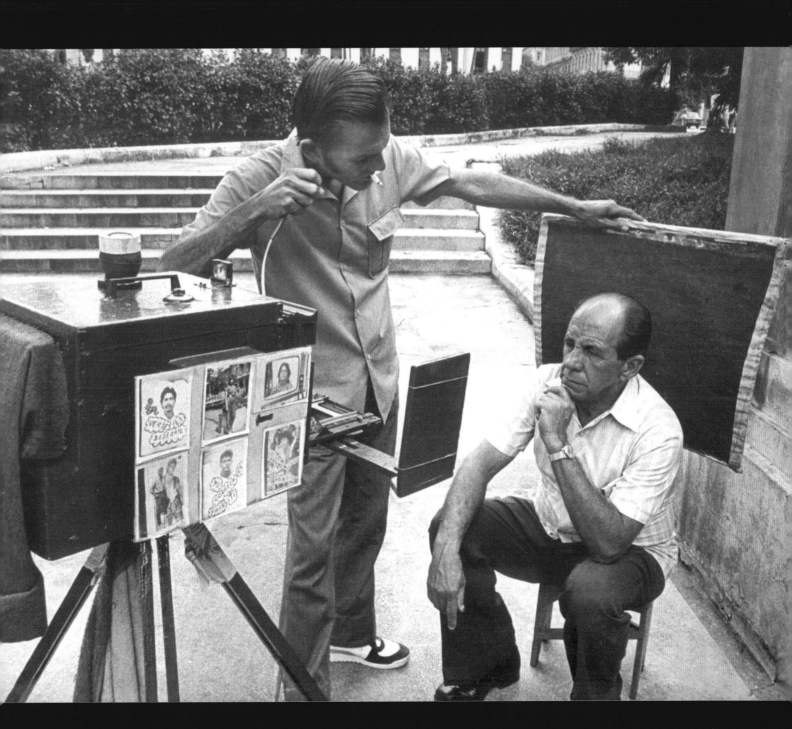

By the 1940s and '50s photography had become a passion in Havana. Photographic enthusiasts met regularly at the store *El Encanto* and grouped together to form the Club Fotográfico. This grew to have an active membership of some 300, and published the *Boletín Fotográfico*, and later the magazine *Foto-Cine*.

Commercial photography also developed in this period. It was at this time that the young Alberto Diaz took the professional name Korda, establishing his own Korda Studios in 1954, specializing in work for the new advertising agencies that set up in Cuba in the early 1950s.

Another group of photographers who were to become famous grouped around Cuba-Sono-Films, an agency belonging to the Popular Socialist Party. These included José Tabio, Raúl Corrales, and Miguel Viñas. They made films and reports on social conditions that were shown at party meetings.

From the beginning, the Revolution of 1959 attracted the interest of Cuban photographers all over the island, professionals and amateurs alike. Photography became the most direct way in which the Revolution became known around the world. Newspapers and magazines were published in far greater runs than ever before, often carrying photographs that occupied whole pages.

During the October Missile Crisis of 1962 the United States declared a naval blockade of the island, and Cubans began to live their most difficult economic years, comparable only with the early 1990s after the Soviet Union collapsed. Even so, Cuban photographers continued to exhibit in galleries around the island and in international exhibitions.

For the first three years of the Revolution, photographers focused on the more direct political changes taking place, and on military resistance to attacks from the United States—especially the failed invasion at Playa Girón (the Bay of Pigs) in 1961— and from anti-revolutionary groups concentrated in the Escambray mountains.

Later, a space opened for wider cultural interests. Cuban photographers discovered aspects of their culture that had been largely hidden from public view, especially Afro-Cuban culture and religion. Photographers began to take more interest in capturing the everyday, the life of the local neighborhoods, the tenements, the factories, and the humor of daily life.

The cultural center Casa de las Américas organized the First Exhibition of Cuban Culture in 1966, which was followed by Salón 70 in the National Museum of Fine Arts in 1970. Cuban photography became much more widely recognized internationally in 1978 with an exhibition in Mexico City, organized by the Mexican Photography Council. For many Cuban photographers of the younger generation it was their first opportunity to participate in a foreign event of this scale, and they became aware of what had been achieved and what they could achieve in the future.

The majority of Cuban photographers live and work from day to day in this remarkable city of contrasts. The people of Havana, its buildings, its energy, its opening out in a wide embrace of the sea—these are the subjects of much Cuban photography.

Cuba is a country that has experienced dramatic change, both painful and exhilarating, since the Revolution of 1959. This revolution has produced an abundance of memorable images that were made known throughout the world through photography rather than the international television networks: it was an extraordinarily photogenic revolution.

And yet daily life has retained a continuity reaching back to the experience of earlier generations, and continues to incorporate social, cultural, and religious traditions with their roots deep in the Cuban psyche. The best photographers understand this and through the images they choose to present, and the way they choose to present them, they provide a valuable key to understanding the life of a dynamic people. The photographic portrait of Havana that emerges is a remarkable tribute to some fine artists who chose to work through a camera's lens.

• THE DISCUSSION OF THE HISTORY OF CUBAN PHOTOGRAPHY DRAWS ON A MONOGRAPH WRITTEN BY THE CUBAN PHOTOGRAPHER MARÍA EUGENIA HAYA (MARUCHA).

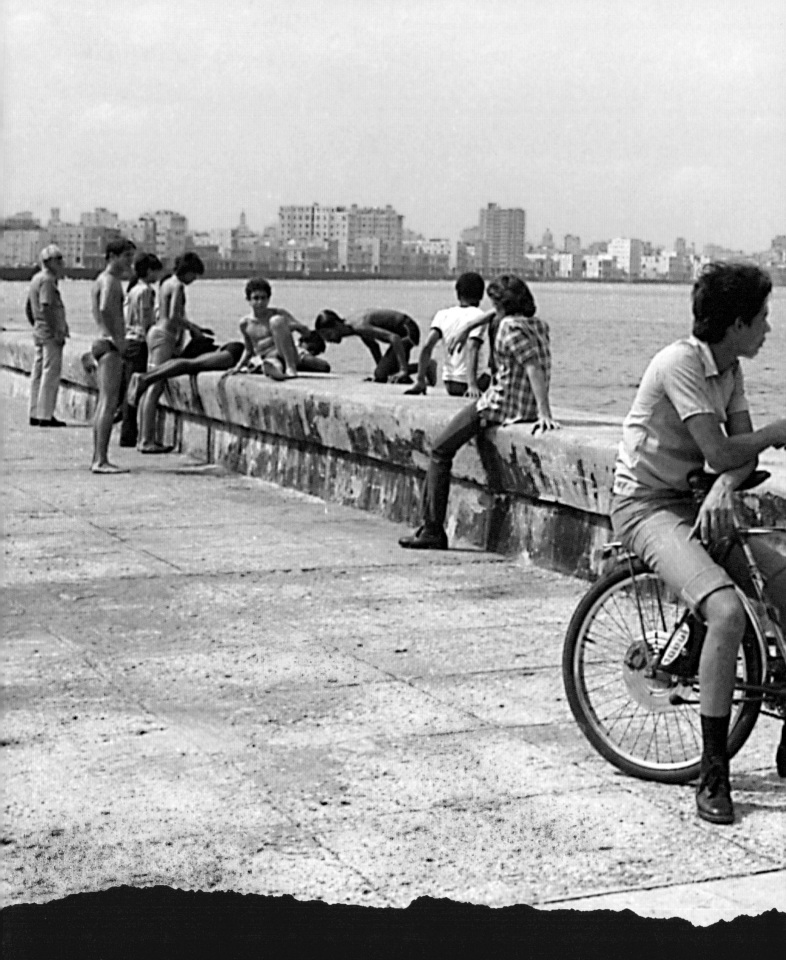

chapter**one**

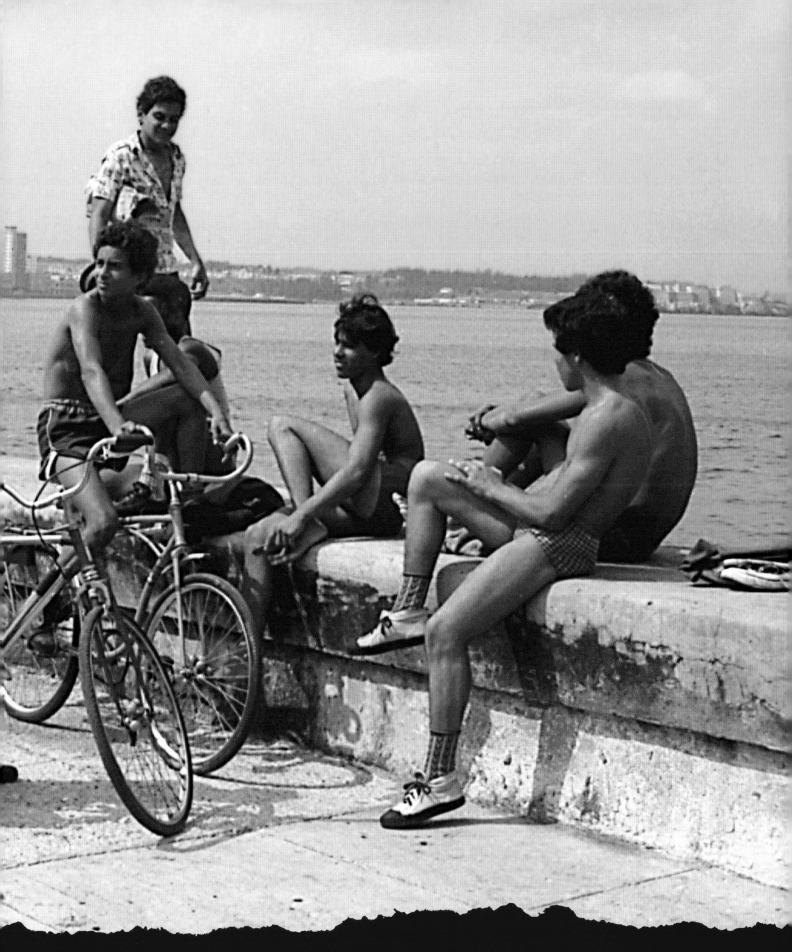

Street Scene

> ... the street was enveloped in babble and laughter. Men met women, kissed them on the cheek, talked, moved on.
>
> MARTHA GELLHORN

street scene

People-watching on the streets of Havana is a serious occupation. People come out of their houses to escape the heat and pass the time in animated conversation. They touch, they kiss, they watch each other. Physical closeness and touching are essential to Cuban culture, and they even have a name—*cubaneo*.

People gather in queues without knowing what is being sold. But it doesn't matter, because they get into conversation, laugh, argue, exchange gossip, and when they get to the head of the queue they are prepared because they have with them their *jaba*, their palm leaf bag, which they fill throughout the day.

Anything can happen on a Havana street. Young boys pass on their way to fish, carrying an inflated inner tube from a truck, bigger than themselves. A musician clutching a double bass goes by, riding postillion on the back of a bicycle. Women hang clothes out to dry from a balcony, or a flag from a window. Kids, lovers, old couples hang out along the Malecón sea wall. A group of old people do morning exercises together in a park. Nearby, old men sit playing dominoes.

Each day is a struggle to put food on the family table, keep a bicycle or car on the road, and make domestic repairs. But people have time for each other, and support each other by elaborate networks of family and friends. Gossip is not just gossip; it reinforces networks, it passes on information that will prove to be useful to someone.

It has been remarkable over the last few years to witness the rebirth of the old city. Many people imagine that its neglect and abandonment date from the revolution of 1959, but in fact the process began a century before.

They also imagine that restoration work is somehow being funded by the United Nations, or by foreign investors. By and large it is not. Old Havana is a remarkable example of inner-city regeneration financed by creating hotels, restaurants, bars, and shops that generate the funds for the work to keep moving forward. Meanwhile the local population remains, and the children attend classes in the restored museums and palaces.

Other less favored parts of the city remain derelict and over-populated, with people living in squalid conditions. Yet, so far at least, Havana has escaped the fate of other large Latin American cities with their sprawling shanty towns, barefoot children, and widespread illiteracy. Havana, for all its troubles, is a city of hope, laughter, simple human kindness, and the surprise of the unexpected.

previous page: MIGUEL VINAS, *Malecón*, 1983

I am a sincere man
From where the palm tree grows
And before I die I wish
To set out the verses of my soul

JOSE MARTI, from *SIMPLE VERSES*

right: OSVALDO SALAS, *José Martí's birth place,* **1974**

Born in this house in 1853, José Martí was a sensitive and prolific writer and poet whose entire adult life was devoted to bringing about the independence of Cuba from Spanish rule. He was the main organizer of the forces who launched the final war against the Spanish on 29 January 1895. Despite shaky physical health, he returned to Cuba from exile in New York to join the guerrillas fighting the Spaniards in the east of the island. He was killed only weeks later, riding a white horse into battle. Martí is known in Cuba as the Apostle, and as Cuba's national hero. His political thinking and personal example were consciously emulated by the revolutionaries who seized power in 1959. He is also claimed by those Cubans in the United States who oppose the government of Fidel Castro—to the extent that the anti-Castro radio and TV stations that beam propaganda at the island from Florida are named for José Martí.

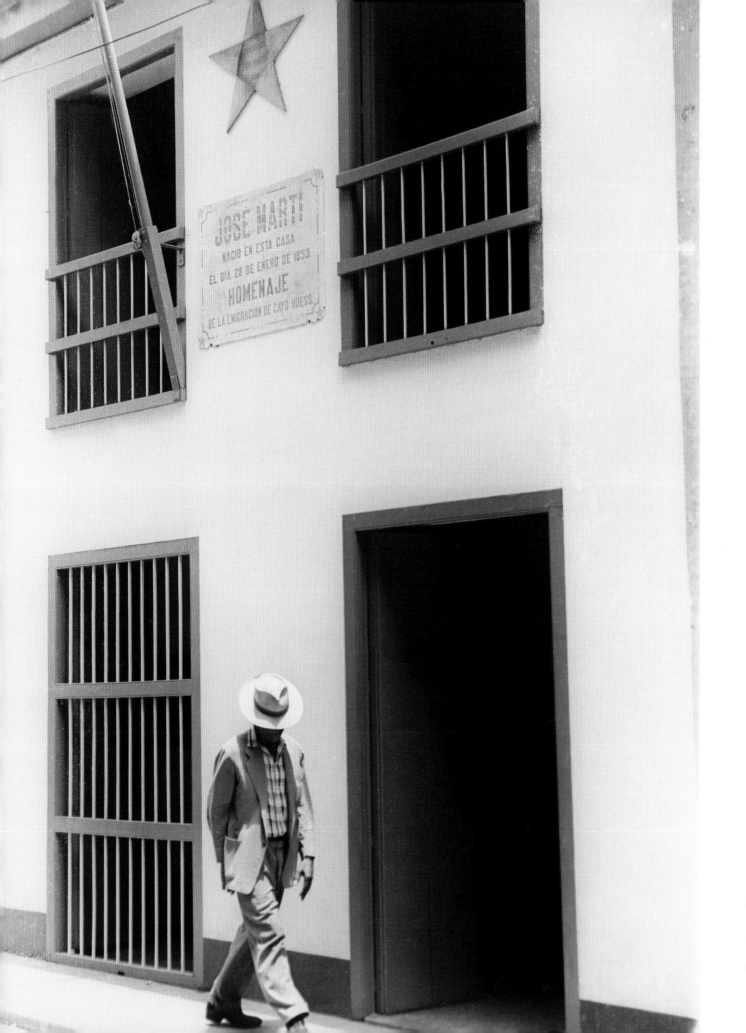

street scene

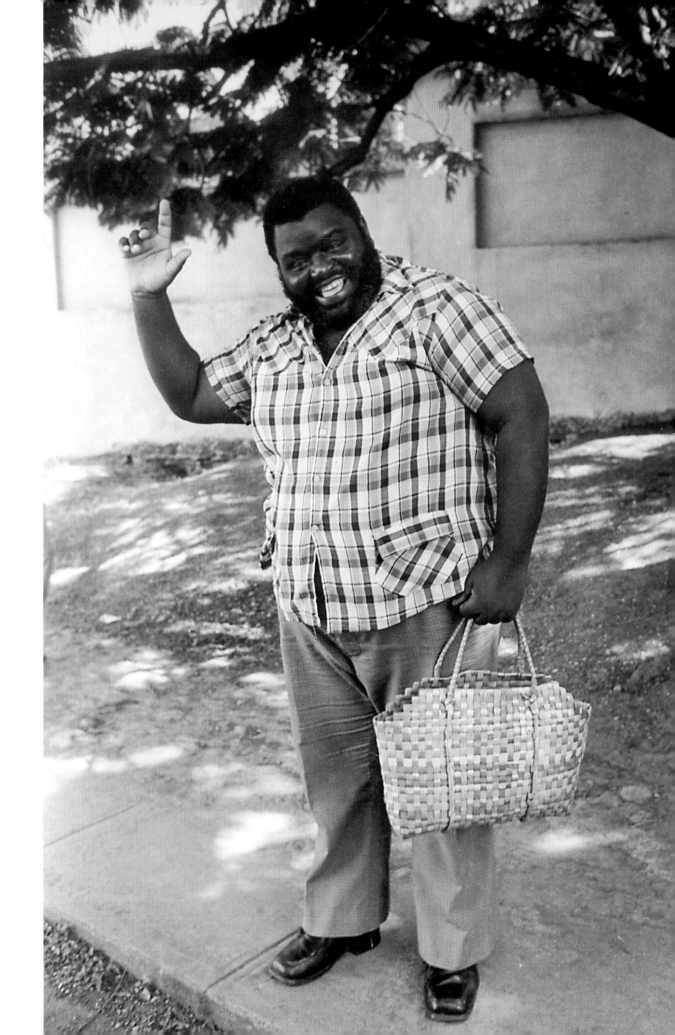

left: LUIS FERNANDEZ (PIROLE), *The fat man*, 1984

There is a joke that says that the body of a Cuban is made up of his head, his trunk, his extremities . . . and his *jaba*. The jaba is nothing more than a bag made of palm leaves that accompanies a Cuban wherever he goes. In the course of the day it is filled with whatever comes his way.

below: ISABEL SIERRA, *The Chinaman*, 1985

Chinese immigrants began arriving in Cuba in the middle of the 19th century to work on railway construction and in the countryside.

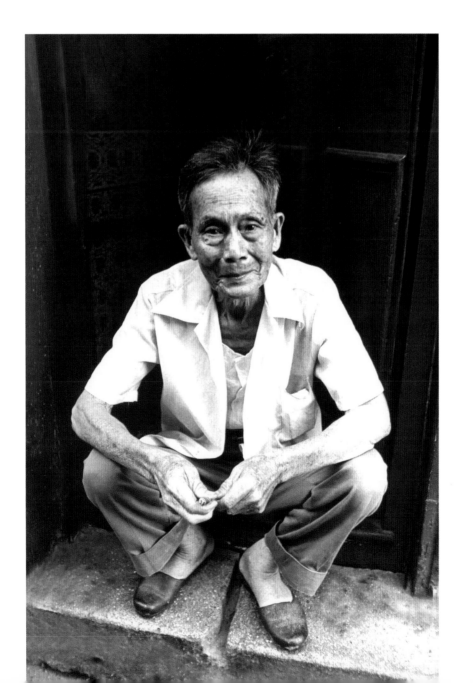

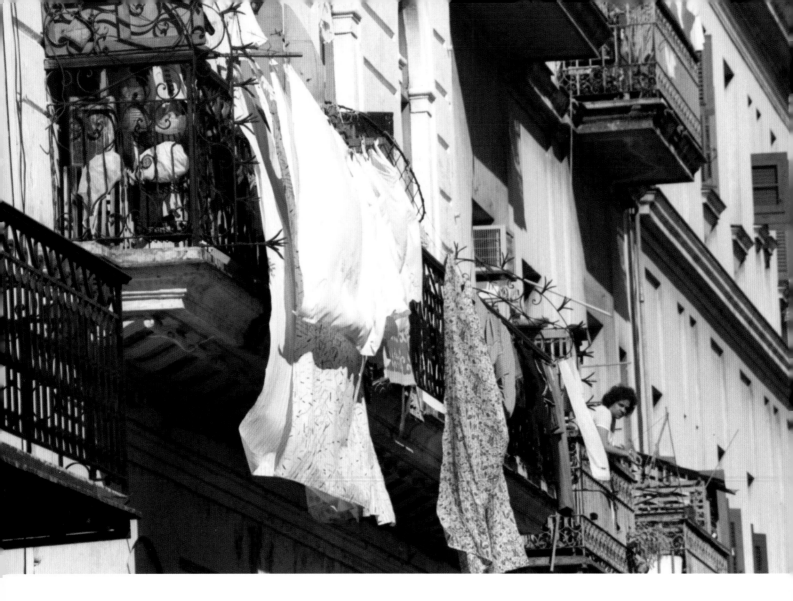

above: CELSO RODRIGUEZ, *Balcony with drying sheets,* 1994

Havana may be crumbling, but it is unique in having escaped the ravages of redevelopment suffered by old cities throughout Europe and the Americas in the second half of the 20th century. The focus on building infrastructure outside the capital city preserved Havana in all its decaying splendor.

right: SERGIO ROMERO, *Balcony in Old Havana,* 1985

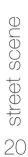

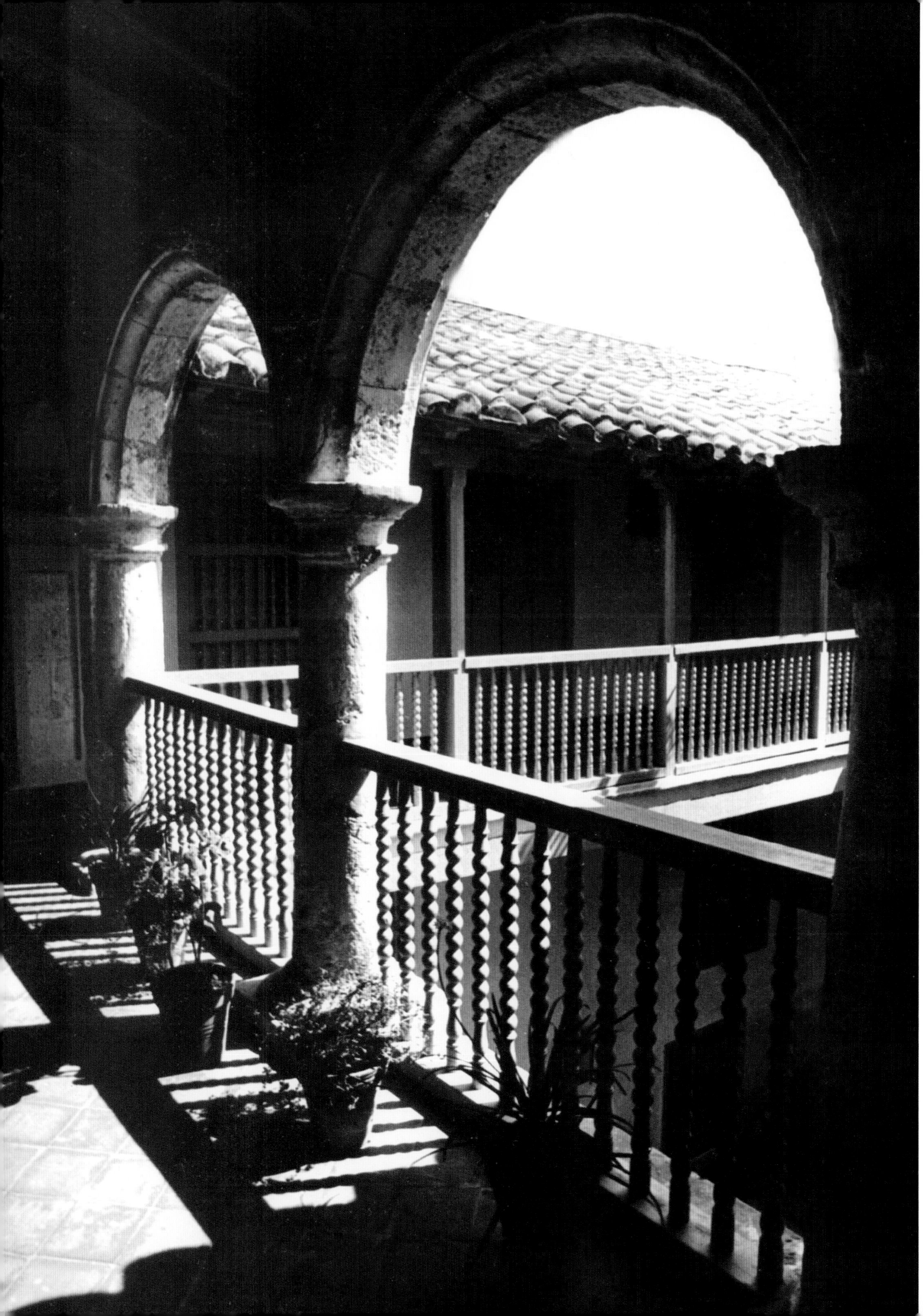

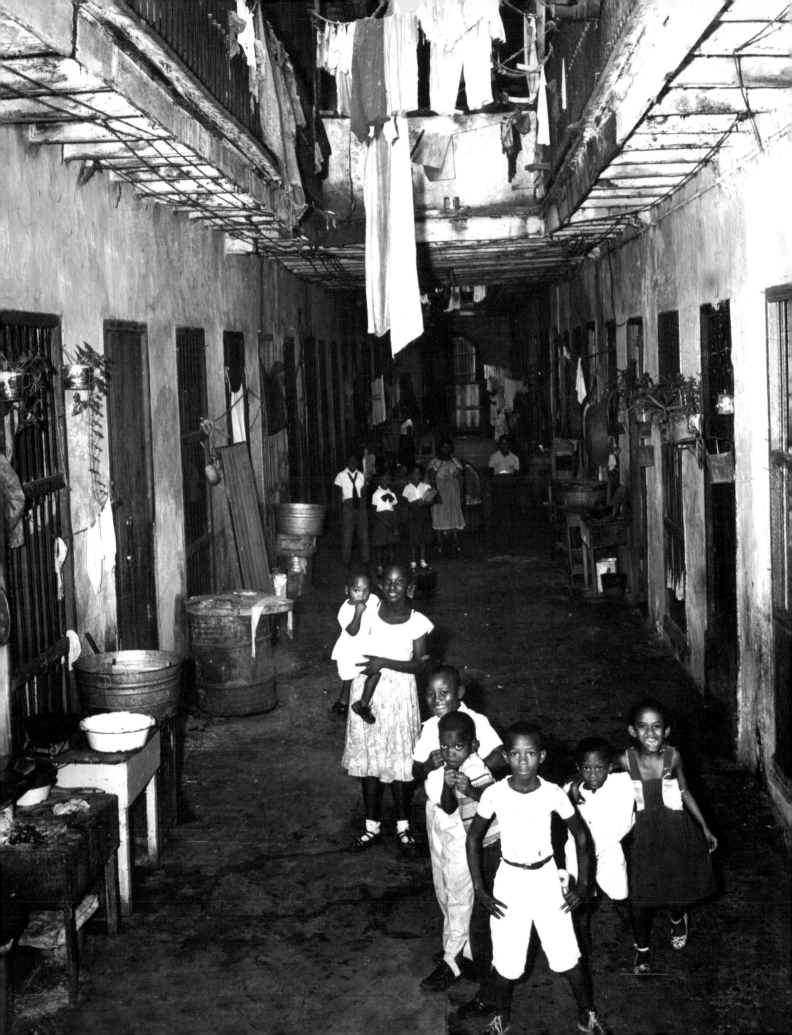

I have, let's see,
that being black
no one can stop me
at the door of a dance hall or a bar.

Or even at the reception desk of a hotel
shouting at me that there are no rooms
not even a tiny room, nor an enormous room
nor a small room where I might rest.

NICOLAS GUILLEN, from "I HAVE"

left: **CONSTANTINO ARIAS,** *Tenement,* **1950**

Every large city of Latin America has overcrowded slums like Old Havana. The
rooms in these buildings often have mezzanines to accommodate additional
families, with the result that the structure of the buildings is overburdened and
in danger of collapse.

next page: **SERGIO ROMERO,** *Young boy,* **1986**

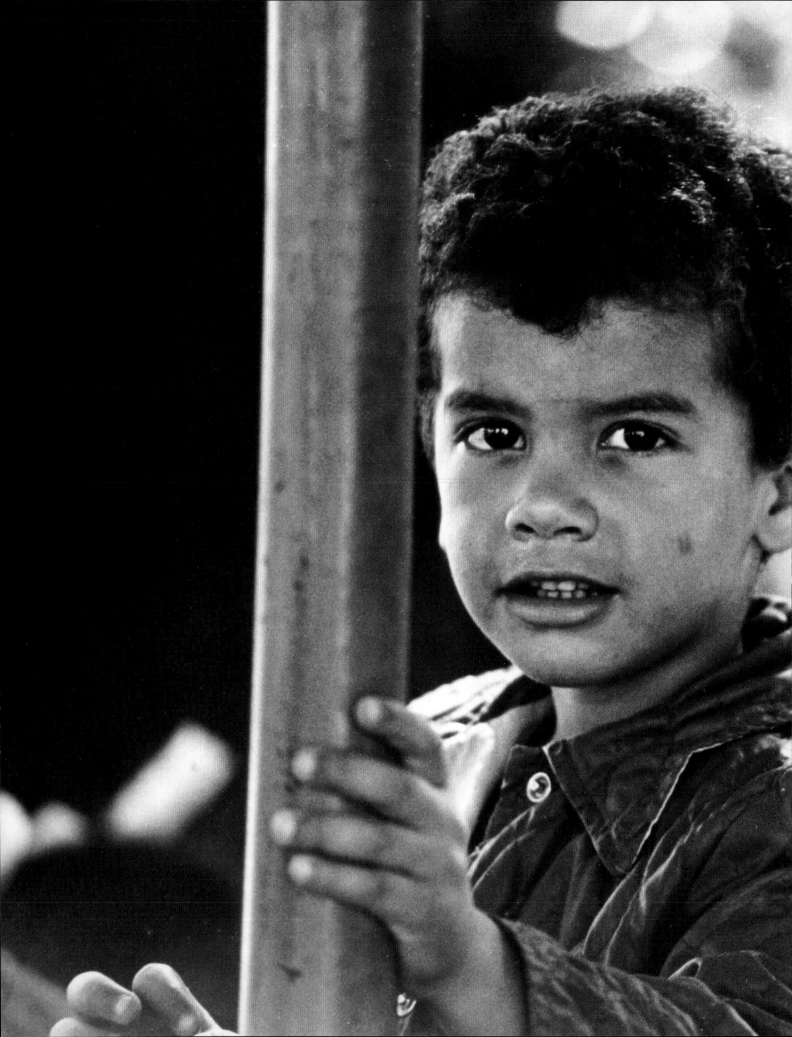

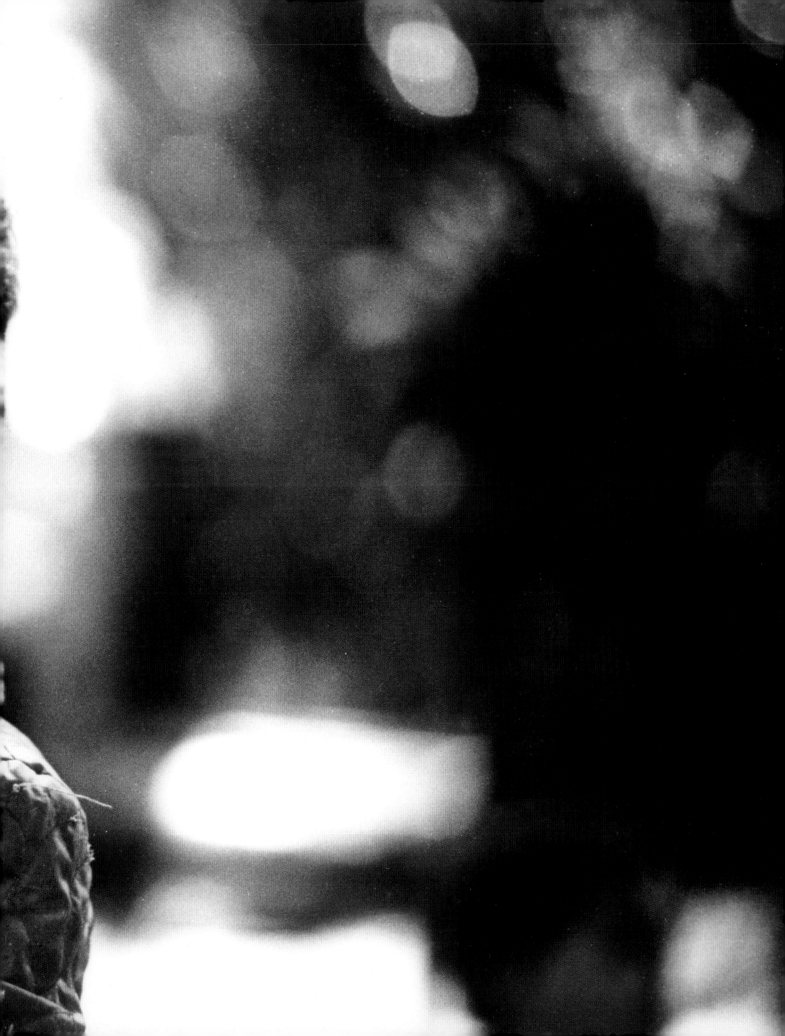

right: SERGIO ROMERO, *Flags draped from windows,* **1987**

Why it is that Cuba is so full of potent symbols? The images of the Revolution one can understand. The heroic, or diabolic, guerrillas—depending on your point of view—who entered Havana triumphantly from victory in the Sierra Maestra mountains epitomized the raw energy and nerve of youth. Camilo Cienfuegos, Che Guevara, and Fidel Castro quickly became icons within Cuba and throughout the world. Today the image of Che is coveted more than ever by those who see in him a pure and noble ideal, and by those marketing everything from vodka to T-shirts.

But the iconography goes much deeper. The ancient American cars that lurch through Havana streets held together by some strange alchemy; heavily built women and shriveled old men puffing on cigars in front of tenement blocks; the Morro lighthouse guarding the entrance to Havana Bay; the Malecón sea wall curving sinuously around the city's bulging shoreline, holding it back from slipping into the Gulf Stream; neo-classical buildings rubbing shoulders with colonial Spanish architecture, art deco with austere modernist apartment blocks from the 1950s. Under the tropical sun, softened by salt sea breezes, infused with life from the infectious smiles on street faces, everything is transformed into an icon.

And then there is the national flag, the most potent symbol of all, designed more than a century ago. A white star set in a red triangle inserted into three blue stripes separated by two white stripes. Simple, unforgettable, and proudly flourished by islanders celebrating independence from "la Yuma," the Monster to the North, and by their hostile cousins across the Florida straits who also claim to represent the nation.

next page: BOHEMIA ARCHIVE, *Street bar outside the Lonja de Comercio,* **1916**

For many years street bars, like this one in the square between the Lonja de Comercio and the Basilica de San Francisco de Asís, disappeared from Havana's streets, along with all other forms of small-scale enterprise. They have started to return, particularly in Old Havana under the patronage of the City Historian's office, which is overseeing restoration work.

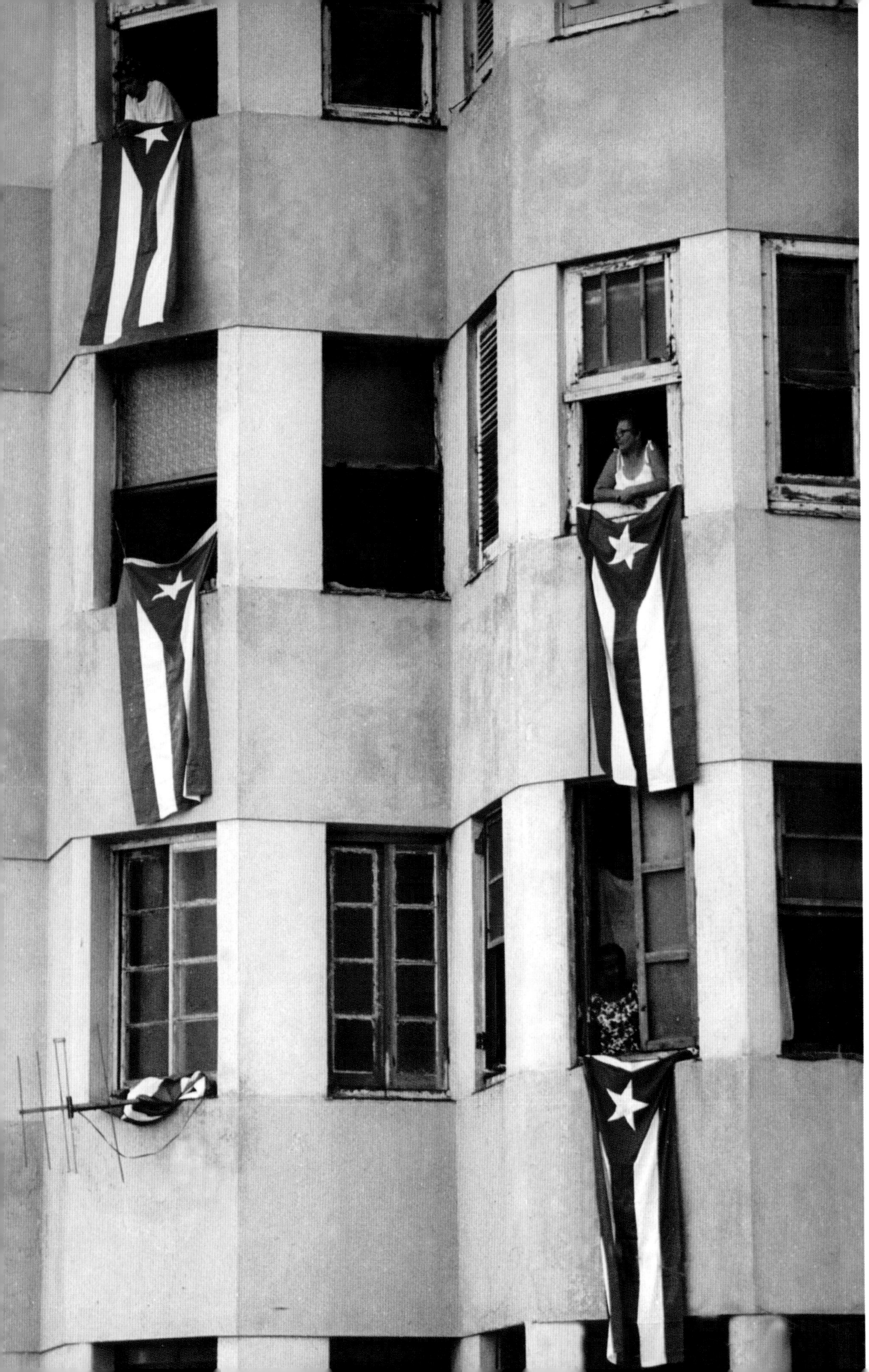

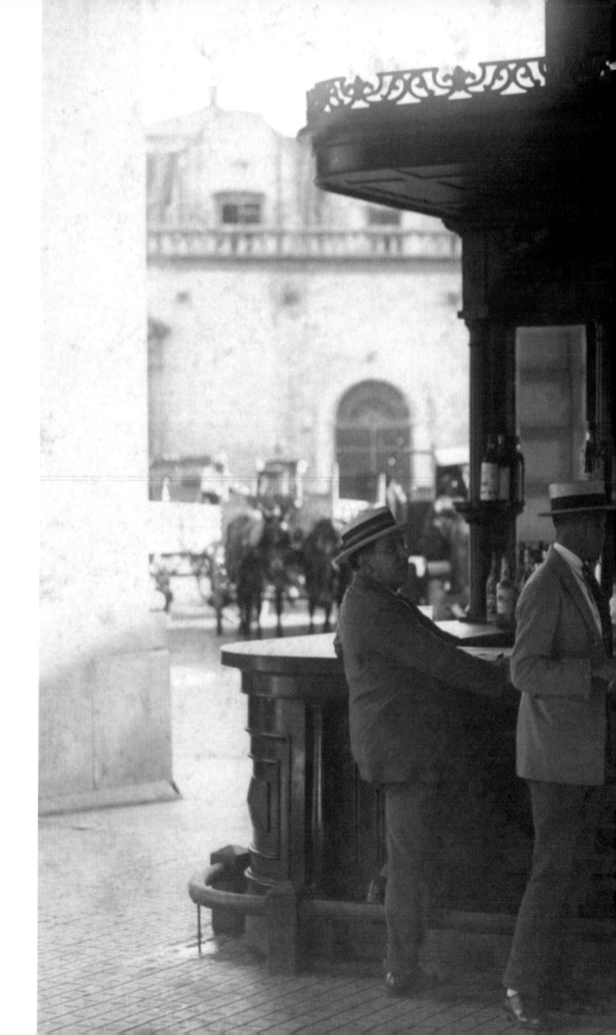

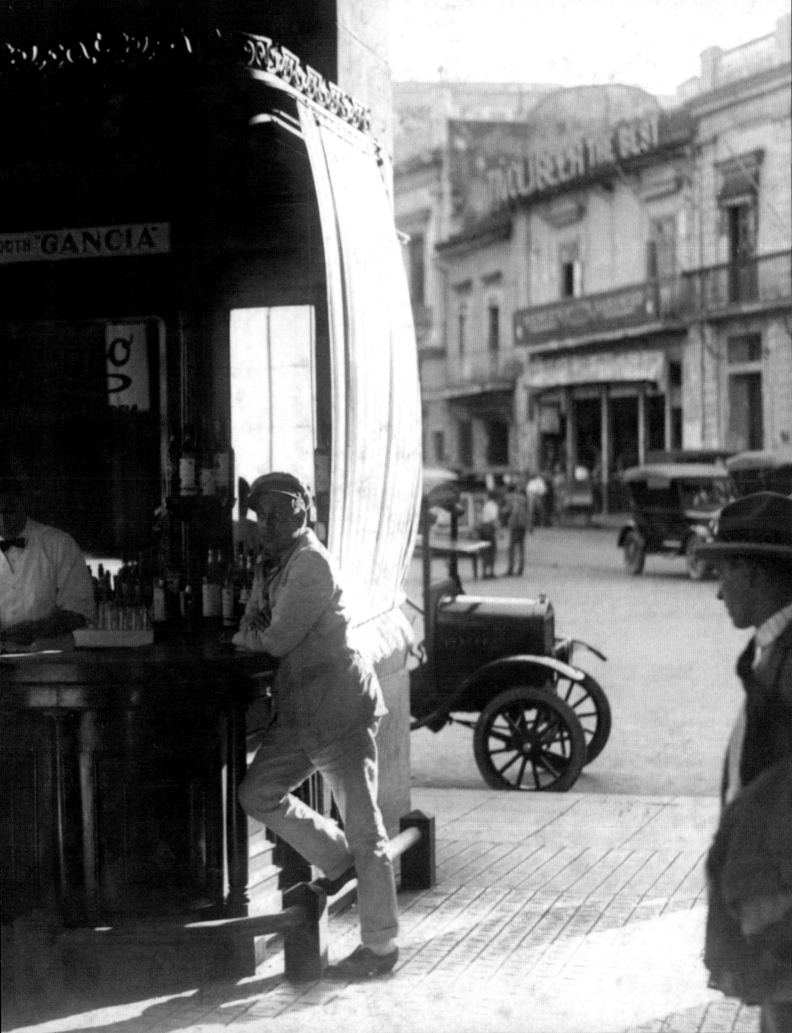

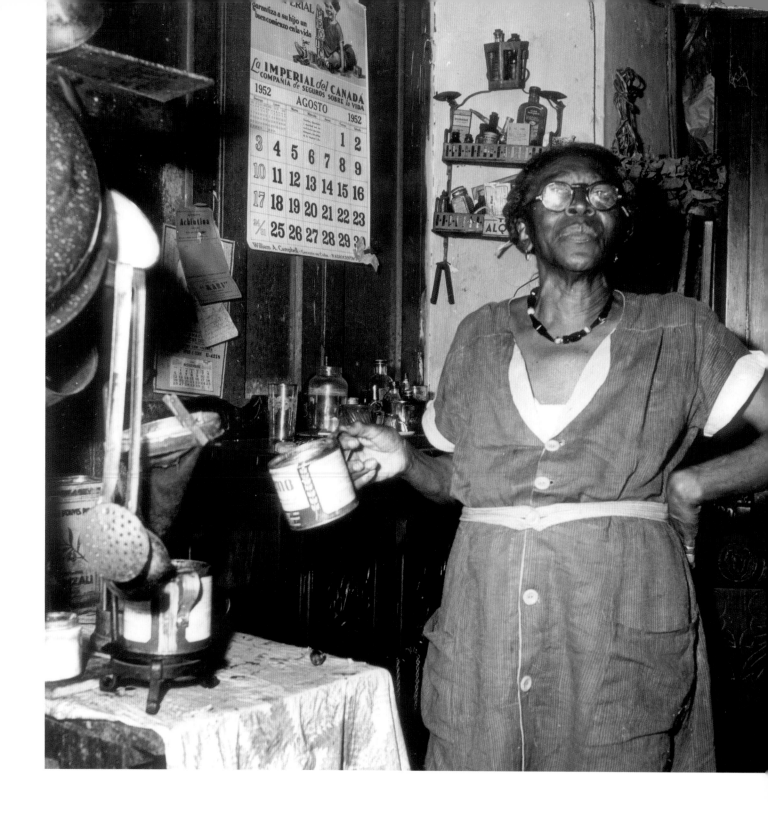

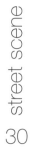
above: **CONSTANTINO ARIAS**, *The black woman*, 1952

Constantino Arias had a great interest in making portraits, situating his subjects within their social group and class. He made a series of portraits of black people, to which this belongs.

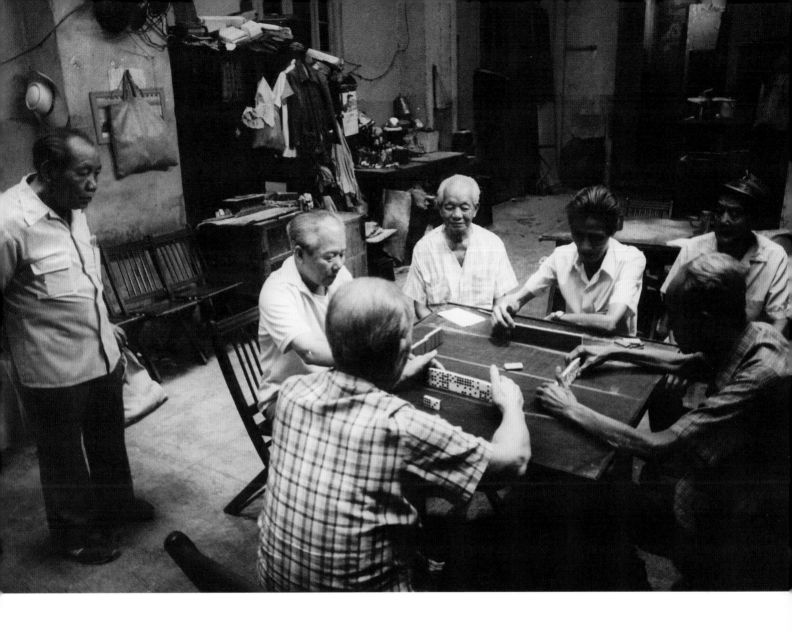

above: **FRANCISCO BOU,** *Old men playing dominoes in the Chinese quarter,* 1992

Gradually many Chinese immigrants, supported by their tight family structures, were able to accumulate capital to create their own small businesses, such as laundries and vegetable stores, and smallholdings for growing vegetables. Those in the Havana region originally settled in the Acueducto district to the south of the city, where there is fertile soil suitable for horticulture. Later they settled into the district around Calle Zanja and Dragones, which is still a Chinatown today.

Despite intermarriage, the Chinese community maintained its independent culture, and even kept its language alive. And yet it identified strongly with national aspirations for an independent Cuba. Thousands of Chinese Cubans died in the independence wars of 1868–78 and 1895–98. A monument to their sacrifice was erected in Havana.

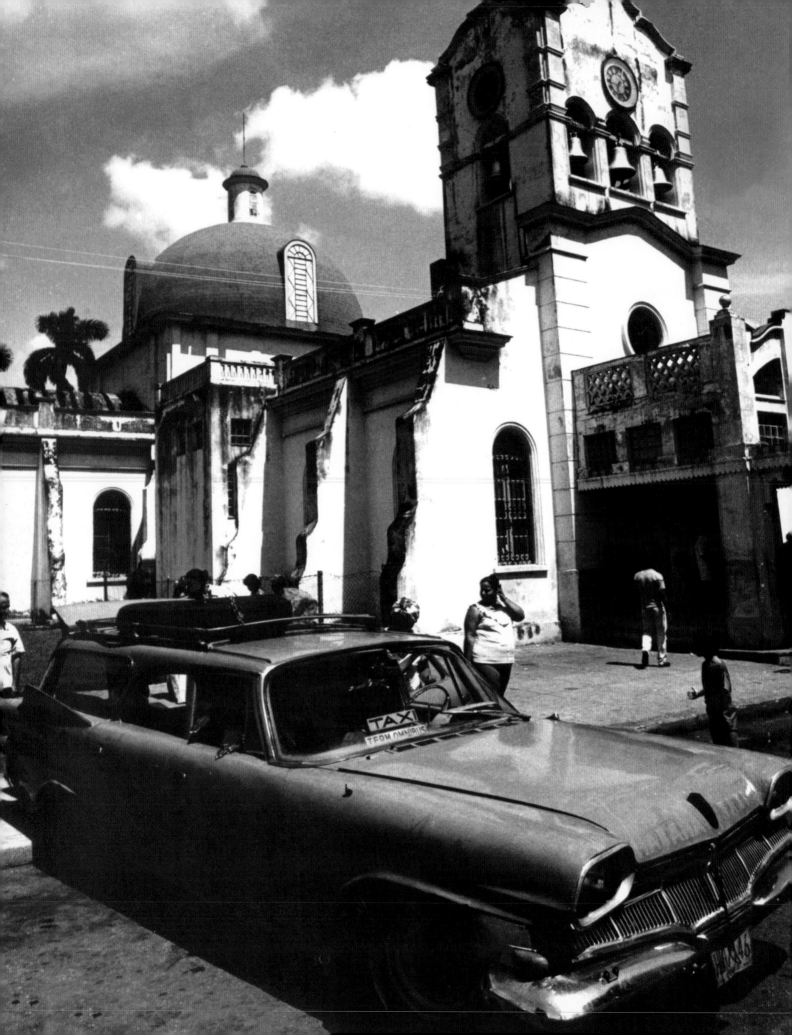

The long city spread along the open Atlantic; waves broke over the Avenida de Maceo and misted the windscreens of cars. The pink, grey, yellow pillars of what had once been the aristocratic quarter were eroded like rocks; an ancient coat of arms, smudged and featureless, was set over the doorway of a shabby hotel, and the shutters of a night-club were varnished in bright crude colours to protect them from the wet and salt of the sea. In the west the steel skyscrapers of the new town rose higher than lighthouses into the clear February sky. It was a city to visit, not a city to live in, but it was the city where Wormold had first fallen in love and he was held to it as though to the scene of a disaster.

GRAHAM GREENE, from *OUR MAN IN HAVANA*, 1958

left: SERGIO ROMERO, *Church of Regla,* **1994**

The Virgin of Regla or Yemayá is, according to the Yoruba religion, the patron saint of sailors, the goddess of motherhood. Her number is always seven. She is portrayed as a black virgin dressed in blue, protecting a boat with three fishermen. According to legend she saved three fishermen and, in commemoration of that deed, every 7th of September all who go to sea pay tribute to her.

next page: PRENSA LATINA ARCHIVE, *Havana street,* **1957**

Before 1959, Havana boasted some of the most splendid department stores in the Americas, with elaborate neon signs hung out across the main shopping streets. Beside them were bars, restaurants, beauty parlors, and every kind of gift shop, many offering air-conditioned comfort.

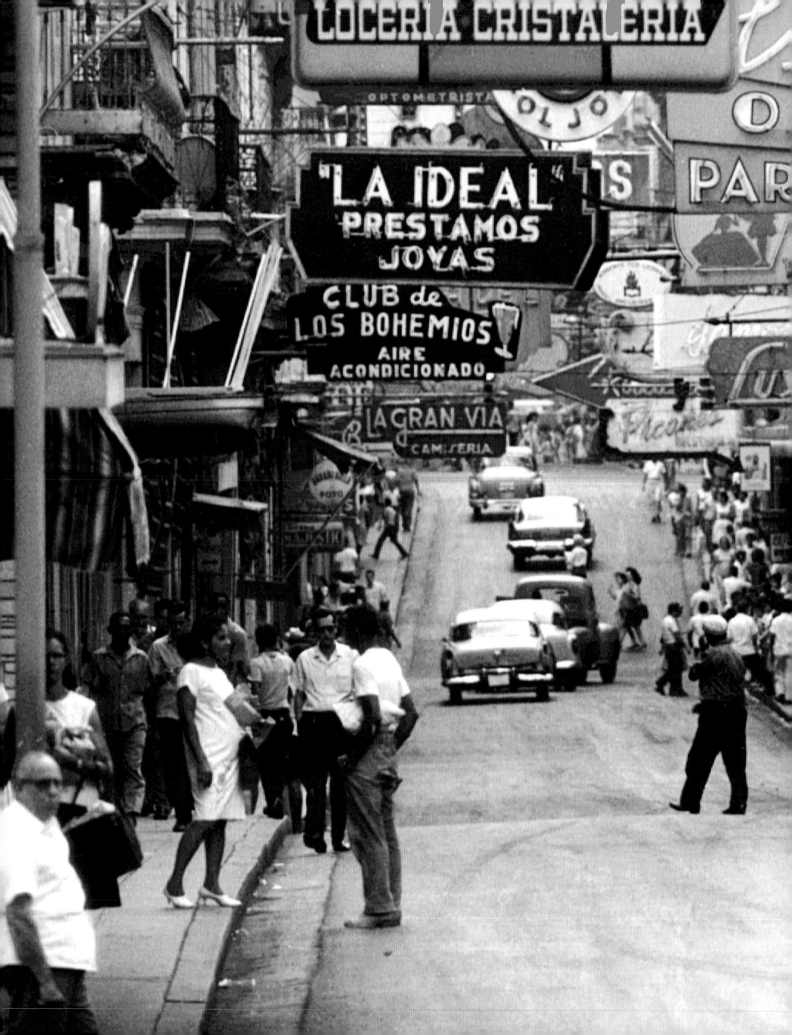

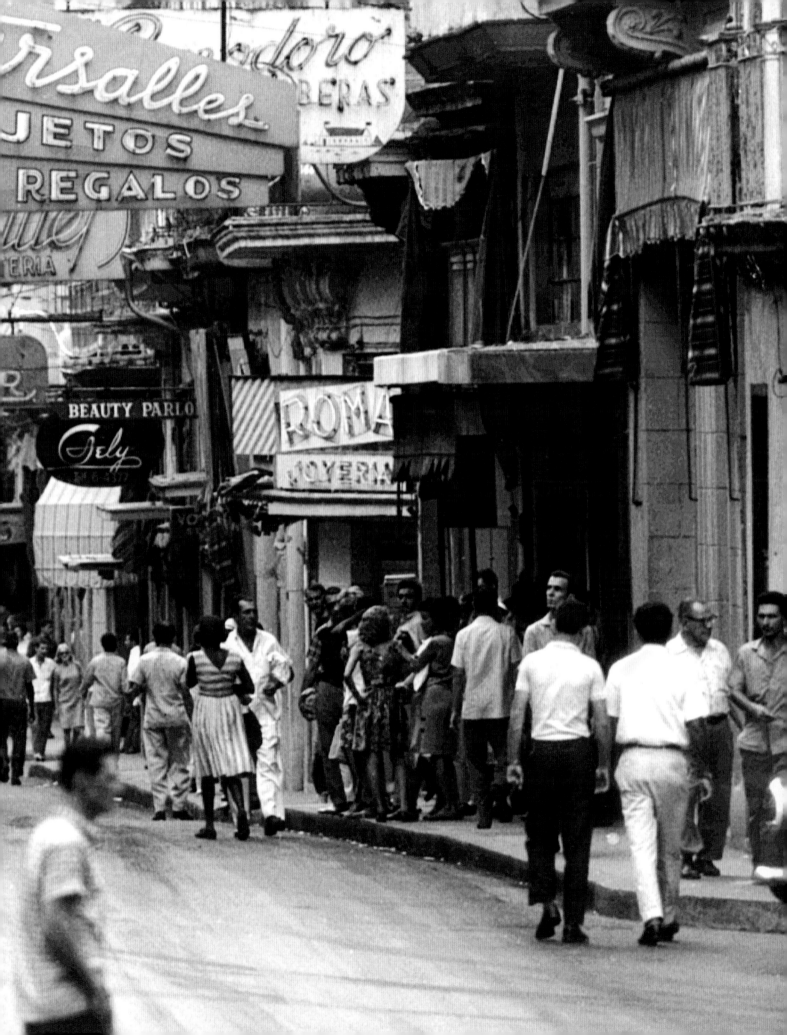

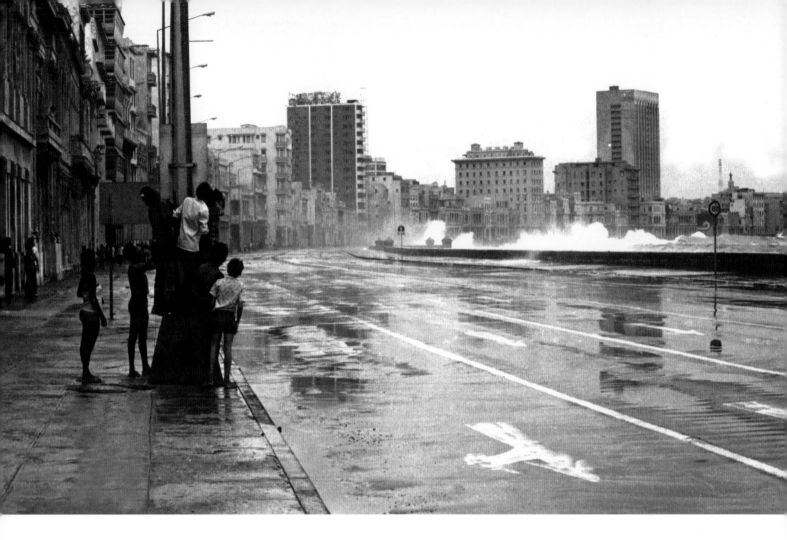

above: SERGIO ROMERO, *Waves breaking on the Malecón*, 1985

The Malecón sea drive curves around the city from the Castillo de la Punta to the Chorrera at the mouth of the Almendares river. It is a place for lovers to meet, for fishermen to fish, for friends to share a bottle of rum. It is also known as the Havana Business Center, a place where deals are made with only the sea as witness.

top right: SERGIO ROMERO, *Malecón with cyclist,* 1993

In the early 1990s, gasoline was virtually unobtainable in Cuba, and the streets were deserted.

bottom right: SERGIO ROMERO, *Double bass transported by bicycle,* 1992

Wherever you go you hear the throbbing rhythms of the rumba, the bolero, the guaguancó, the conga, the cha cha cha, Afro-Cuban jazz, salsa, and a variety of peasant song forms. The artists who create this musical cornucopia often have to travel long distances on the erratic Havana buses to their rehearsals—or transport their instruments on the back of a bicycle.

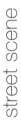

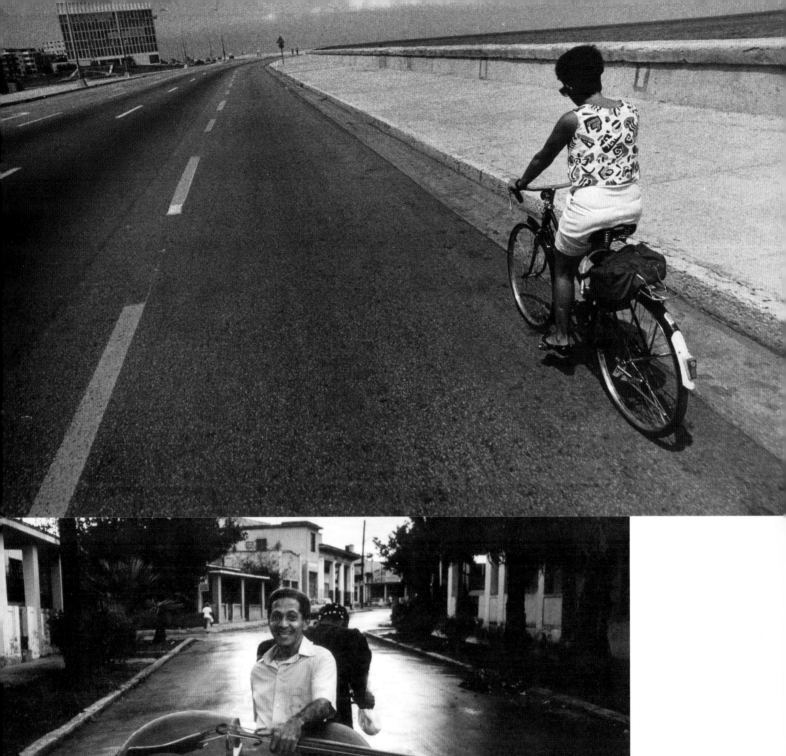

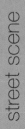

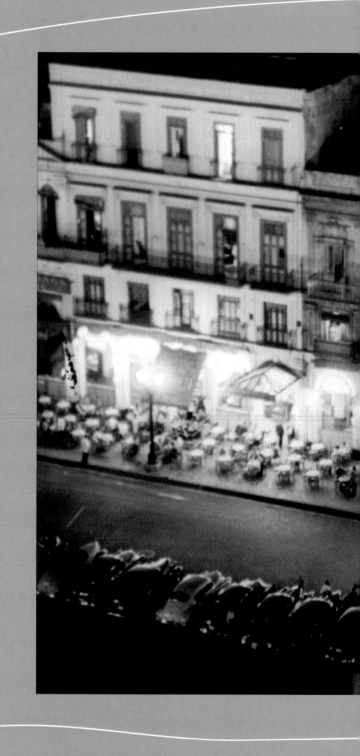

above: CONSTANTINO ARIAS, *Paseo de Prado restaurant terrace by night,* 1950

A vibrant night life is returning to the streets of the old town. Prado, the elegant boulevard that runs from the Castillo de la Punta, at the mouth of the harbor, past the Central Park and the Capitolio, is being restored to its former glory.

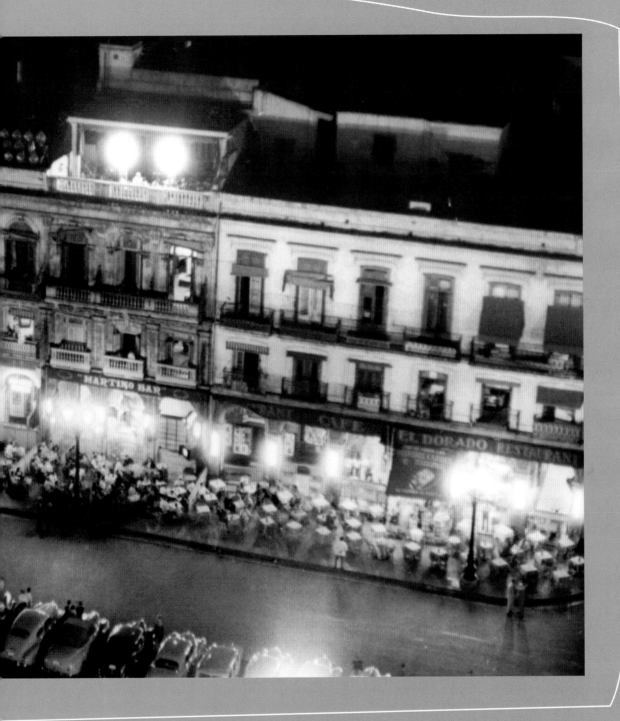

below: TITO ALVAREZ, *Children*, 1976

right: RIGOBERTO ROMERO, *The patio of my house is not private,* 1986

Physical closeness and touching are part of Cuban culture. People live on the street, coming out of their houses to escape the heat, and pass the time in lively conversation. The experience of queuing for everything enhances social cohesion even more. People join a queue without knowing what it is for, and stock up with as much as possible. In the Coppelia ice cream park it is quite normal to see someone walking away with three ice cream cones, licking each in turn.

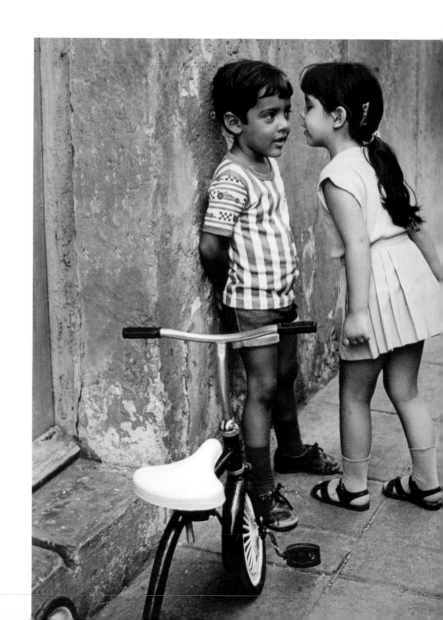

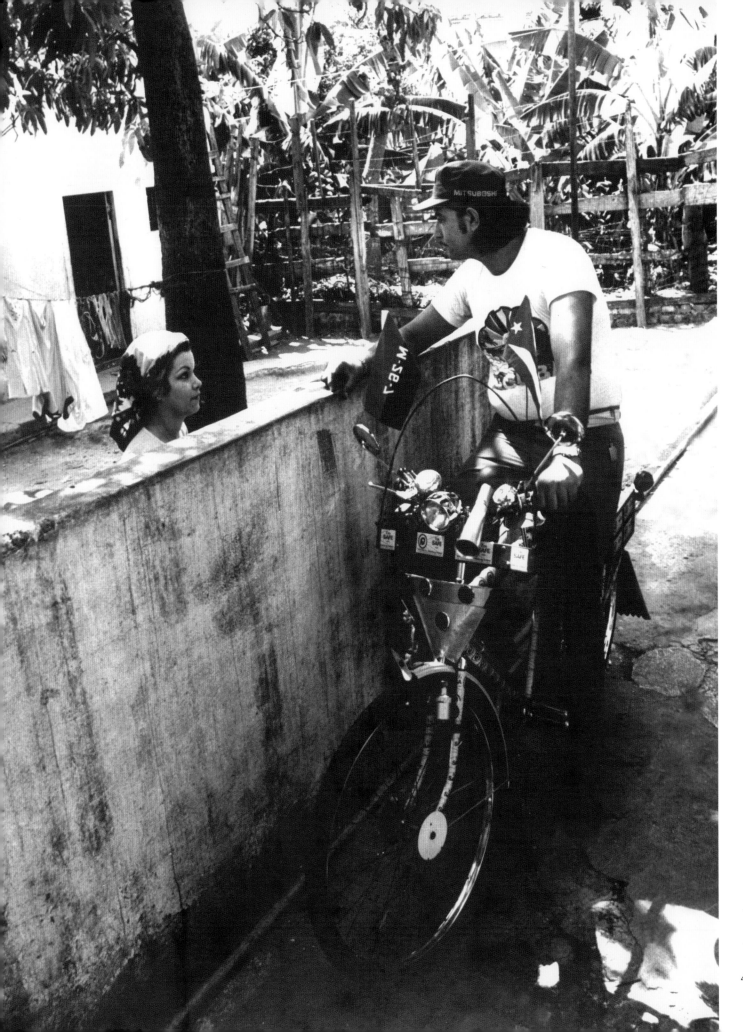

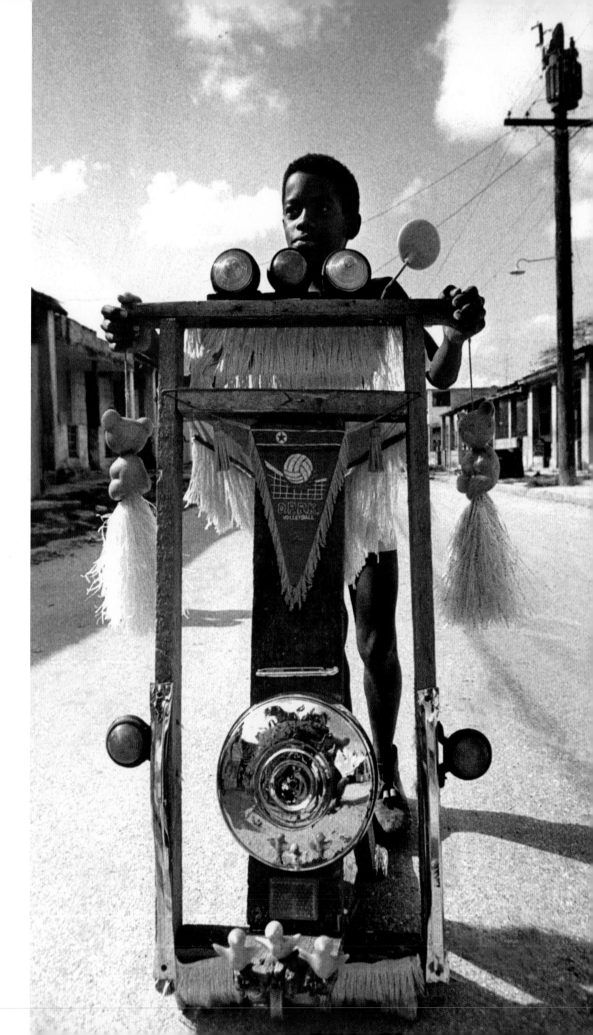

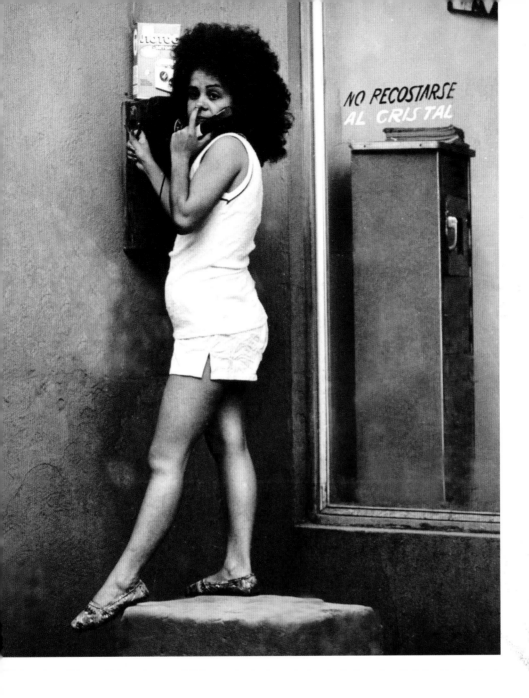

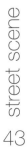

left: **SERGIO ROMERO,** *Boy with scooter,* 1991

above: **SERGIO ROMERO,** *Woman making a phone call,* 1984

In the early days of the Revolution, many services were provided free, including telephone calls. This did not encourage short phone conversations, and on street corners throughout Havana queues would form of people waiting their turn to use the phone. Of course, everyone would take a great interest in the conversation, joining in the discussion of family problems, expressions of love, and so on.

next page: **LIBORIO NOVAL,** *Veteran,* 1971

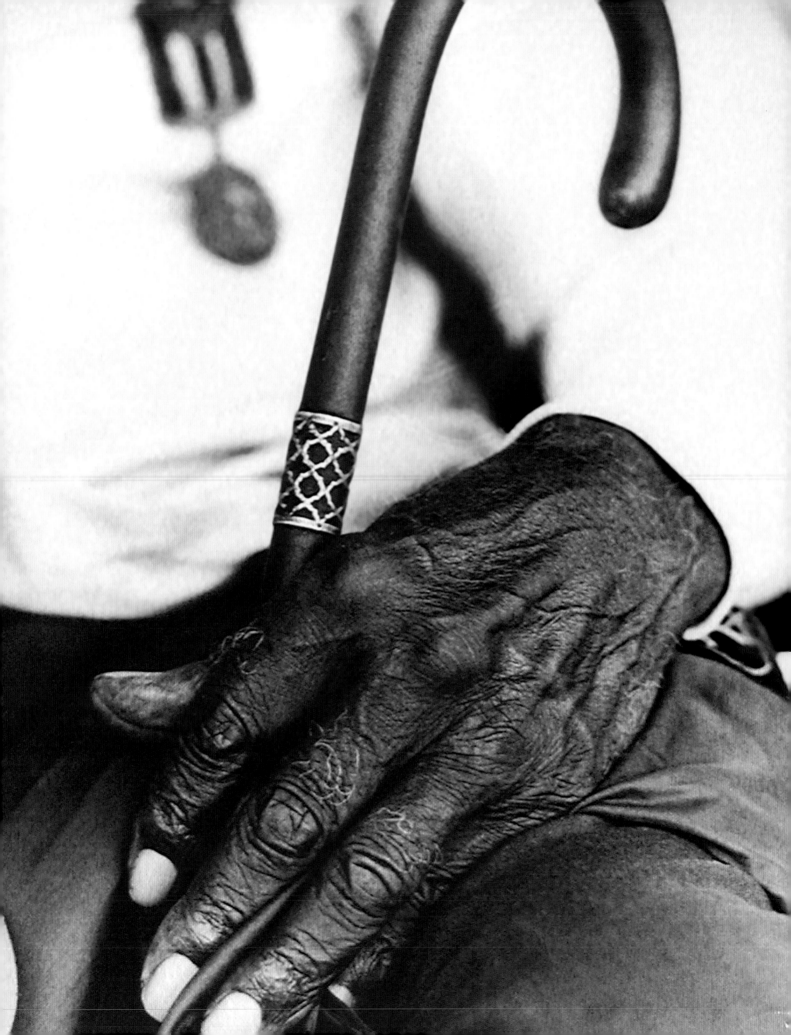

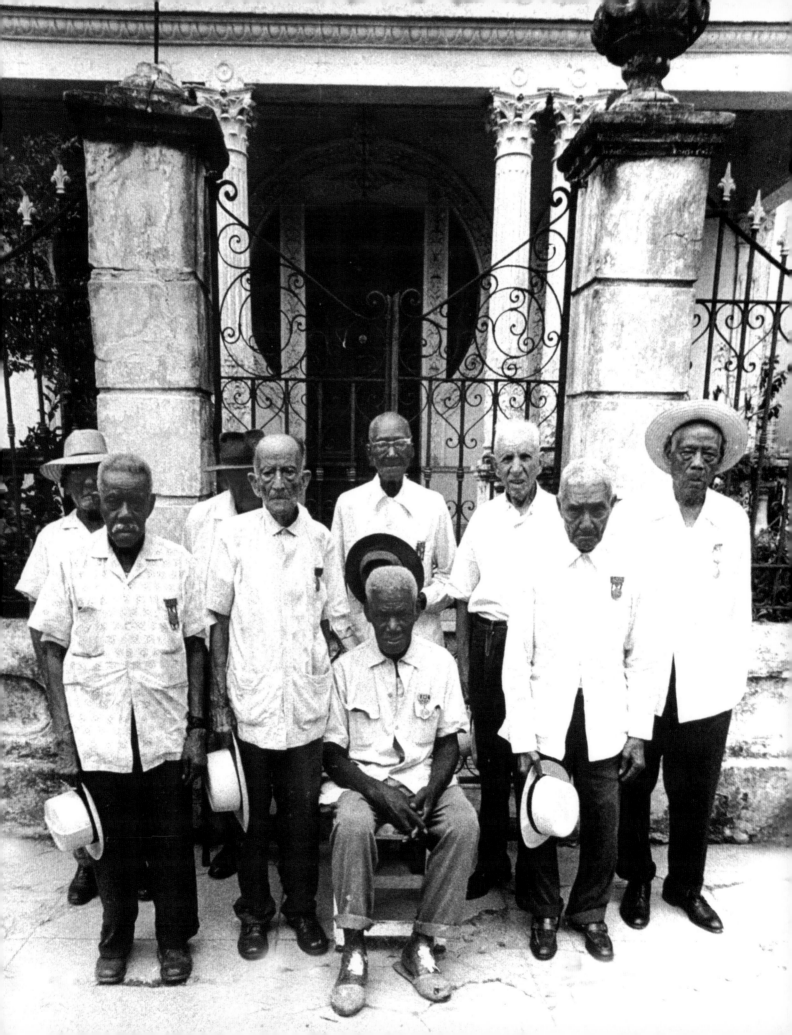

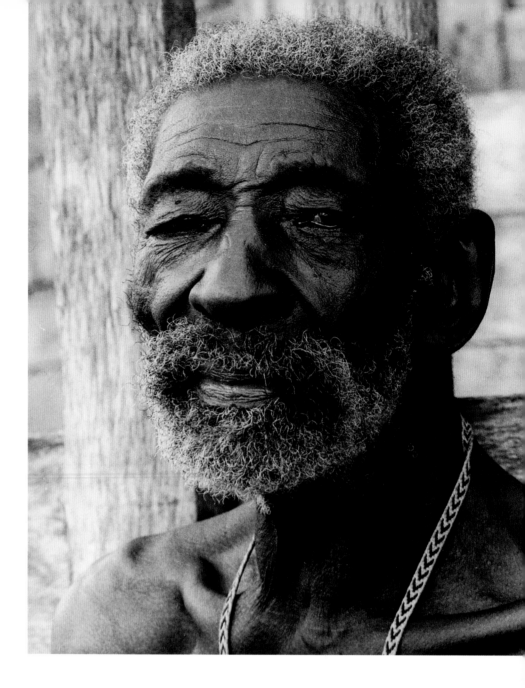

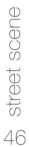
previous page: **IVAN CANAS,** *Veterans,* **1980**

History is etched in the lines of these old faces, the firmness of their gaze, the confidence of their stance. All participated in the War of Independence, 1895–98.

above: **FRANCISCO BOU,** *Portrait of an old man,* **1992**

right: **LEOVIGILDO GONZALEZ,** *Grandparents' club,* **1986**

Each district of Havana has its Third Age club, affectionately known as a grandparents' club. The old people of the district meet to chat and socialize, and many take part in exercises together.

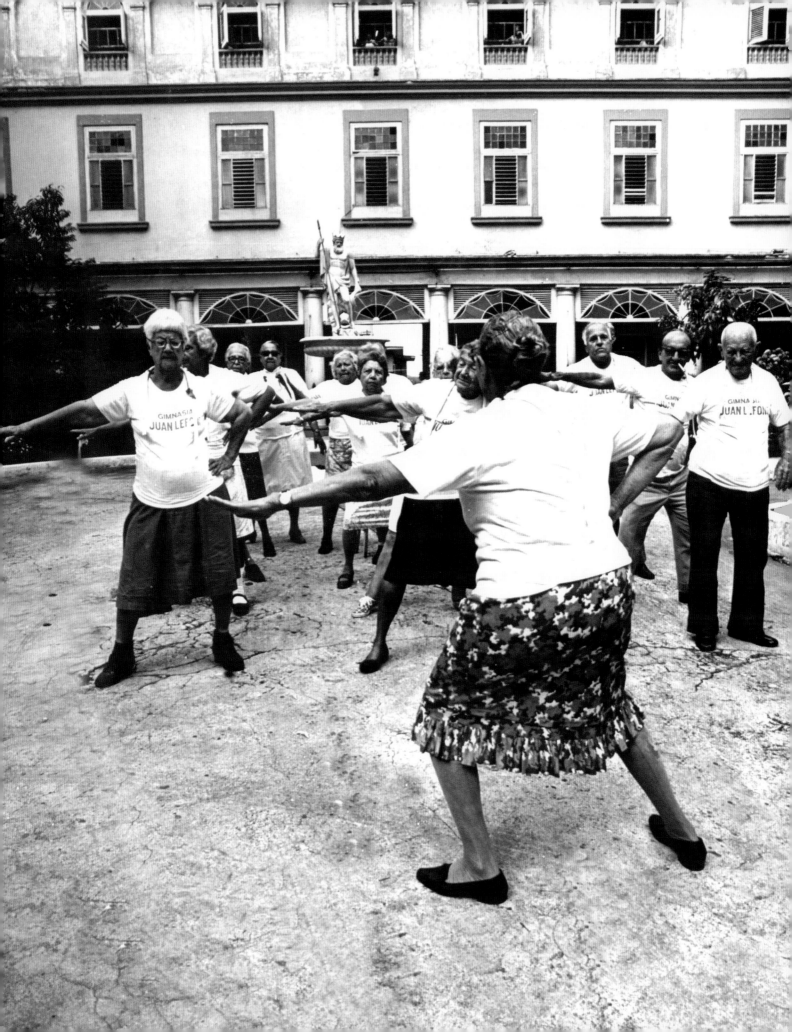

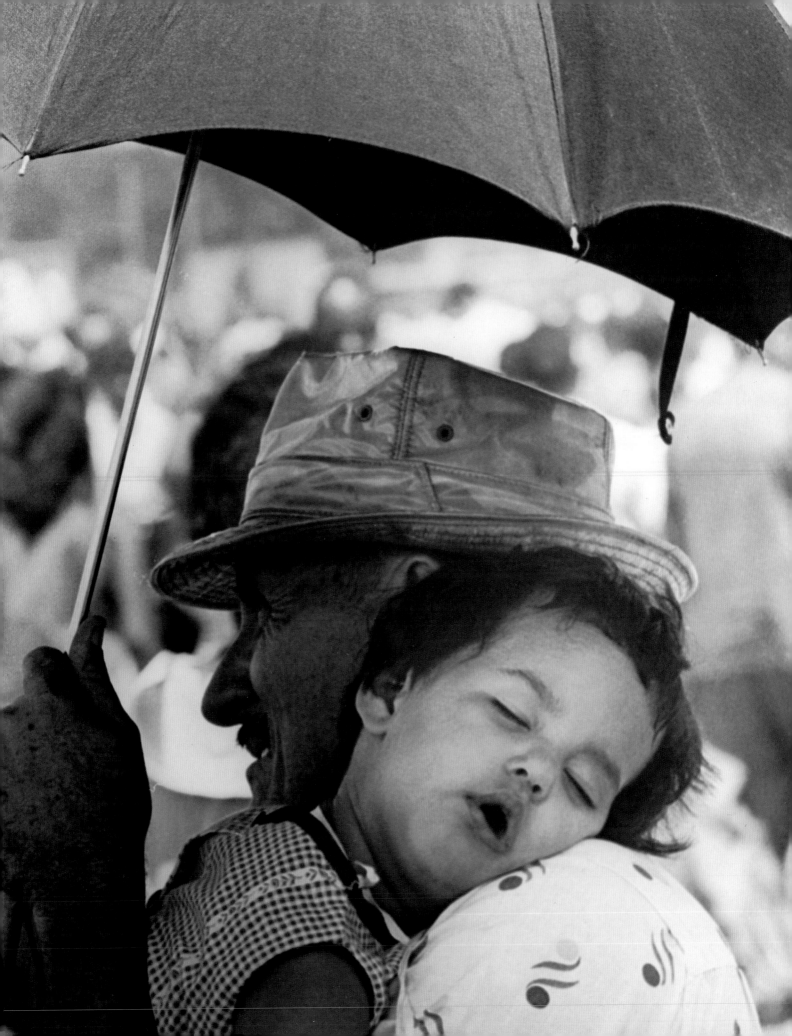

left: OSVALDO SALAS, *Siesta,* 1974

The closeness between generations became even more important in the
1970s and '80s. The traditional family exploded under the pressure of social
demands—the introduction of universal education, the incorporation of
women into the labor force, participation in the militia, the proliferation of
meetings of every kind, mobilizations of city dwellers for the sugar harvest,
international military missions to Angola. . . . Grandparents assumed a new
role in holding the family together, stepping in to take care of the children
and often proving more indulgent than the parents.

... Let us walk through Havana, my love
keeping close to the sea
the day is dawning and the city
wishes to rise ...

IRENO GARCIA, from "WALKING THROUGH HAVANA"

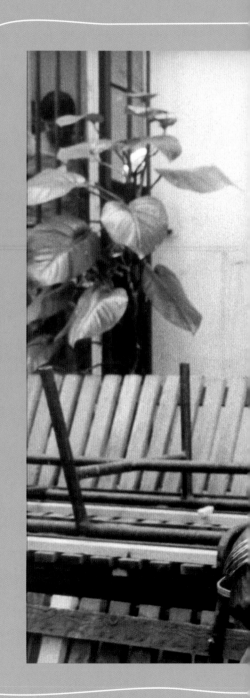

right: MARIO DIAZ, *Portrait of woman with old man,* 1985

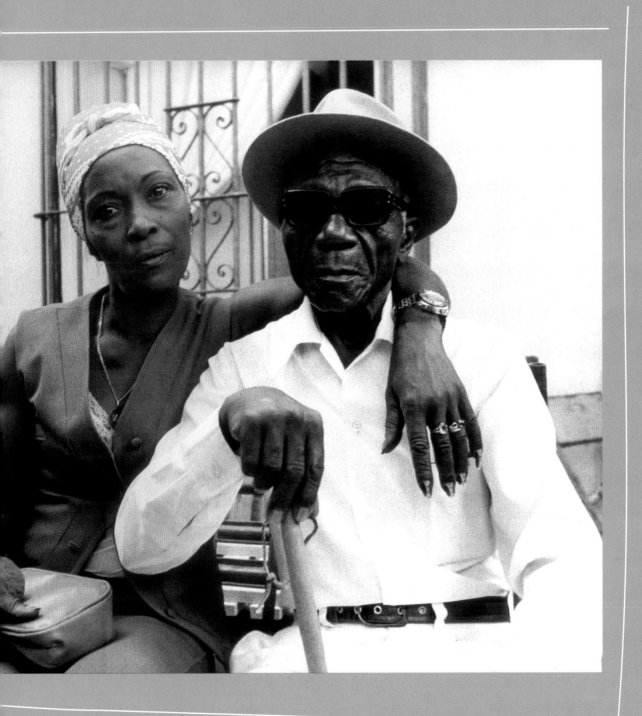

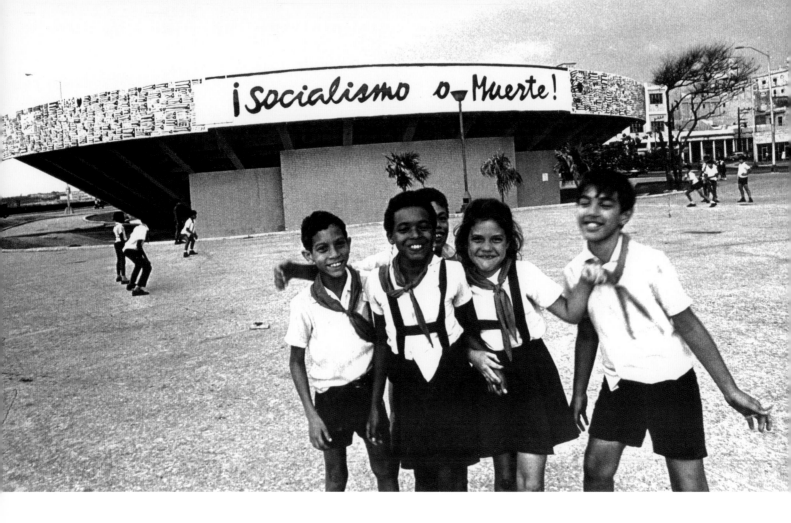

¡socialismo o Muerte!

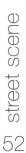
above: SERGIO ROMERO, *Pioneers in the Plaza Antonio Maceo,*
1985

Slogans continue to be prominently displayed in public places all over the
island. The children in their red school uniforms and neck scarves are known
as pioneers.

right: JOSE ALBERTO FIGUEROA, *Children outside the Capitolio*
building, **1986**

The Capitolio is the principal building of the republican period (1902–1959).
Conceived as the seat of government under President Mario García Menocal,
it was built between 1928 and 1931 to a design by the architects Covantes
and Cabarrocas. Directly beneath its cupola, set in a marble floor, was
placed a diamond-encrusted rock, from which all distances in Cuba are
measured—just as distances in France are measured from the Arc de
Triomphe.

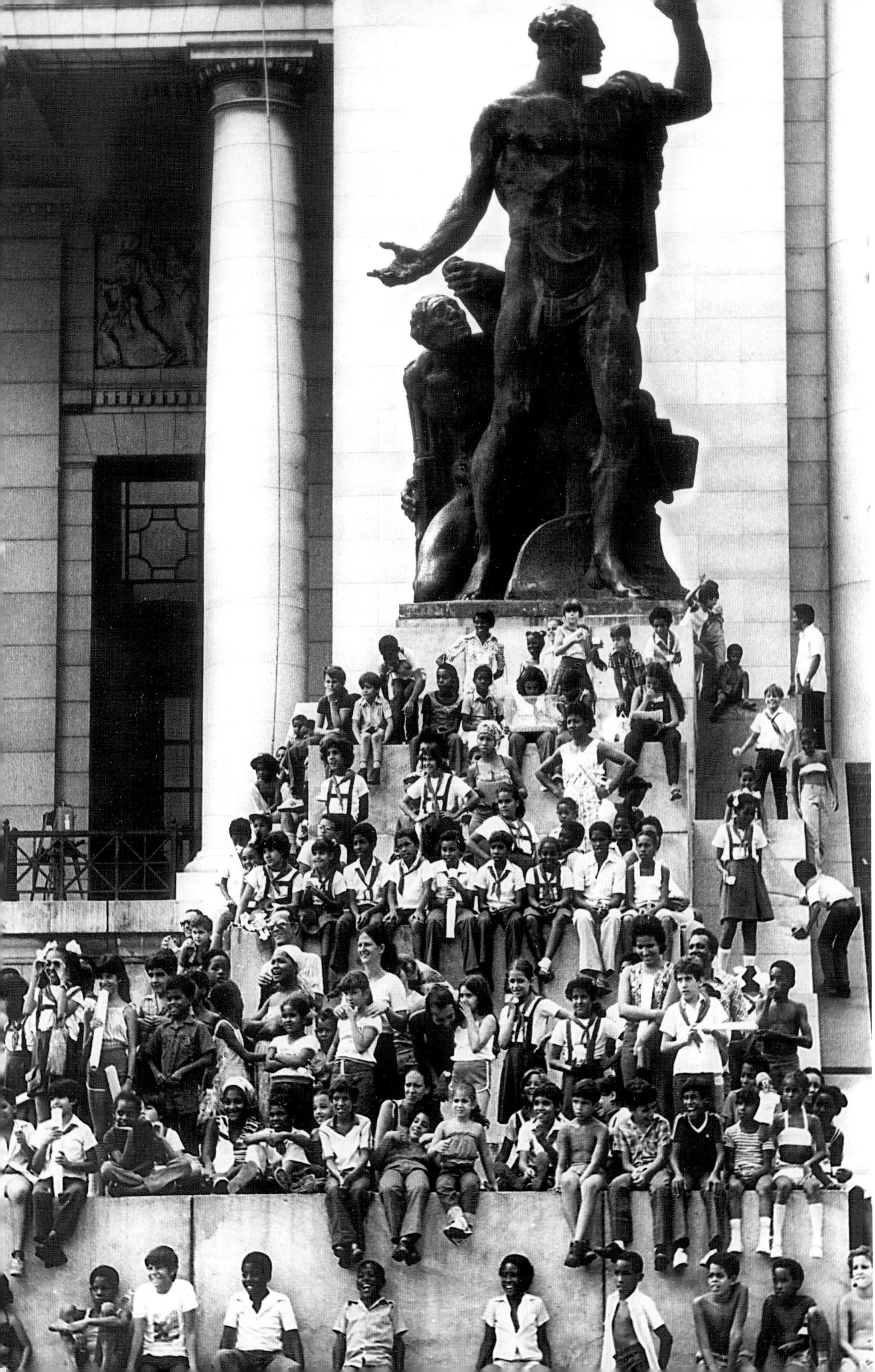

right: OSVALDO SALAS, *Policeman with five boys on a motorcycle*, 1975

For many years the government sought to make the police more accepted through a publicity campaign on television. A child would come up to a policeman and ask, "Policeman, policeman, are you my friend?" The policeman would reply by picking the child up and making a fuss of him. The campaign was so successful that whenever a child was asked what he wanted to be when he grew up, he would most likely reply either that he would like to be like Che, or that he wanted to be a policeman.

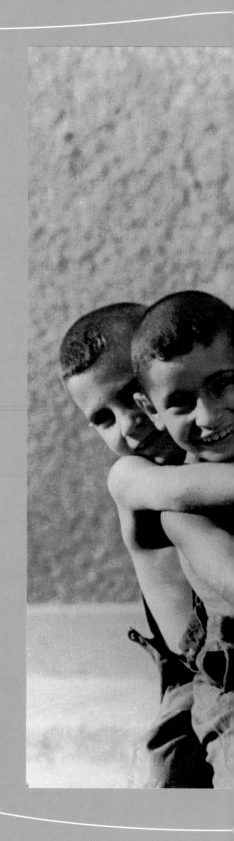

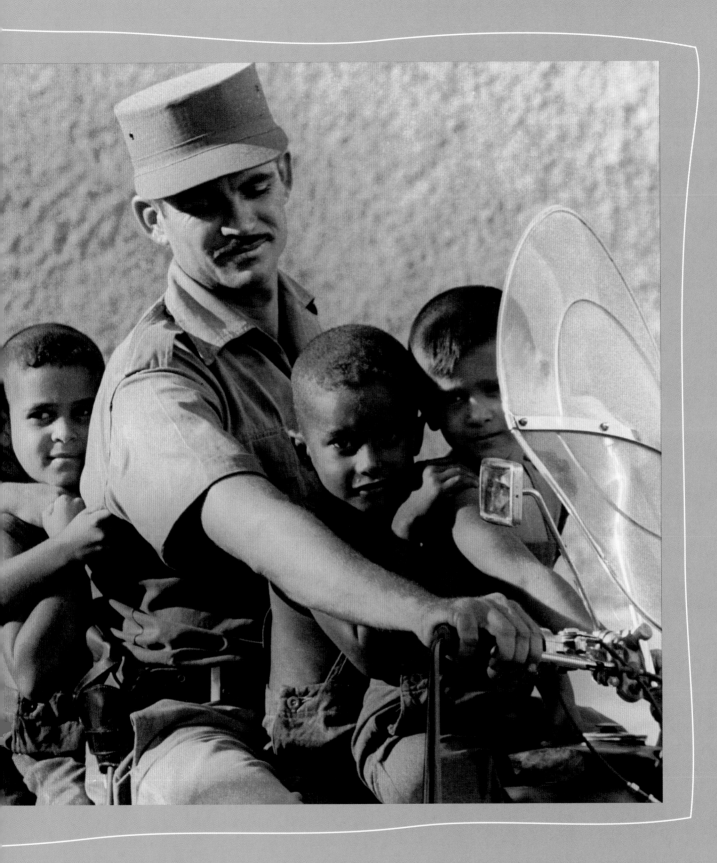

City of my loves in the dust,
  beautiful city of decay and wings,
in you I truly was born one month of January
    when hope struck you in your breast.
  If I lived a great love it was in your streets,
      if I live a great love it has your face,
  city of the loves of my life,
      my woman forever without distance.
  If you did not exist I would invent you,
my city of Havana.

FAYAD JAMIS, from "I OPENED THE IRON GATE"

top right: NATIONAL LIBRARY ARCHIVE, *Paseo del Prado,* **1904**

The Paseo de Prado was built toward the end of the 19th century and was the first street to break with the architectural traditions of Old Havana. Its redevelopment in the 1920s was strongly influenced by the French landscape architect Jean-Claude Forestier.

Returning to Havana from a foreign trip in the early 1960s, the novelist Alejo Carpentier was struck by the endless proliferation of columns. The awnings, which had previously hung between the columns to shade the colonnades, had rotted away, bringing the columns into sharp relief. And so Carpentier named Havana the City of Columns.

bottom right: NATIONAL LIBRARY ARCHIVE, *Manzana de Gómez,* **1933**

Havana for a long time had a reputation for being at the forefront of fashion. American companies would test new products there before releasing them in the United States. Chewing gum was first chewed in Havana, and houses in Havana were lit with electric lights before anywhere else in the world. In the 1950s Cuba was the first Latin American nation to have television.

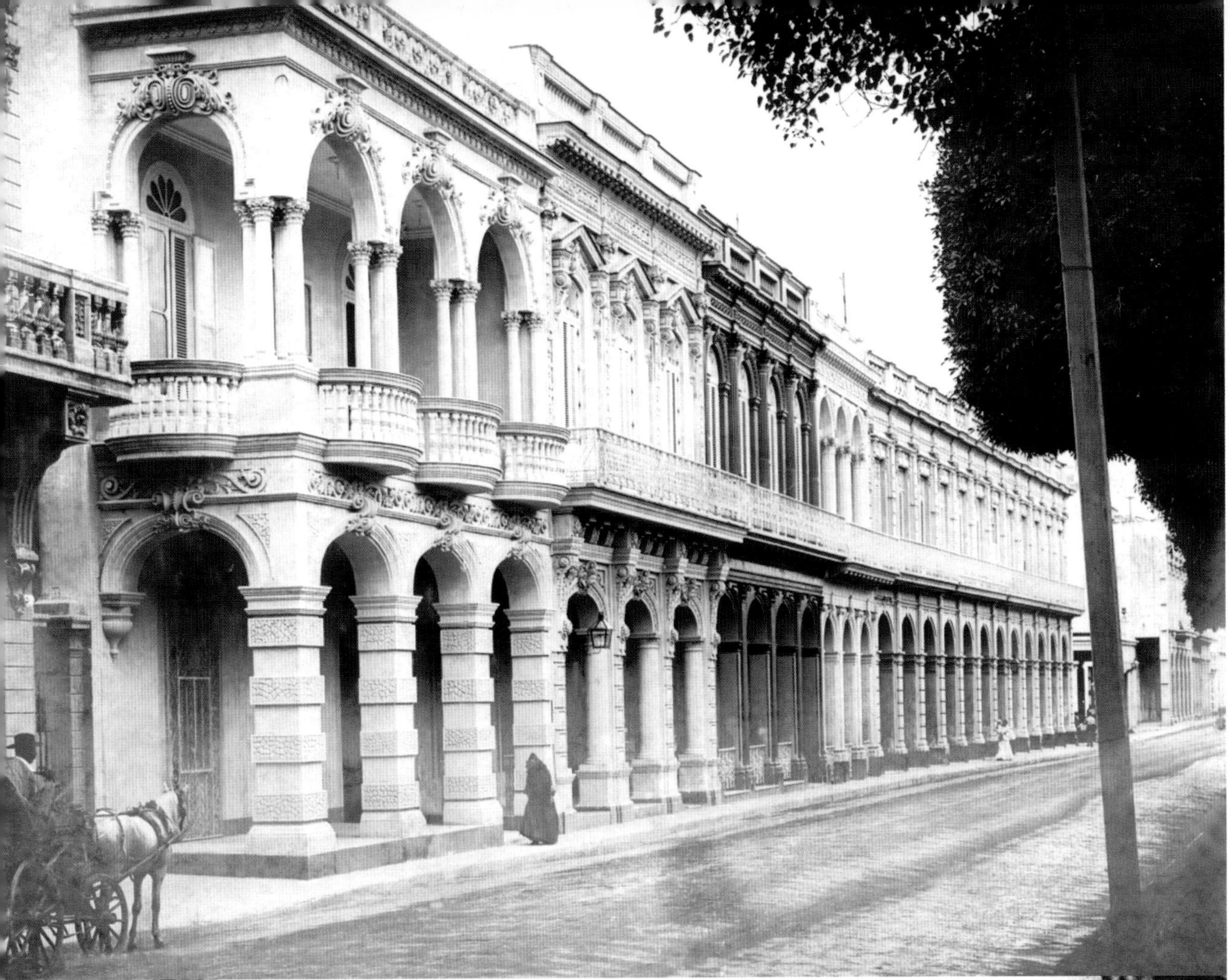

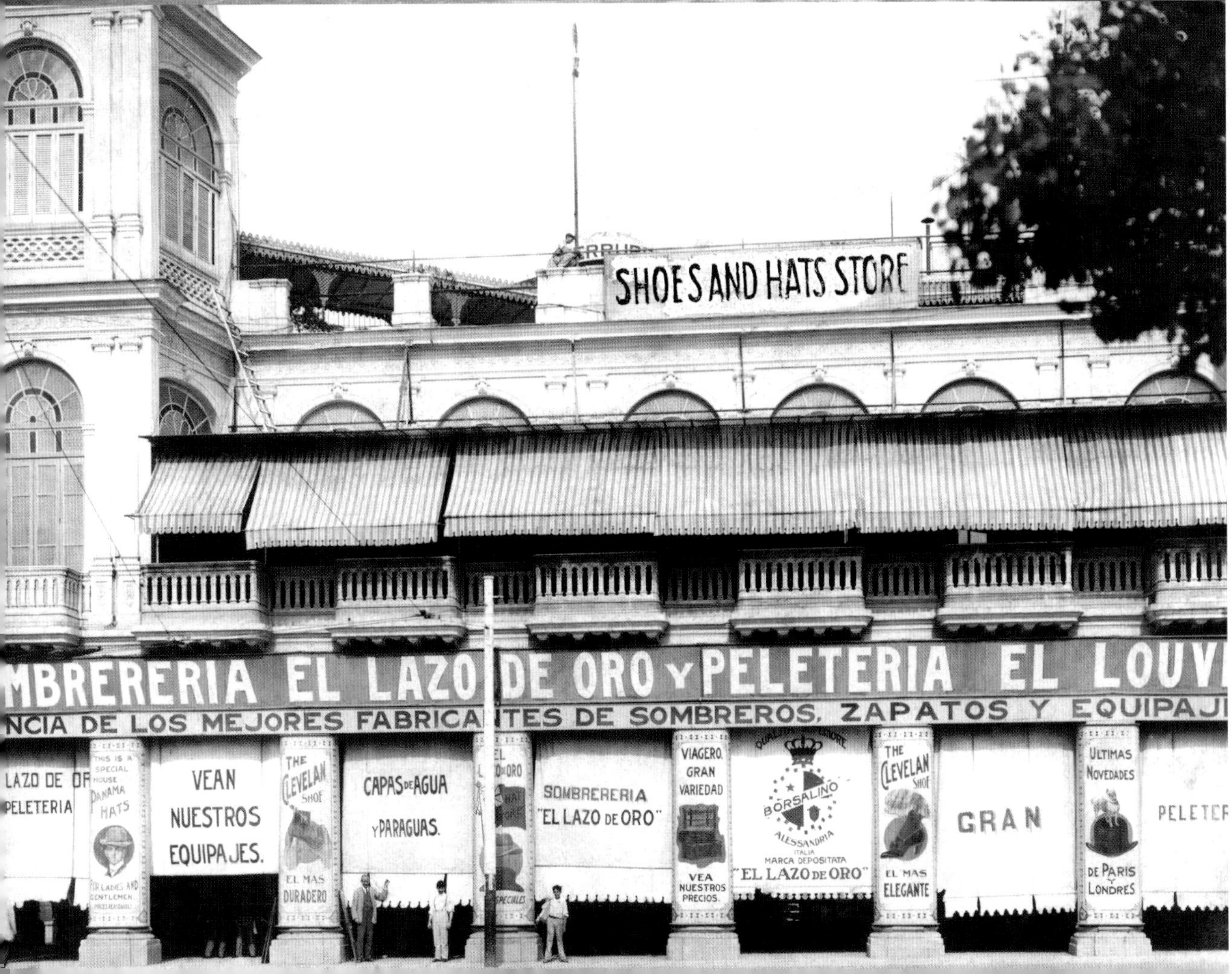

SHOES AND HATS STORE

SOMBRERERIA EL LAZO DE ORO y PELETERIA EL LOUVRE

NCIA DE LOS MEJORES FABRICANTES DE SOMBREROS, ZAPATOS Y EQUIPAJI

LAZO DE OR
PELETERIA

THIS IS A
SPECIAL
HOUSE
PANAMA
HATS

FOR LADIES AND
GENTLEMEN

VEAN
NUESTROS
EQUIPAJES.

THE
CLEVELAN
SHOE

EL MAS
DURADERO

CAPAS DE AGUA
Y PARAGUAS.

EL
LAZO
DE ORO

SPECIALES

SOMBRERERIA
"EL LAZO DE ORO"

VIAGERO,
GRAN
VARIEDAD

VEA
NUESTROS
PRECIOS.

BORSALINO
ALESSANDRIA
ITALIA
MARCA DEPOSITATA
"EL LAZO DE ORO"

THE
CLEVELAN
SHOE

EL MAS
ELEGANTE

GRAN

ÚLTIMAS
NOVEDADES

DE PARIS
Y
LONDRES

PELETER

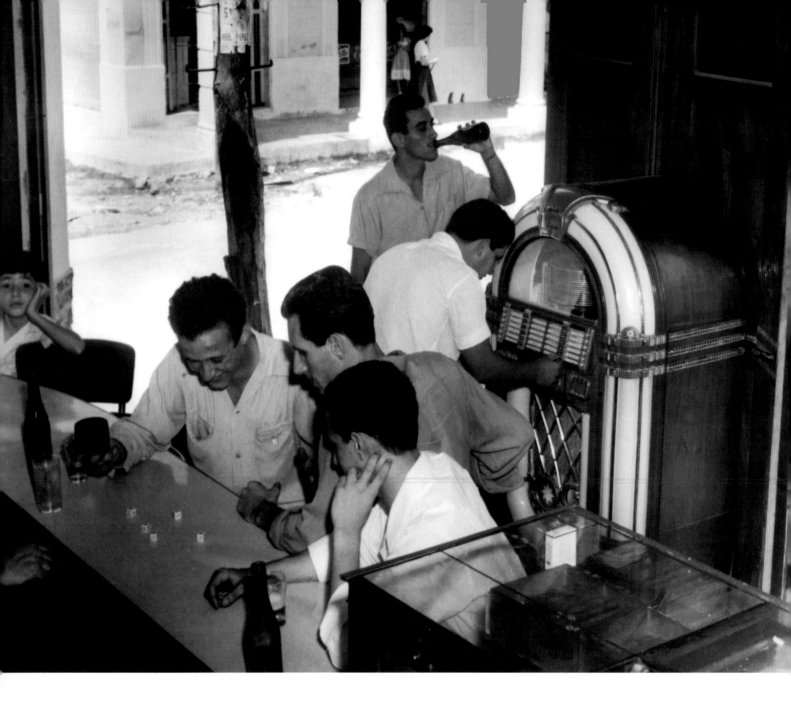

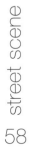
above: **BOHEMIA ARCHIVE,** *Bar with jukebox,* **22 April 1950**

This workers' bar could as well be in contemporary Havana as in the Havana of half a century ago.

right: **SERGIO ROMERO,** *Man juggling with empty boxes,* **1987**

Nothing seems abnormal on a Havana street.

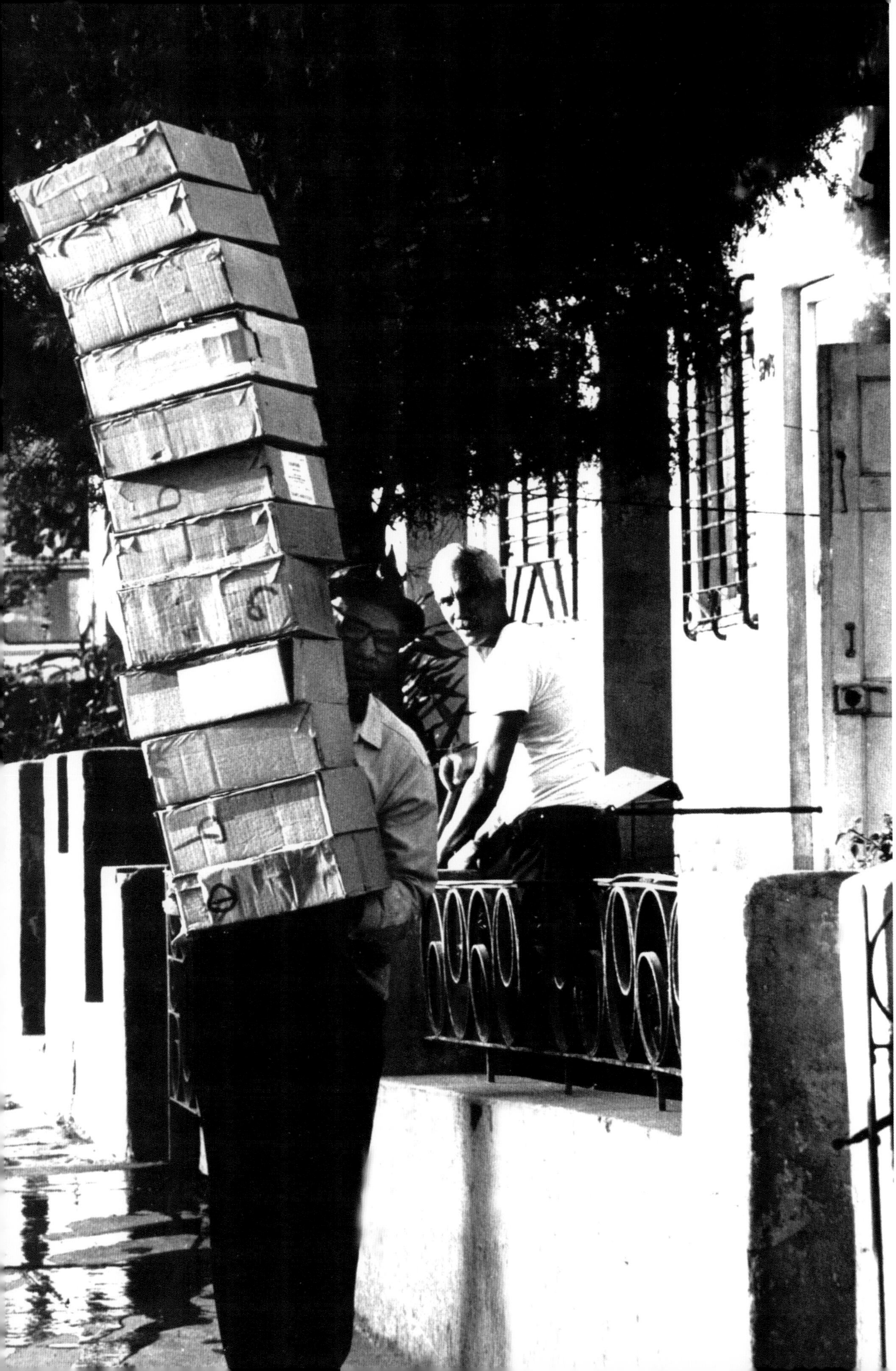

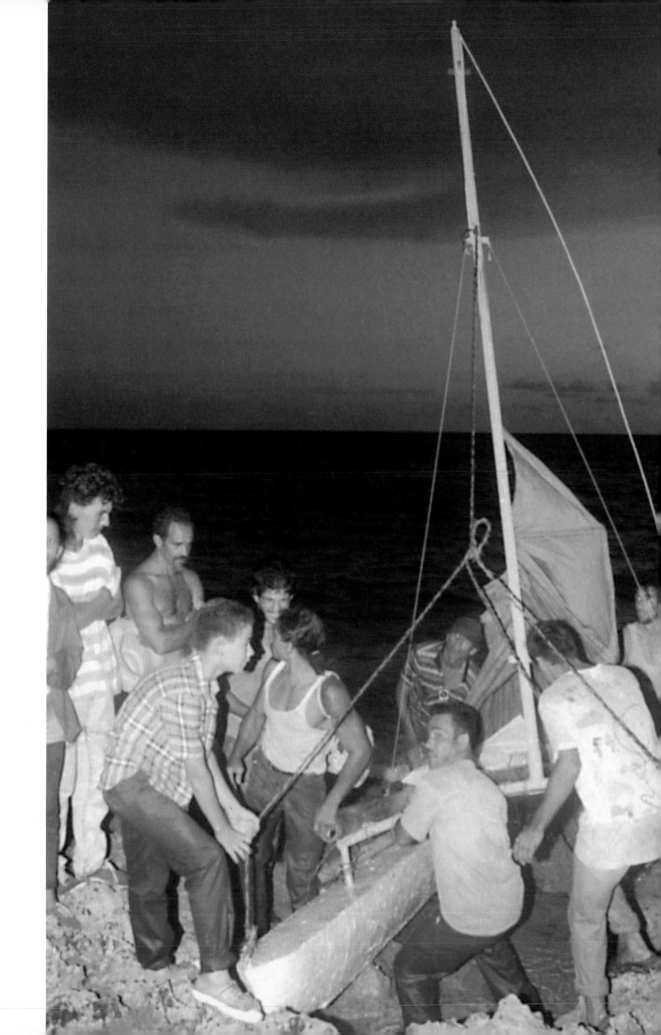

left: MIGUEL VINAS, *Rafters,* 1994

The "Rafters Crisis" of the summer of 1994 was one of the saddest moments in
recent Cuban history. Tens of thousands of Cubans set off for the coast of Florida
on makeshift rafts, seeking an escape from the difficult economic conditions at the
time and a new future in the Promised Land. An unknown number, certainly
several thousand, perished in the attempt, dying of hunger and exposure at sea,
or eaten by sharks.

In 1994 the pressure to leave the island had been growing for some time, and
many were building rafts hoping for an opportunity to leave. Finally, the Cuban
government responded to taunts coming from the United States by withdrawing
the coast guards who had been preventing the departure of most would-be
emigrants.

So many would not have risked their lives if it had not been for the 40-year-old
U.S. Cuban Adjustment Law. This promises the right to stay and work and,
subsequently, U.S. citizenship to any Cuban who arrives on U.S. territory directly
after leaving Cuba. No other immigrant group receives such treatment.

In all, hundreds of thousands of Cuban families were touched by this crisis.

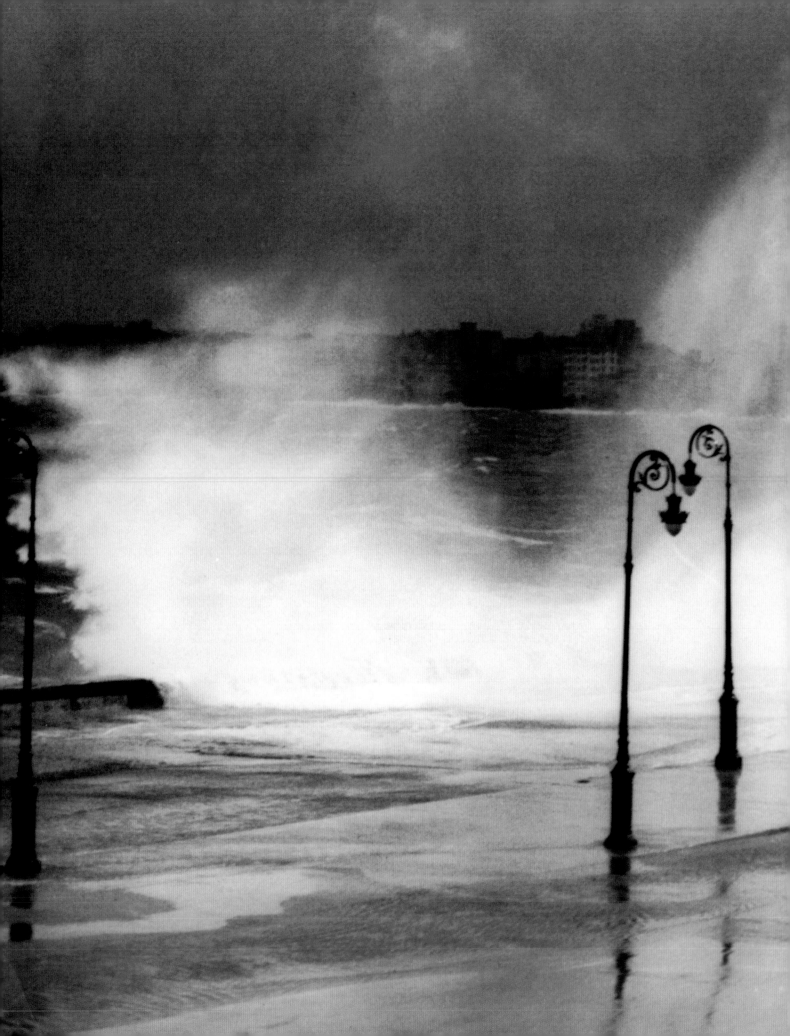

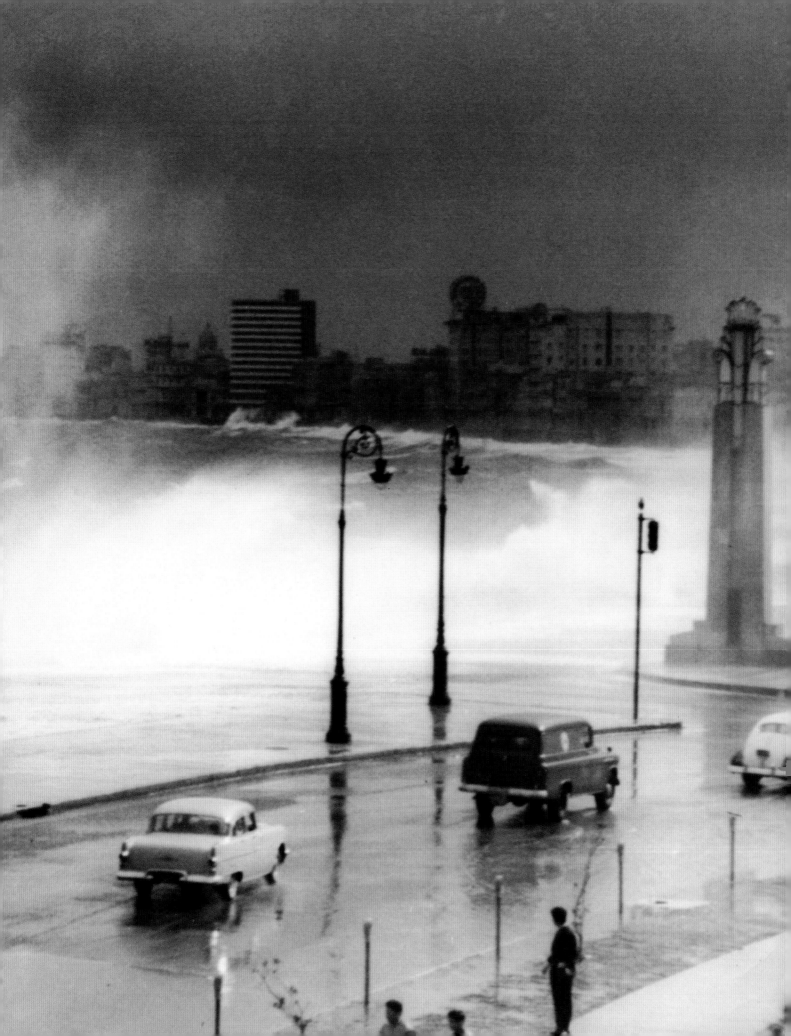

Getting up to close the shutter you look across the harbor to the flag on the fortress and see it is straightened out toward you. You look out the north window past the Morro and see that the smooth morning sheen is rippling over and you know the trade wind is coming up early.

ERNEST HEMINGWAY, from "MARLIN OFF THE MORRO: A CUBAN LETTER," 1933

previous page: **BOHEMIA ARCHIVE,** *North Front on the Malecón,* **12 January 1958**

right: **PRENSA LATINA ARCHIVE,** *Fishing opposite the Morro lighthouse,* **1986**

The fishermen on the Malecón have their own psychology, almost a Zen approach to life. They often fish until after dawn, yet even if they catch nothing one can see them leaving contented after exchanging stories throughout the night. They form an exclusive men-only club, and sit with a bottle of rum discussing their troubles and exchanging hooks and bait, linked by a special bond.

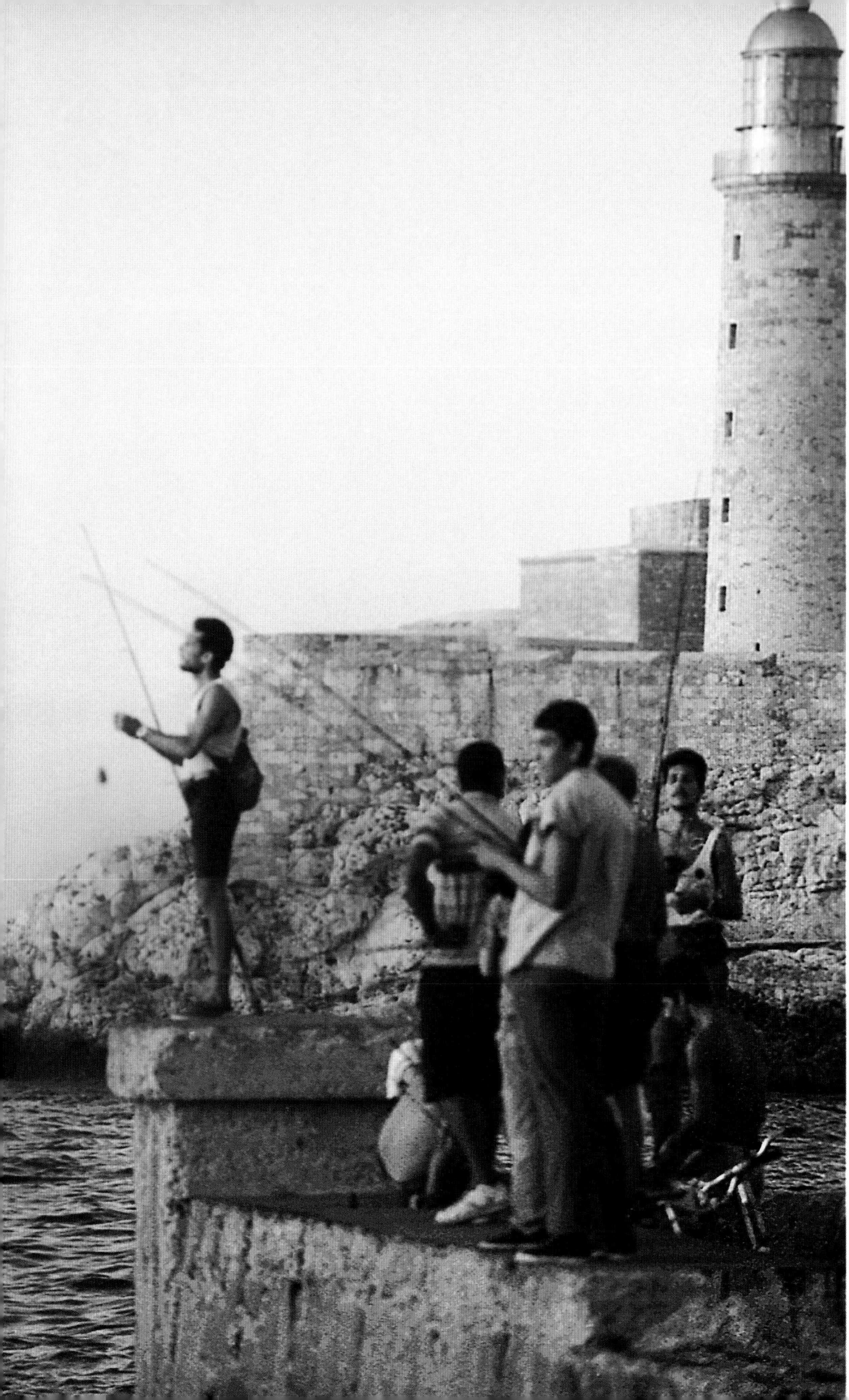

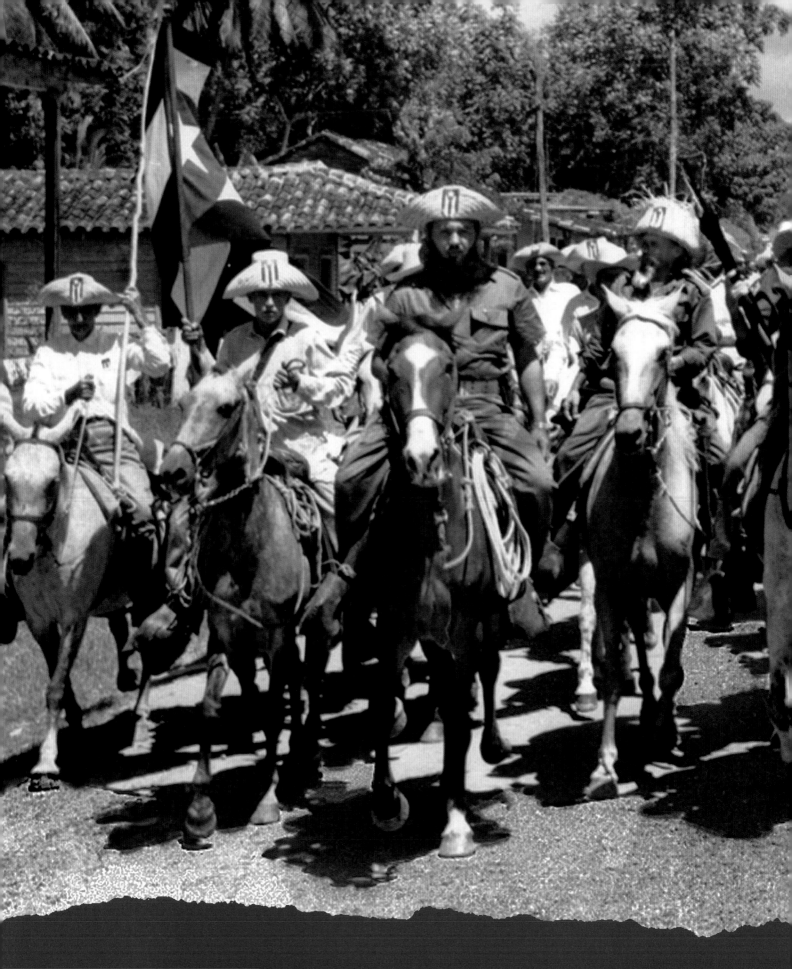

chapter**two**

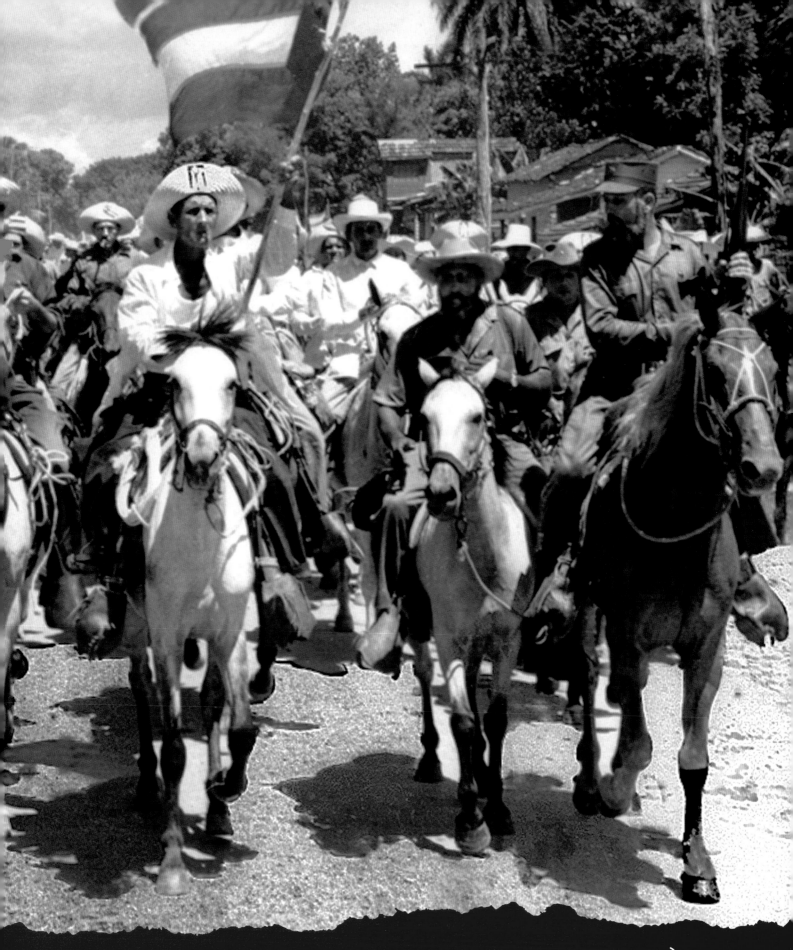

revolution

revolution

The images of Cuba's Revolution of 1959 are etched deep in the psyche of the Cuban people. But not only of the Cuban people. All over the world people watched amazed as this little country, barely 90 miles from U.S. shores, abruptly broke its links with the United States and continued to go its own way in subsequent decades—exhilarating for its supporters and wildly frustrating for its opponents. The images that were to become so familiar reached the world largely through the lenses of Cuban photographers, particularly Alberto Korda, Raúl Corrales, Osvaldo Salas, and Perfecto Romero. The artistic judgment of these men very directly helped to shape the way the world has viewed the Revolution.

The most famous of all these images is Alberto Korda's photograph of Che Guevara, "The Heroic Guerrilla," wearing his beret with its star, staring fixedly into the distance. Korda and a handful of other photographers accompanied Fidel Castro and the other leaders at public events throughout the early years of the Revolution and produced a remarkable record of a society undergoing profound social change.

There are the images of young, bearded guerrillas fighting in the mountains of the Sierra Maestra, and making their way in triumph across the island; of a sombrero-wearing peasant cavalry entering Havana; of a peasant sitting nonchalantly atop a lamp post at a political rally; of a bespectacled Fidel Castro on a tank confronting the U.S.-backed invasion at the Bay of Pigs; of crowds in their hundreds of thousands holding high Cuban flags as they cheer speeches; of Che Guevara in earnest conversation with Simone de Beauvoir and Jean-Paul Sartre; of Fidel Castro cutting sugar cane. The photographic archive of these years is remarkable for the power of the imagery it contains.

During October 1962 the whole world watched in dread as the United States and the Soviet Union faced off over the installation of Soviet nuclear missiles in Cuba. A country previously known mainly for its sugar, its hot dance rhythms, its rum, cigars, and casinos, a playground for the wealthy, was suddenly at the center of the world stage.

Cuba has continued to make political waves. Its army fighting in Angola in the 1980s played a decisive role in the defeat of the South African army and the subsequent collapse of apartheid. In the year 2000 the confrontation between Havana and the Cuban émigré community in Miami over the return of the shipwrecked boy Elián González dominated U.S. news for the best part of a year, and the issue played a role in the Presidential election contest between Al Gore and George Bush.

Revolutions arise out of a long accumulation of social pressures, and as they transform society, new norms are established. Cuba is once again being transformed, as it adapts to the post–Cold War world.

But this is happening in a context radically different from the Cuba of the 1950s. The Revolution has established a strong national identity, it has educated the population and given them a new confidence. Which is not to say that Che Guevara's ideal of creating the 'New Man' has been realized, only that Cuba today is, and will continue to be, a very different place than it would have been without the Revolution.

The images that follow remind us of the support ordinary Cubans gave to their Revolution, their hard work on its behalf, and the sacrifices they made—but also the sense of fun, and the pride that they brought to it. It was, after all, a very Latin and a very Caribbean revolution, and one during which its participants never ceased to crack jokes about its shortcomings.

previous page: **PERFECTO ROMERO**, *Cavalry,* **1959**
The Cuban Revolution created epic images that surprised the world.

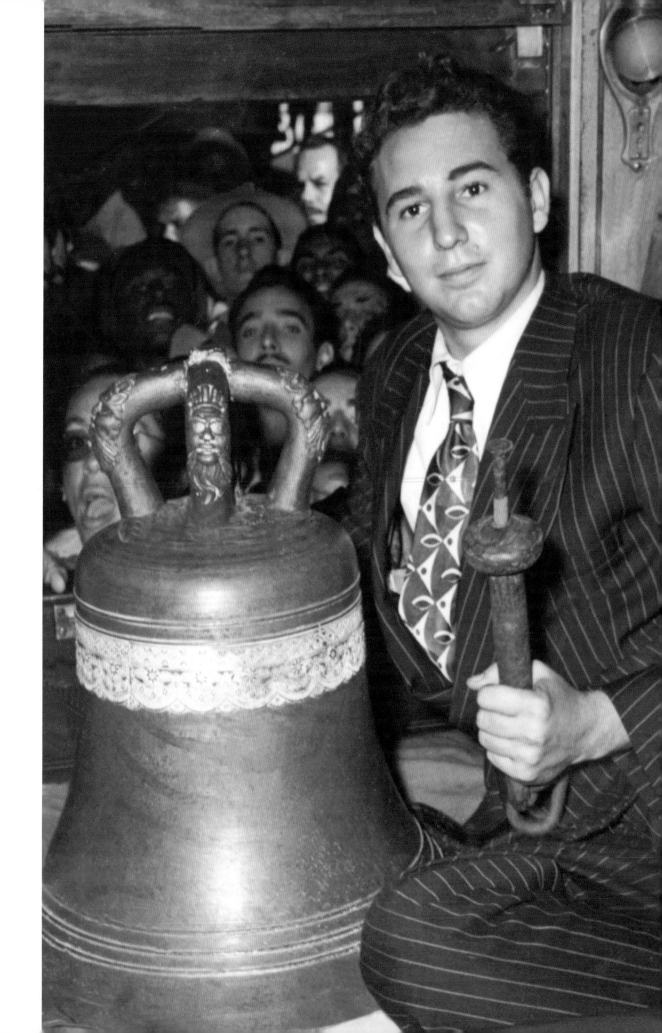

left: **BOHEMIA ARCHIVE,** *Fidel Castro and the bell of*
Demajagua, **6 November 1947**

The bell of Demajagua was Cuba's equivalent of the U.S. Liberty Bell. It was
struck by Carlos Manuel de Céspedes at his sugar estate of Demajagua,
near the eastern port of Manzanillo, to mark the opening of the 1868
War of Independence against Spain. The town of Manzanillo subsequently
maintained the bell as part of the national heritage.

As a student activist against the government of President Grau San
Martín, Fidel Castro had the idea of bringing the bell to Havana and
organizing a mass rally at which it would be rung.

Castro and his friends were successful in persuading the citizens of
Manzanillo to lend their bell, and set off back to Havana with it by train. They
drove with it from the railway station to the university in a parade lasting two
and a half hours.

The bell was left overnight in the university, next to the chancellor's office,
and in the morning it was discovered that the bell had disappeared. Castro
denounced the theft in a radio interview and led a mass rally at the university
campus. He hadn't brought down the government, but he had confirmed his
role as a new political star.

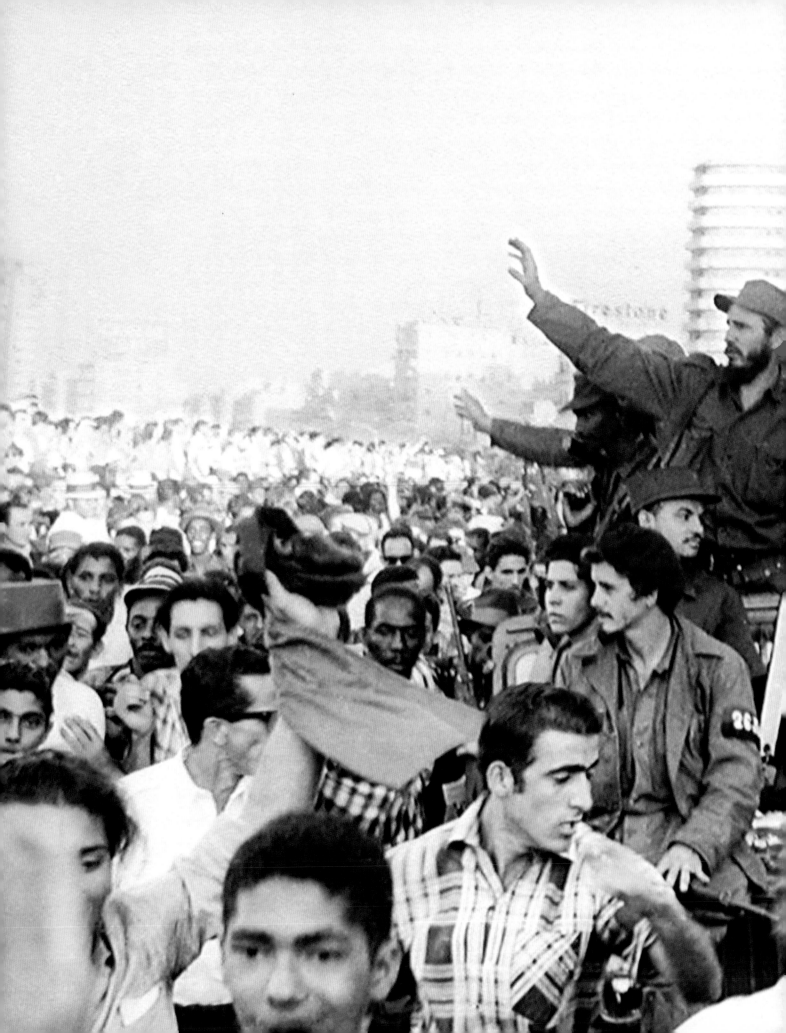

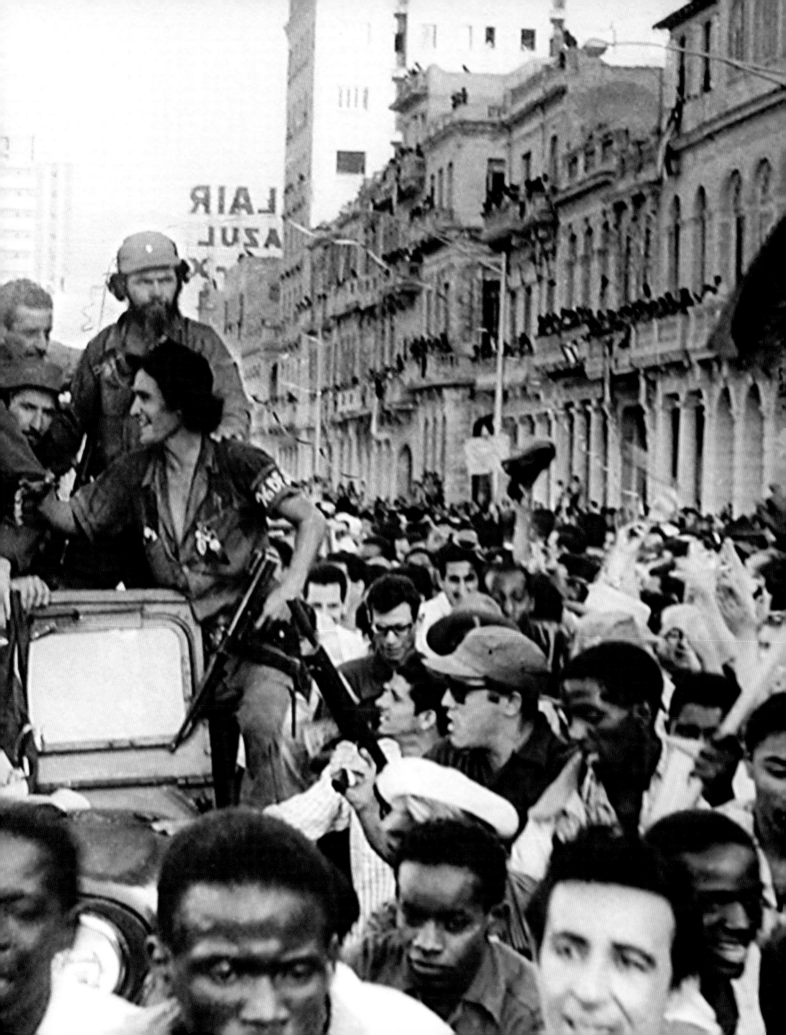

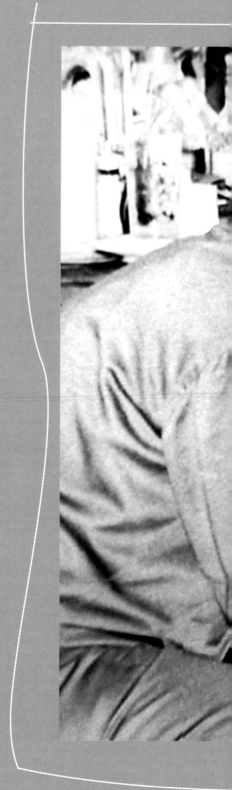

previous page: PERFECTO ROMERO, *Fidel Castro's entry into Havana,* 8 January 1959

What is so striking about many of the photographs of crowds in the early years of the Revolution is the lack of concern for personal safety of the new political leaders. Three days after President Fulgencio Batista fled the island amid the New Year festivities on the last evening of 1958, Fidel Castro set out on a leisurely triumphal parade by road from the east of the island, reaching Havana after five days. Security was always tight, but there must have been many occasions when a determined attacker could have made a successful attempt on Castro's life.

right: PERFECTO ROMERO, *Fidel Castro and Che Guevara in the Cabaña fortress,* 8 January 1959

Che Guevara had reached Havana with his column of guerrillas on 3 January 1959, and took over command of the Cabaña fortress overlooking the Havana bay. When the third of the columns, led by Fidel Castro, entered the city on 8 January, Guevara's instructions were to bring his men down to join the victory parade. But on that day he was suffering from a severe asthma attack and could not leave his room, so as soon as the parade was over Castro went straight to the Cabaña to see him.

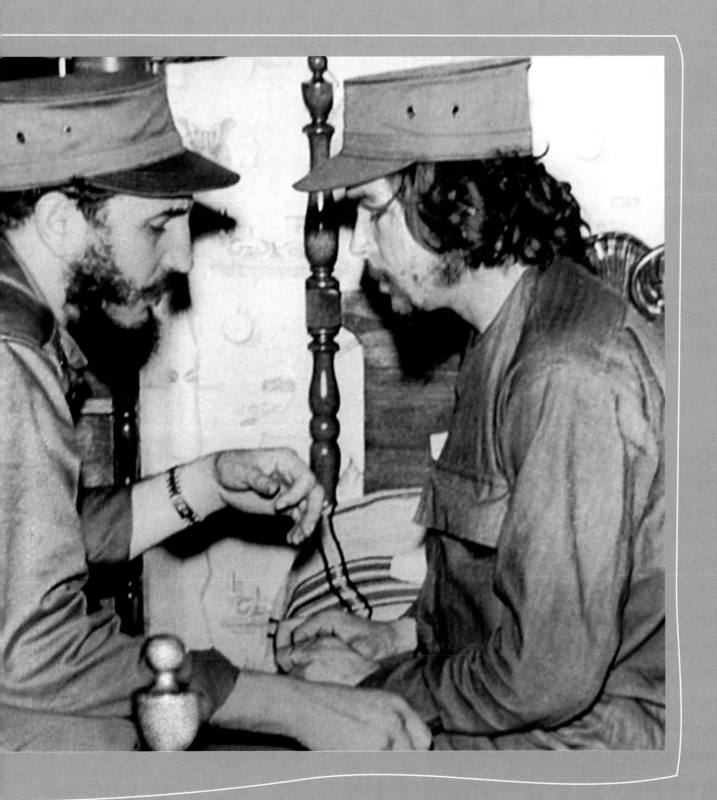

right: ROBERTO SALAS, *The First Day,* January 1961

In January 1961 the United States broke diplomatic relations with Cuba. This demonstration was held outside the U.S. Embassy, on the Havana waterfront. It marked the end of two years of uneasy relations.

How much was the Revolution improvised, and how much was it planned? There was without doubt a strong element of improvisation, but it is just as certain that the new leaders realized from early on that a confrontation with the United States would eventually come. Their desire for national independence was scarcely possible without a program of social reform—an agrarian reform and a campaign to improve the living conditions, education, and cultural level of the population. This in turn meant breaking the power of the large companies dominating the economy, which had supported and profited from the old regime. These companies were by and large U.S.-owned.

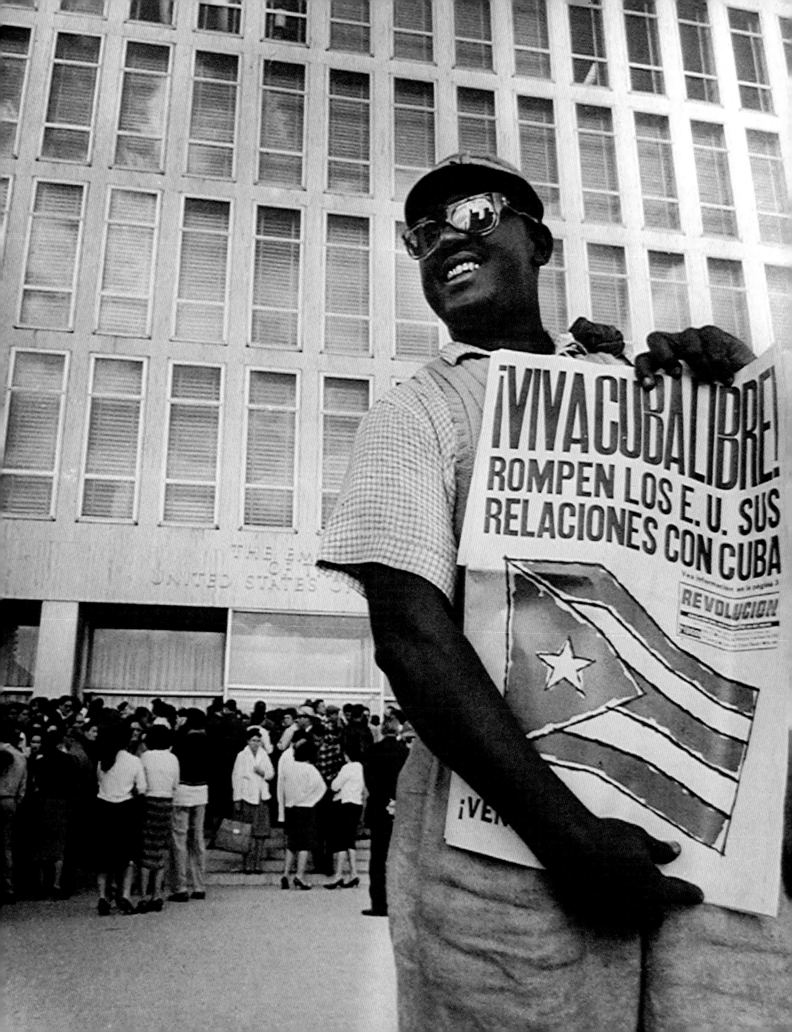

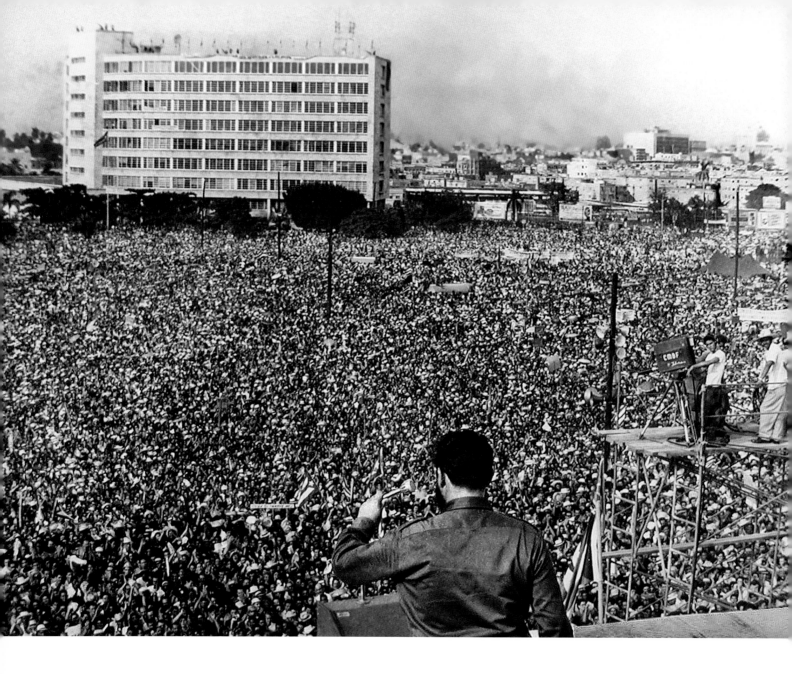

above: **PERFECTO ROMERO,** *The Second Declaration of Havana,* 1962

The "First Declaration of Havana" was made by Fidel Castro in September 1960. He announced that Cuba would establish relations with China and accept the Soviet Union's offer of missiles. By the time of this Second Declaration, Cuba was firmly within the Soviet camp.

right: **JOSE ALBERTO FIGUEROA,** *Demonstration against the Vietnam War,* 1974

This massive demonstration during the Vietnam War targeted President Nixon as "the Hitler of our age," portraying him with a little Hitler moustache.

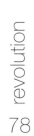

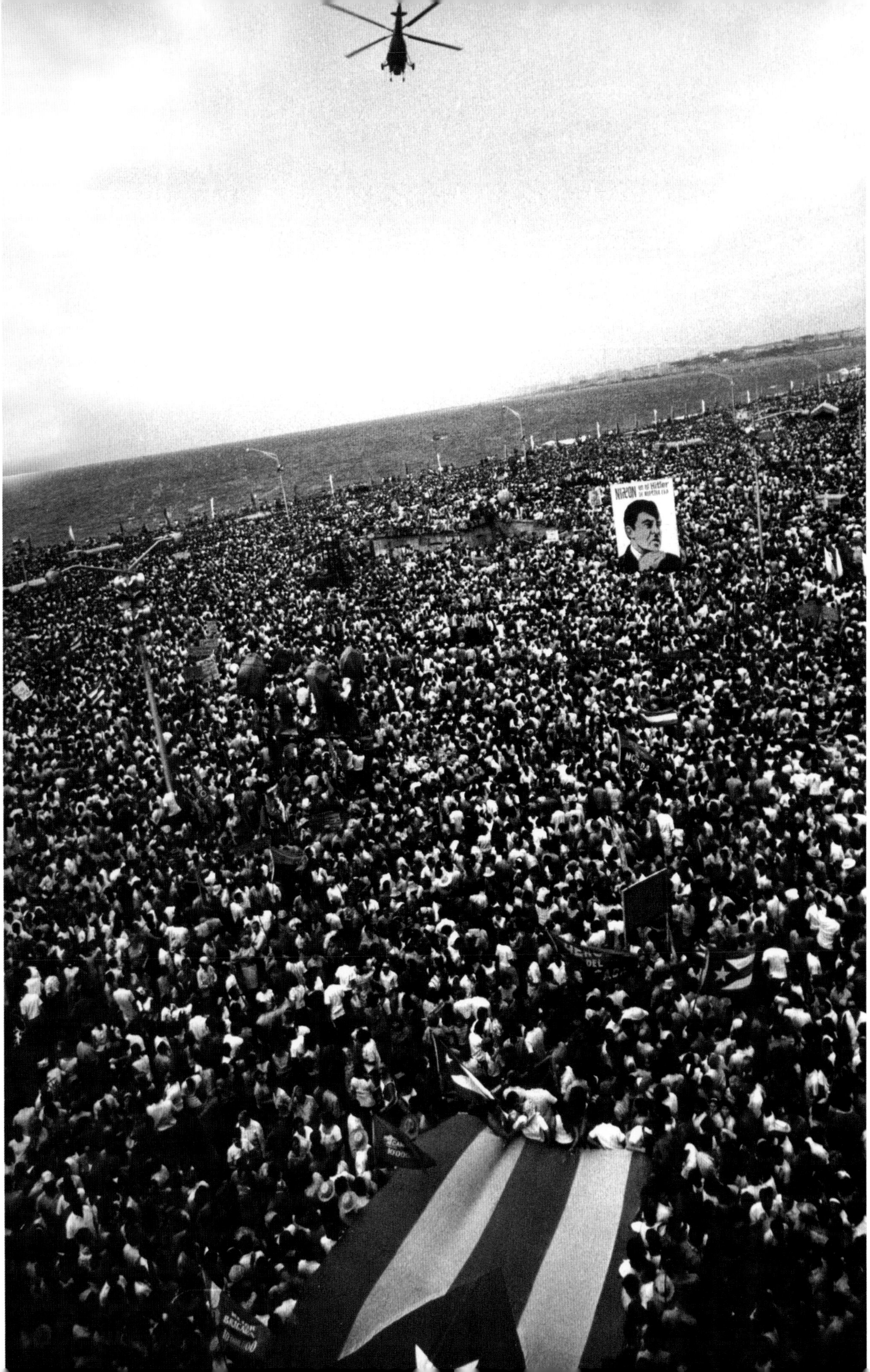
Hitler

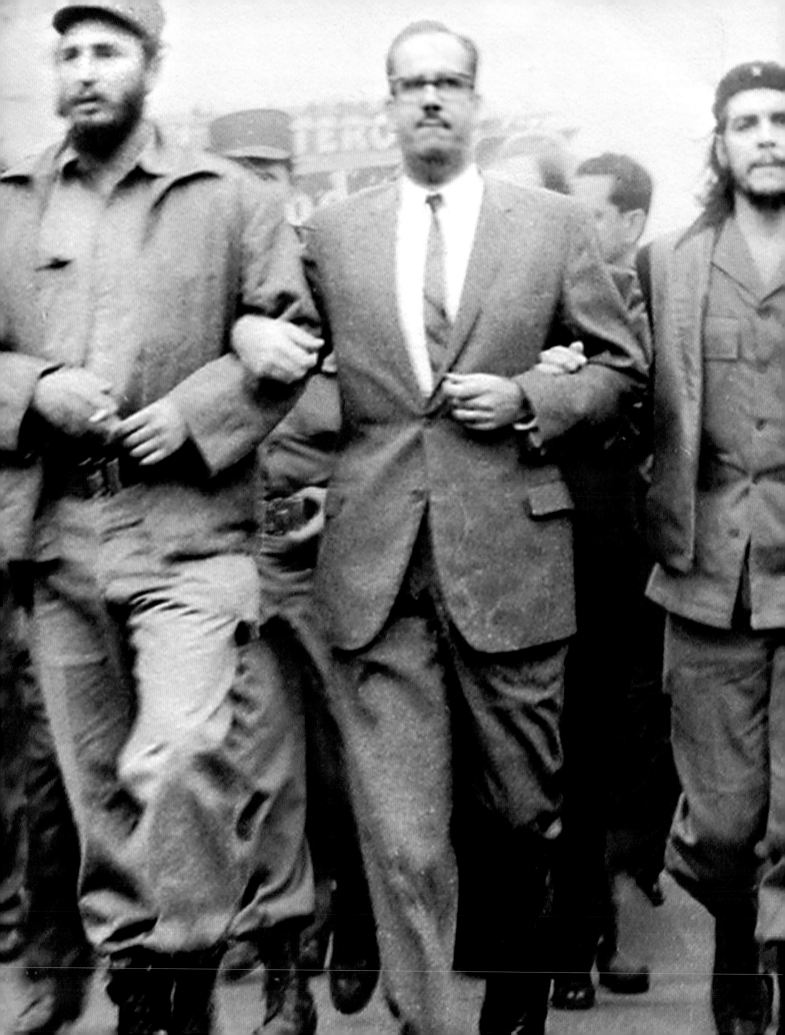

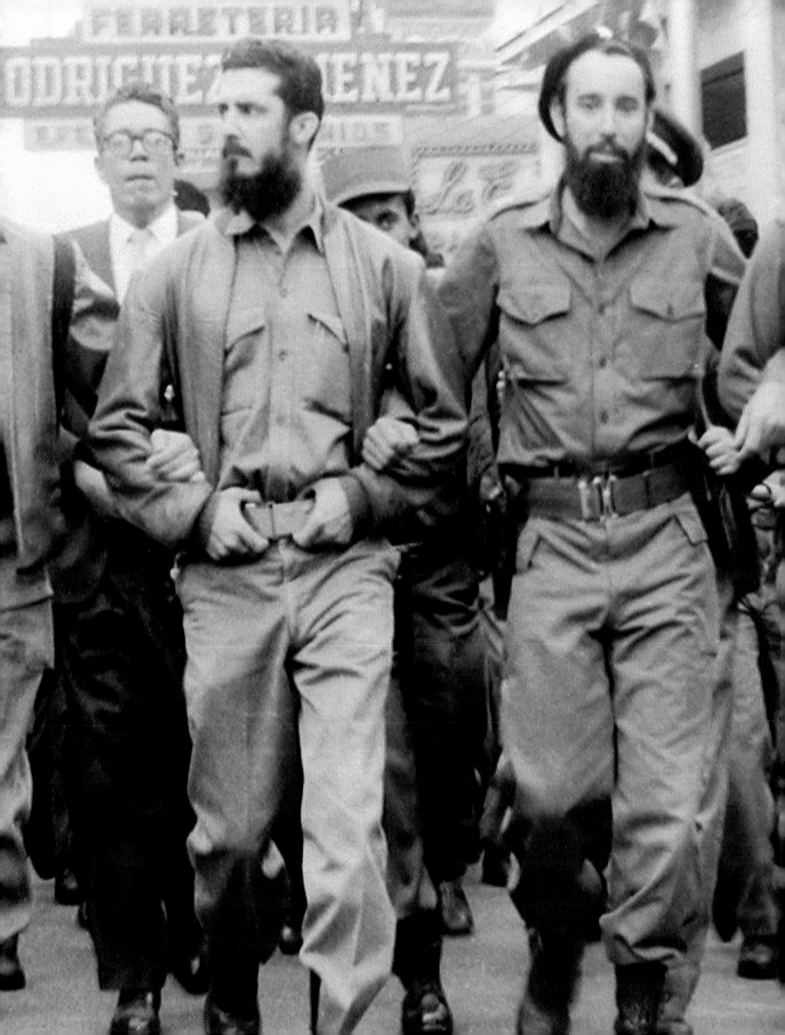

previous page: PERFECTO ROMERO, *March to commemorate the victims of La Coubre,* **5 March 1960**

This march was held to commemorate those who died when the French freighter *La Coubre* exploded in Havana harbor. It is led, from left to right, by Prime Minister Fidel Castro, President Osvaldo Dorticós, Industry Minister Che Guevara, and Labor Minister Augusto Martínez Sánchez. Osvaldo Dorticós remained President until a new constitution was finally adopted in 1976, after which Fidel Castro became both head of government and head of state.

right: PRENSA LATINA ARCHIVE, *Explosion of the French ship La Coubre,* **4 March 1960**

The French freighter *La Coubre*, with a cargo of Belgian weapons, exploded in a dock in Havana harbor on 4 March 1960. The blast was heard all over the city, and was followed by an even bigger second explosion. As many as a hundred people were killed—sailors, soldiers, dock workers—and several hundred others injured. The photograph was taken by an unknown Cuban who happened to be passing by.

Fidel Castro and Che Guevara both rushed to the port when they heard the first explosion, and were within a hundred yards when the second explosion occurred. Castro immediately accused the CIA of sabotage and coined the slogan Patria o Muerte!—Fatherland or Death!

next page: ALBERTO KORDA, *Che Guevara with Simone de Beauvoir and Jean-Paul Sartre,* **March 1960**

Che Guevara was President of the National Bank of Cuba at this time, and this photograph was taken in his office. A massive new building was under construction to house the Bank when the Revolution occurred, but Guevara had no interest in moving into it, saying that it could be better used as a hospital. It continues to be a hospital to this day—the Hermanos Ameijeras hospital, set back from the Malecón sea drive midway between the Hotel Nacional and the entrance to the harbor.

Jean-Paul Sartre, a fashionable French philosopher, was impressed by his meeting with Che Guevara, which lasted for several hours. After Guevara's death in Bolivia seven years later, Sartre wrote that he was "not only an intellectual but also the most complete human being of our age."

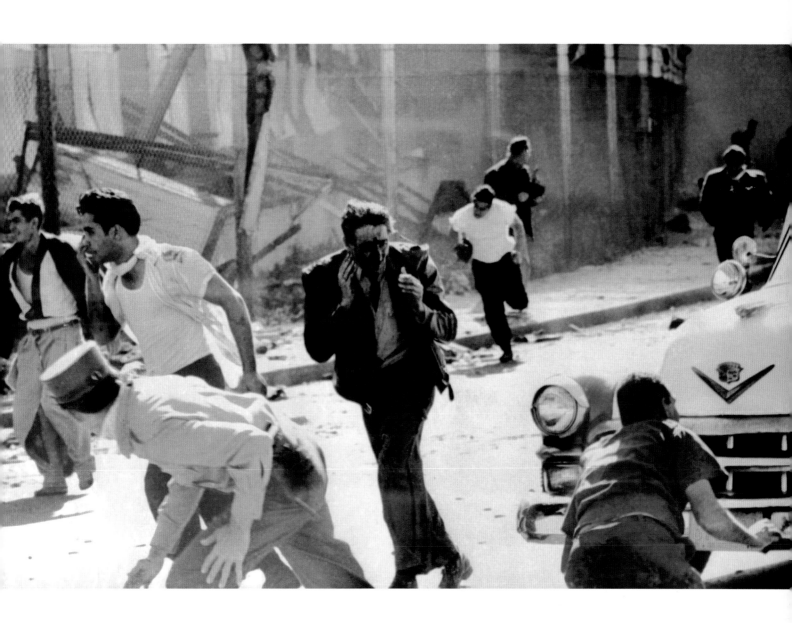

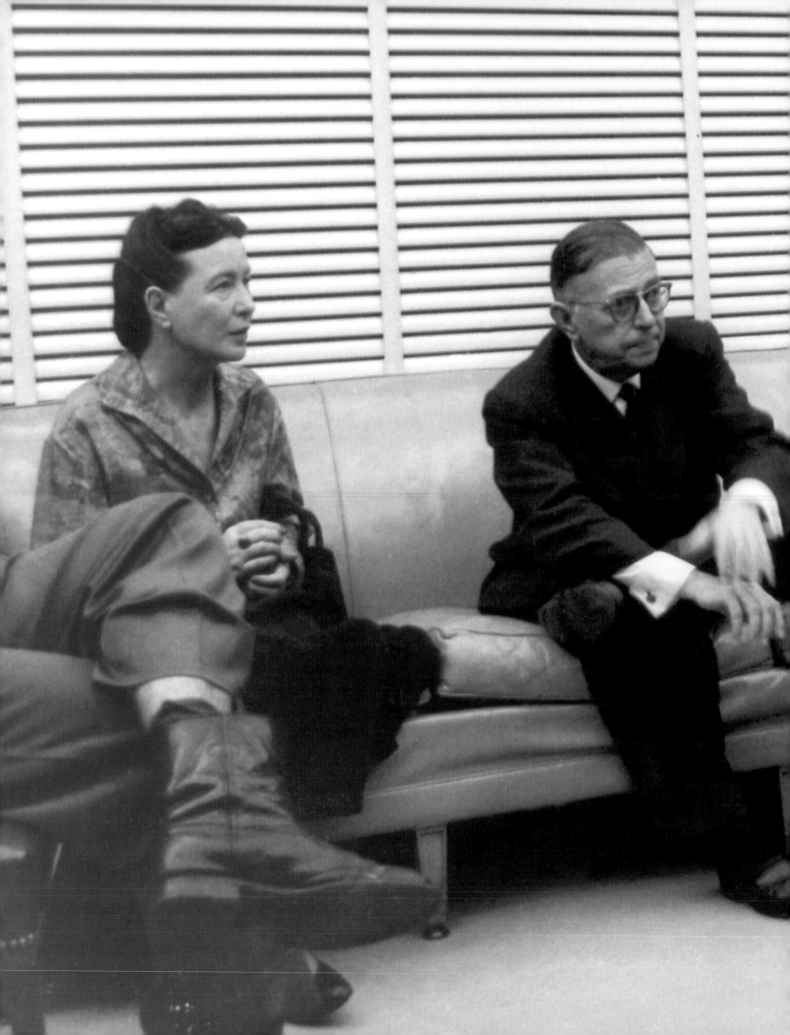

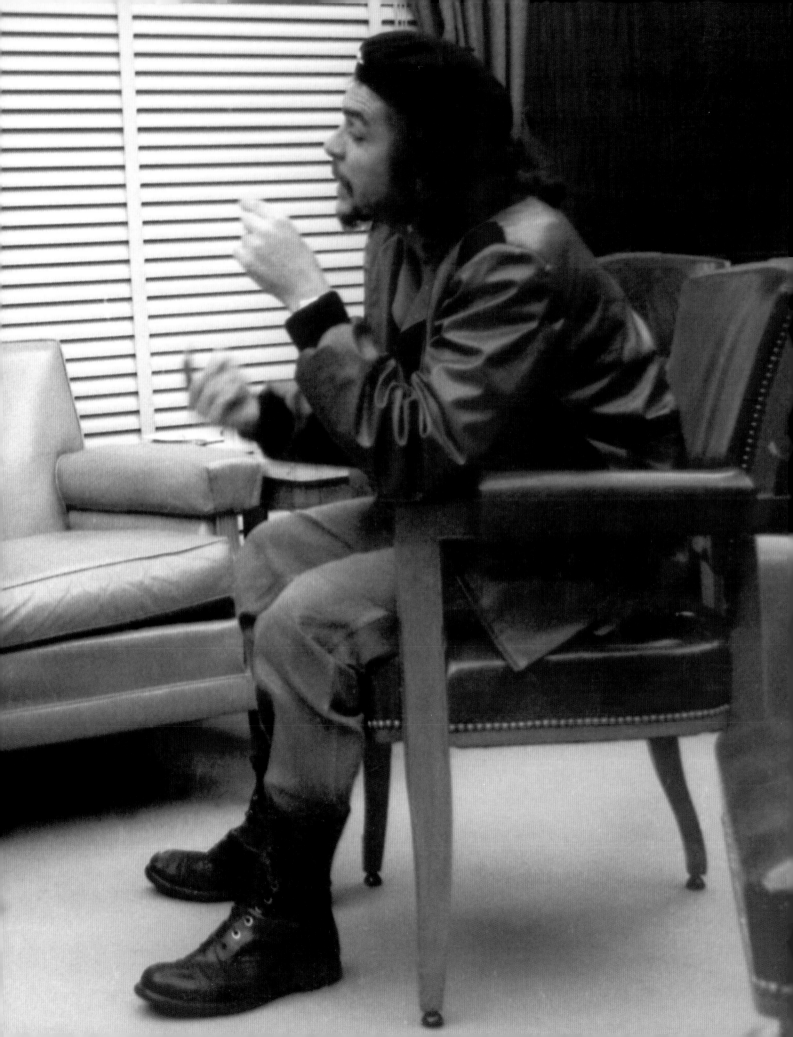

below: ALBERTO KORDA, *Fidel Castro with Simone de Beauvoir and Jean-Paul Sartre,* March 1960

Jean-Paul Sartre and his companion Simone de Beauvoir were among the earliest foreign intellectuals to visit Cuba, interested to witness a revolution in action. Their writings about Cuba encouraged many others to see it for themselves. Simone de Beauvoir was enchanted by the mood of the people.

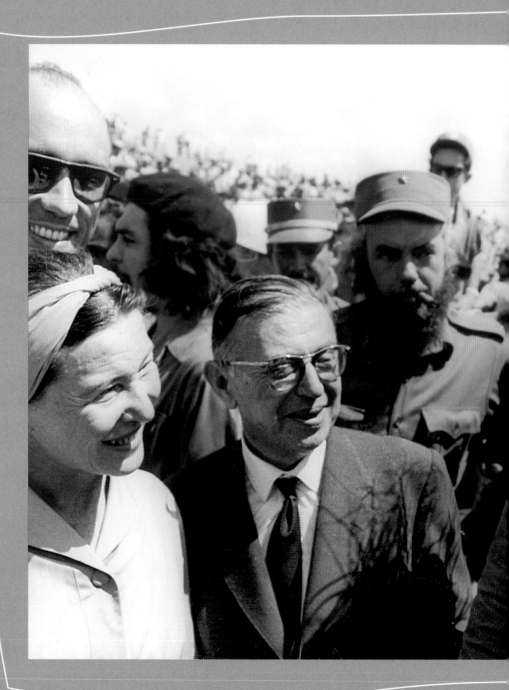

Young women stood selling fruit juice and snacks to raise
money for the State. . . . No machinery, no bureaucracy,
but a direct contact between leaders and people, and a
mass of seething and slightly confused hopes.

SIMONE DE BEAUVOIR

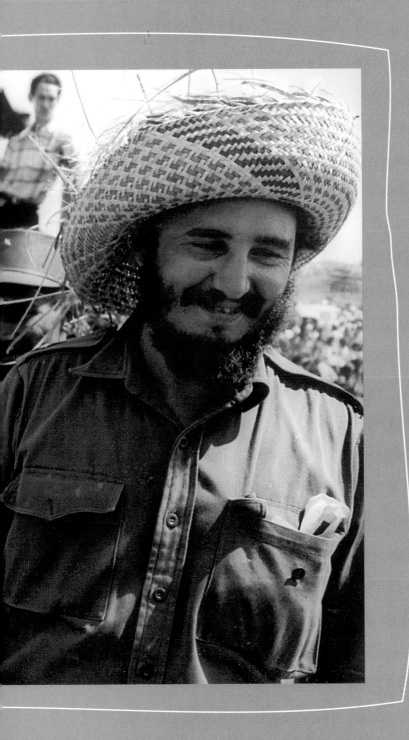

Once more I feel beneath my heels the ribs of Rosinante, I return to the path with my shield on my arm. . . . It is almost ten years since I last wrote you a farewell letter. . . . This could be my last embrace.

ERNESTO "CHE" GUEVARA, comparing himself to Don Quixote in his last letter to his parents, 1967

right: **ALBERTO KORDA**, *Quixote of the Lamp Post,* **17 May 1959**

The nonchalant figure atop this Havana lamp post is a peasant who quite probably had never visited the city before. How did he get there? One can only guess that he was used to climbing royal palm trees to harvest the fruit, which was traditionally fed to pigs to give their meat a special flavor. During the years when the Soviet Union sent industrially produced animal feeds to Cuba, climbing royal palms was a skill in danger of disappearing. But now once again royal palms all over the island are being climbed, and pigs are tasting as they should.

Why Quixote? Cervantes' novel was the first book published by the revolutionary government and was used in the mass literacy campaigns of the early 1960s. Che Guevara compared himself to Don Quixote in his last letter from Bolivia before he was killed. Perhaps it was the medieval ideal of honor the novel portrays that appealed so much.

The photograph was taken at the rally of peasants in the Revolution Square when the Agrarian Reform Law was announced. This law nationalized the large plantations, which were mostly foreign-owned.

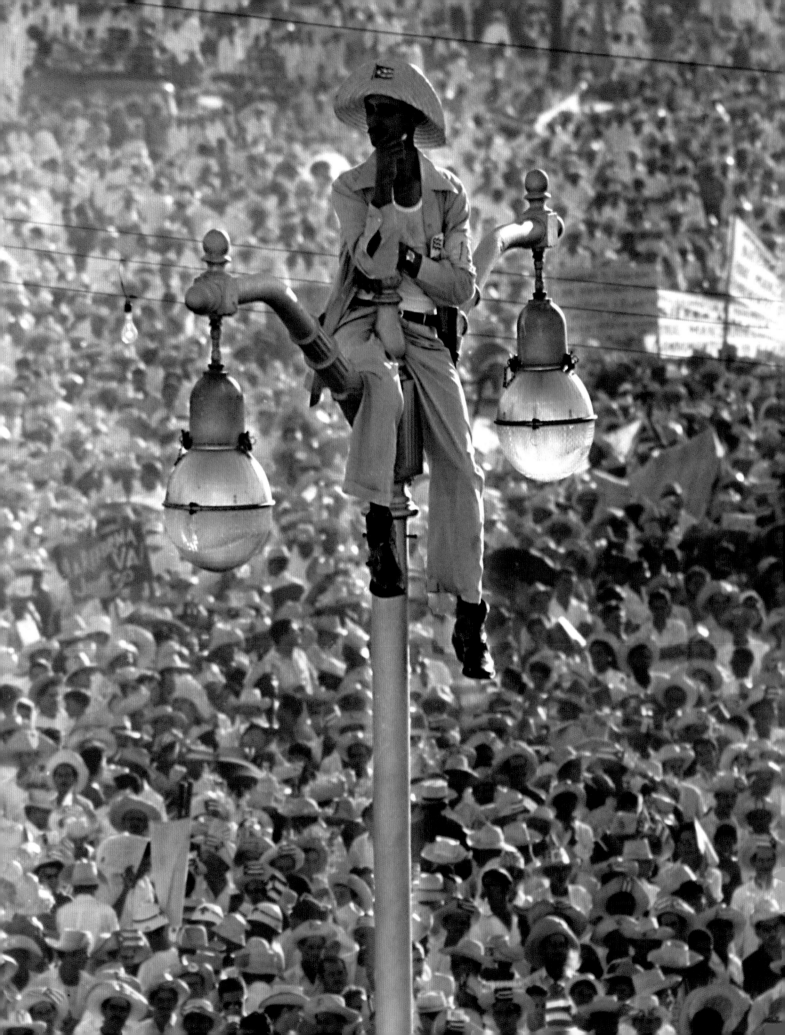

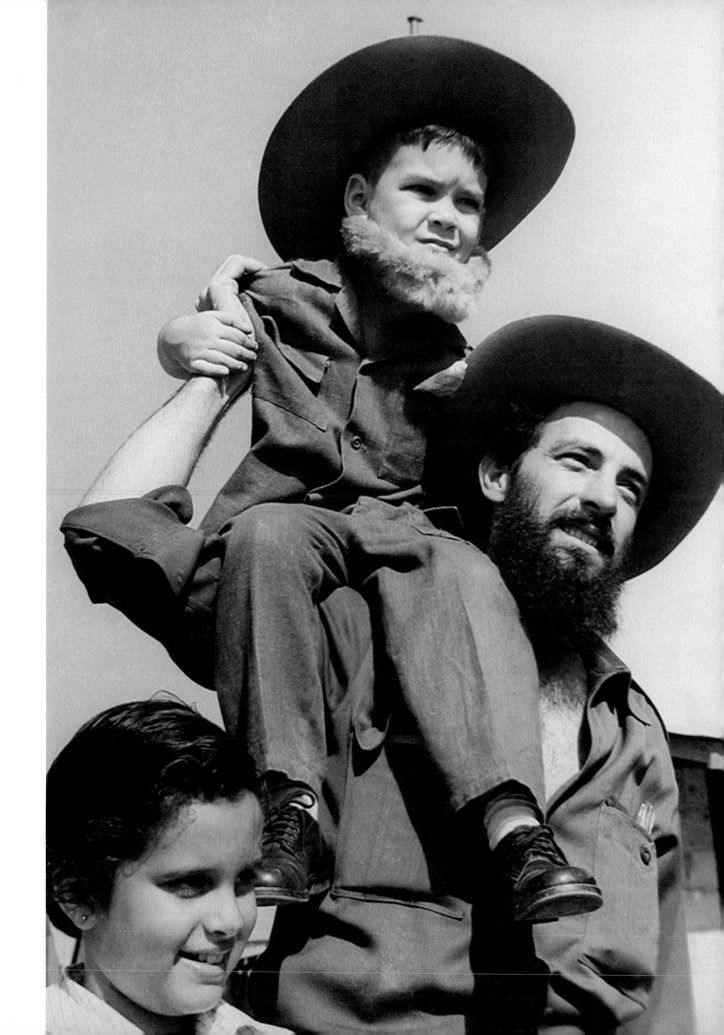

left: PERFECTO ROMERO, *Camilo Cienfuegos with children,* 1959

Camilo Cienfuegos was the son of exiles from the Spanish Civil War and was active in working-class protests against the Batista government from the mid-1950s, being wounded by police gunfire in one rally in December 1955. He left Cuba for California, where he married an American, but by August the following year he was in Mexico with Fidel Castro, planning an invasion of eastern Cuba.

As Fidel Castro's guerrillas consolidated their position at the end of August 1958, Camilo Cienfuegos, with a column of 82 men, and Che Guevara, with a column of 148 men, were despatched on foot to Las Villas province in the center of the island, a march that took six weeks. When they later moved on to Havana, it was Camilo Cienfuegos who entered the city first, on 2 January 1959. After the Revolution he held the role of army chief of staff, until the plane he was flying in went missing in October 1959. Neither the wreckage nor his body were ever found. Each year his death is marked by a ceremony throughout the island. Children throw flowers into the sea, or into a river, lake, or pond.

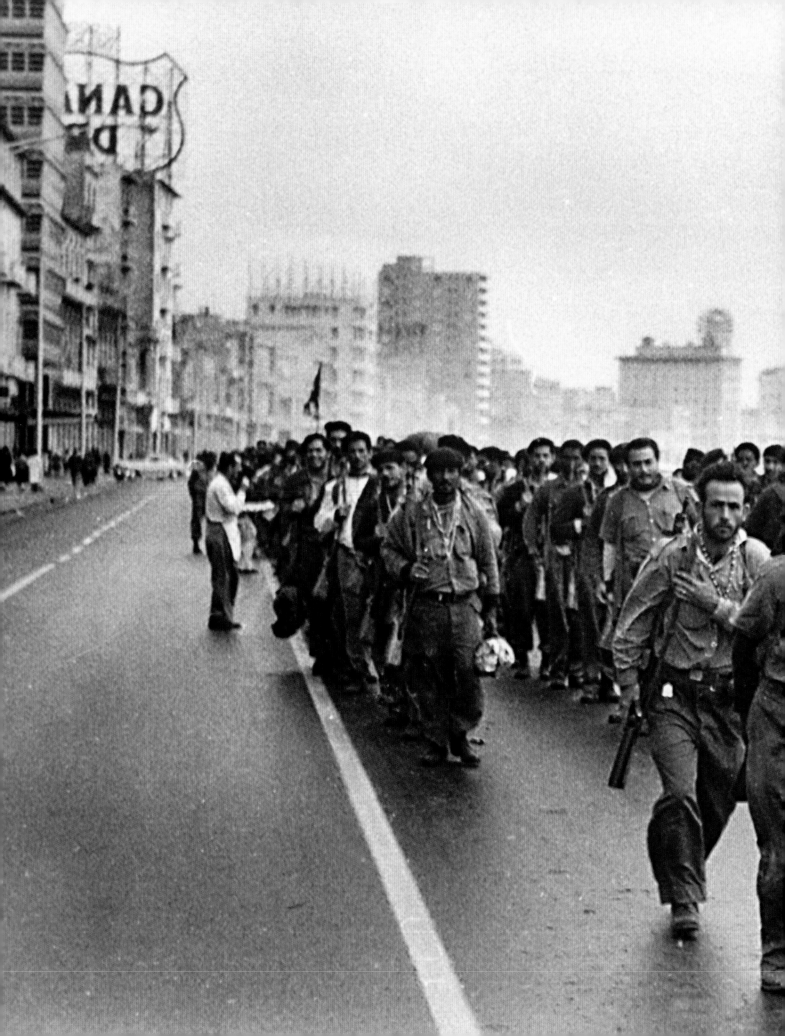

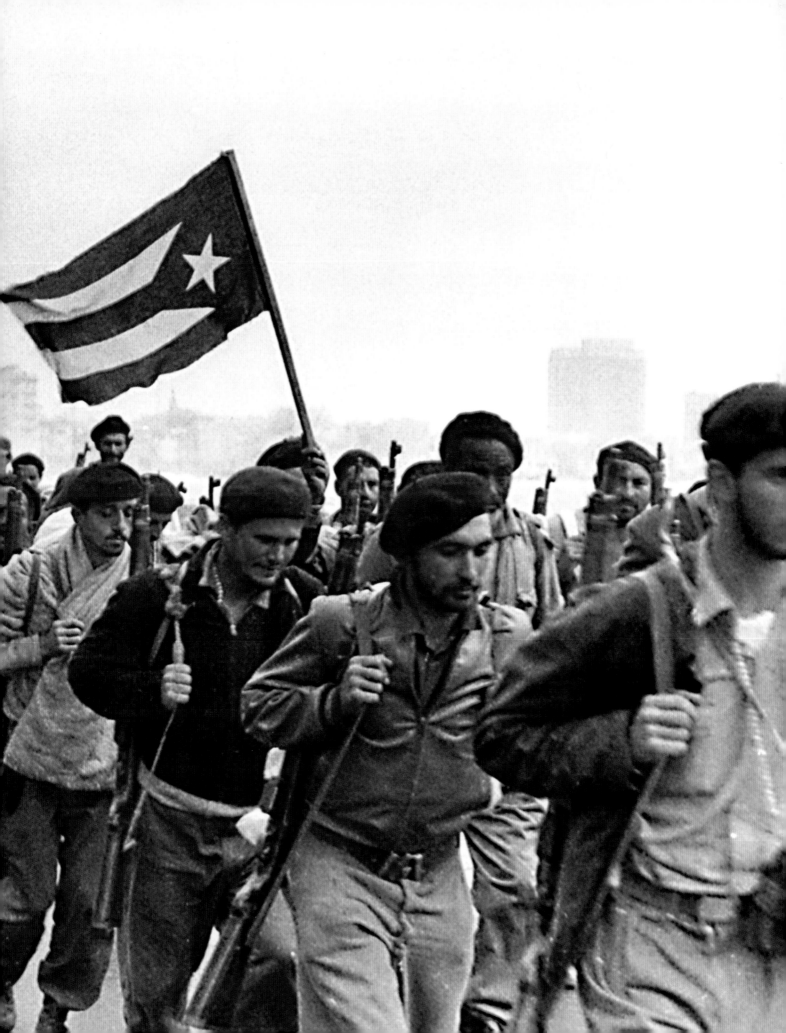

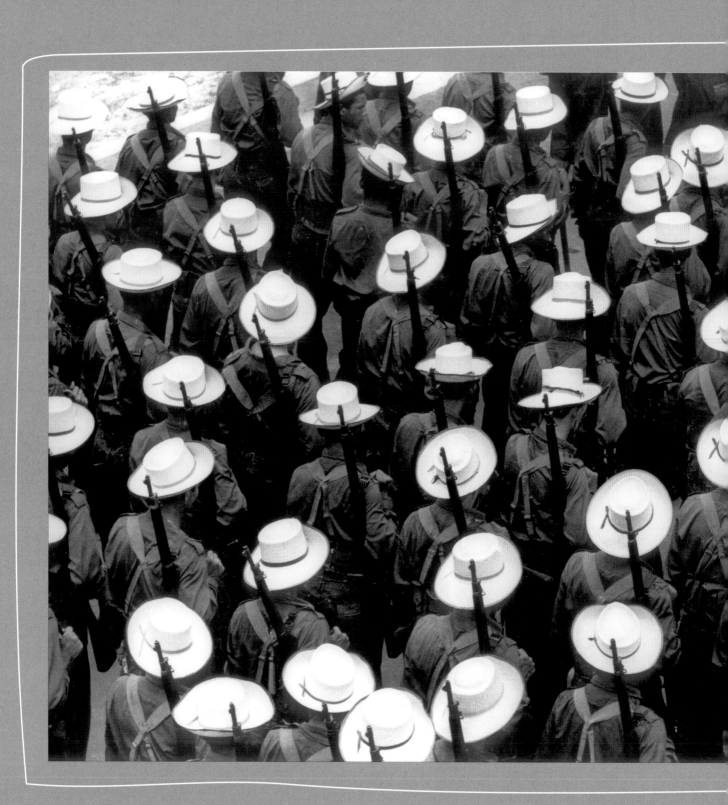

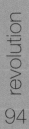

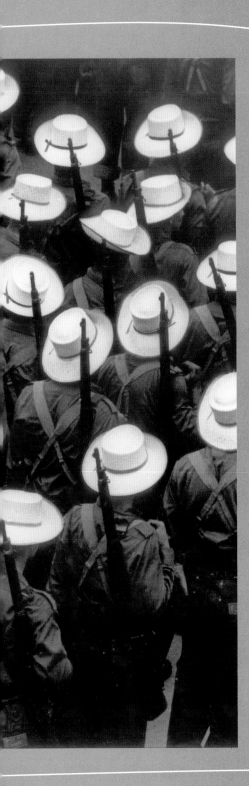

previous page: RAUL CORRALES, *Mobilization*, January 1961

January 1961 was the month the United States finally imposed its economic blockade, and Cubans realized that they had to survive as best they could. The militia was mobilized and placed on permanent alert. It was not long before they saw action.

On 15 April, eight U.S. planes bombed Cuban military bases. At the funeral the following day, Fidel Castro declared the Revolution socialist. As many as ten thousand men and women massed at the cemetery. The next day the invasion at Playa Girón on the edge of the Zapata Swamp near Cienfuegos (the "Bay of Pigs invasion") began. A ragged group of Cuban exiles and mercenaries supported by the CIA launched a half-hearted assault on Cuban government forces. Within three days 1,197 troops had been rounded up and captured. The Cuban government called the episode "the first defeat of U.S. imperialism in the Americas."

left: RAUL CORRALES, *Little Hats,* 1960

These militiamen wore sombreros as part of their uniform.

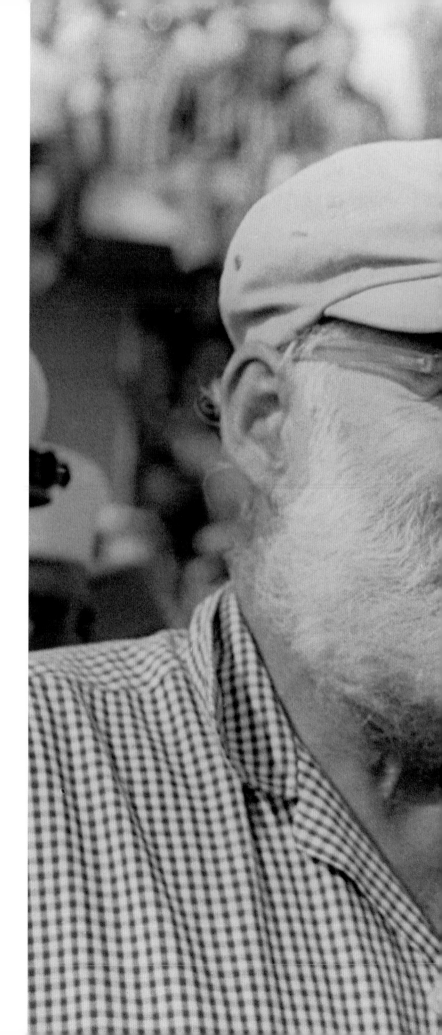

right: OSVALDO SALAS, *Fidel Castro and Ernest Hemingway,* **15 May 1960**

Fidel Castro was a great admirer of Ernest Hemingway but, although Hemingway lived in Havana, the two men met only once. At the award ceremony for the annual Ernest Hemingway Fishing Tournament in 1960, held at Havana's Barlovento Yacht Club, Fidel Castro was presented by Hemingway with the individual prize for catching the biggest blue marlin.

   Hemingway visited Cuba after he returned from the Spanish Civil War, and from 1939 he lived on and off at Finca Vigía in San Francisco de Paula, a suburb to the southeast of Havana. He kept himself apart from the internal politics of the country, and spent all of 1959, the year following the Revolution, outside Cuba. However, in a letter to a friend early in 1960 he wrote, "I believe completely in the historical necessity of the Cuban revolution. I do not mix in Cuban politics but I take a long view of this revolution and the day by day and the personalities do not interest me. . . . In the present situation there is nothing I can say that would not be misinterpreted or twisted. I have a terrible amount of work to do and want to be left alone to do it."

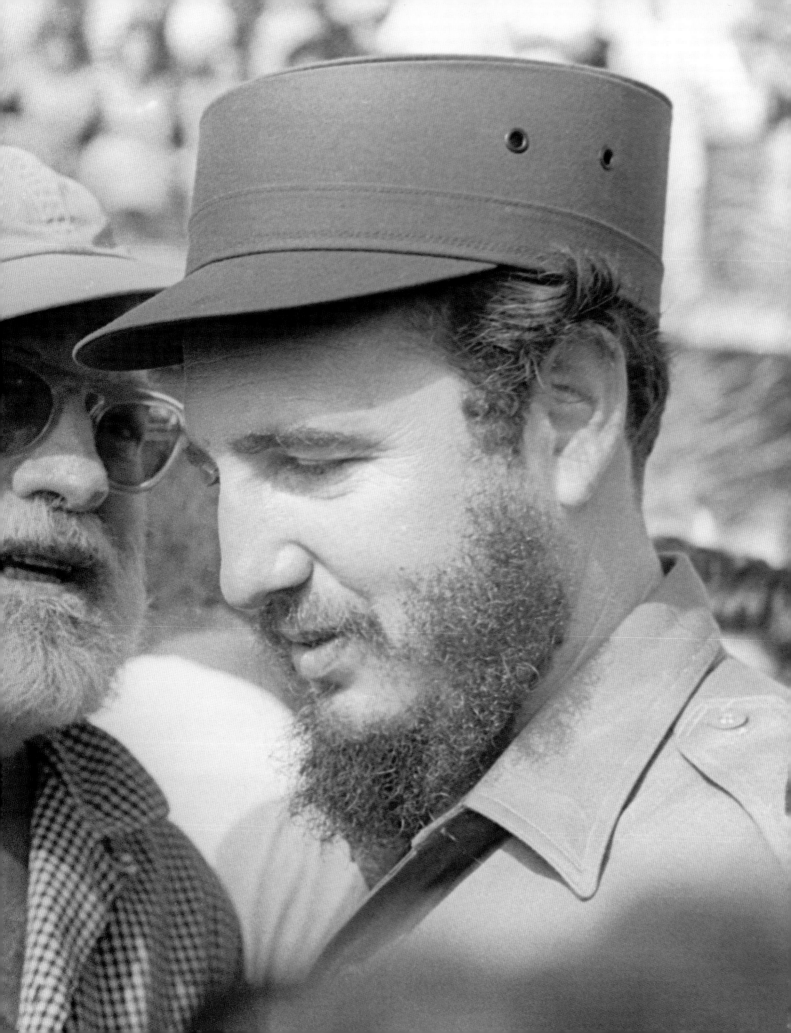

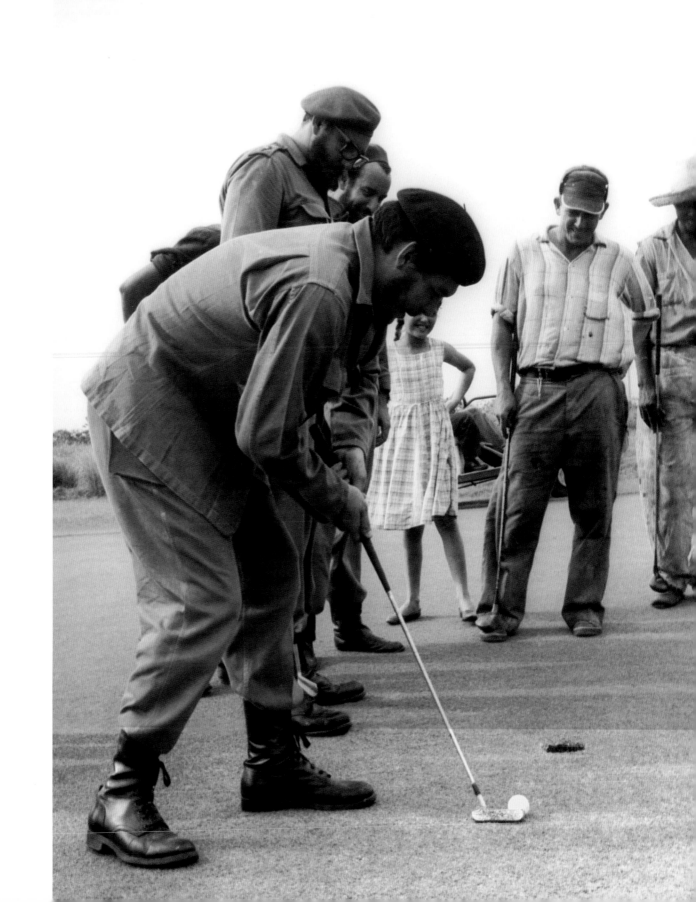

left: **ALBERTO KORDA**, *Che Guevara and Fidel Castro playing golf,* May 1960

This image of revolutionary guerrillas playing golf was intended to shock. The previous month Fidel Castro had taken an entourage of one hundred politicians and advisers to the United States, where he was the guest of U.S. newspaper editors. The visit was a public relations success. In New York Castro toured the United Nations, addressed a crowd of 30,000 in Central Park, and lunched with publishers, businessmen, and financiers.

But during the five days that Castro spent in Washington, President Eisenhower was out of town playing golf, and Castro had to content himself with meeting with Vice-President Nixon.

On his return to Cuba, Castro, who had never played golf before, organized a game with Che Guevara, who had played a little as a youth in Argentina. They invited the magazine *Revolución* to send their photographer Alberto Korda to record the event.

Korda clicked away happily until Che Guevara asked why he was wasting so much film. When Korda replied that he had plenty of stock, Guevara suggested that he should be more frugal in future, because he might find it hard to replace. Eight months later the United States imposed a trade embargo on Cuba.

next page left and right: **RAUL CORRALES**, *The New Rhythm Band,* 1962

These militiamen were not professional musicians, but workers who were mobilized during the October Missile Crisis and formed a band that gave concerts in the evenings.

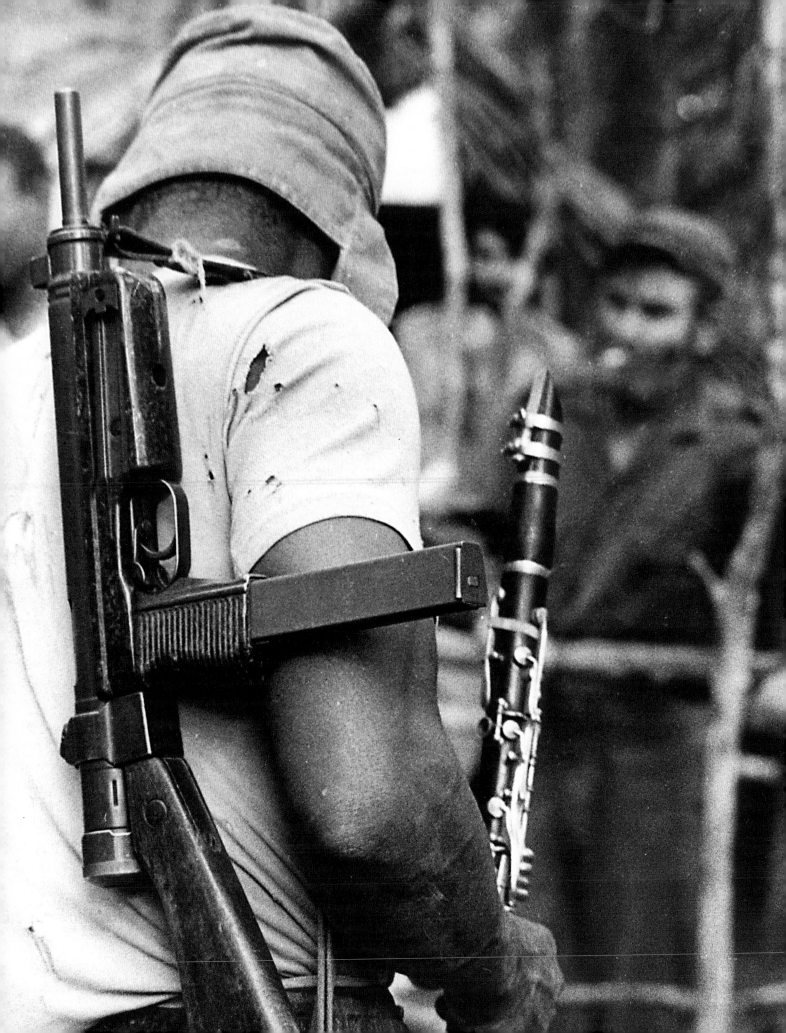

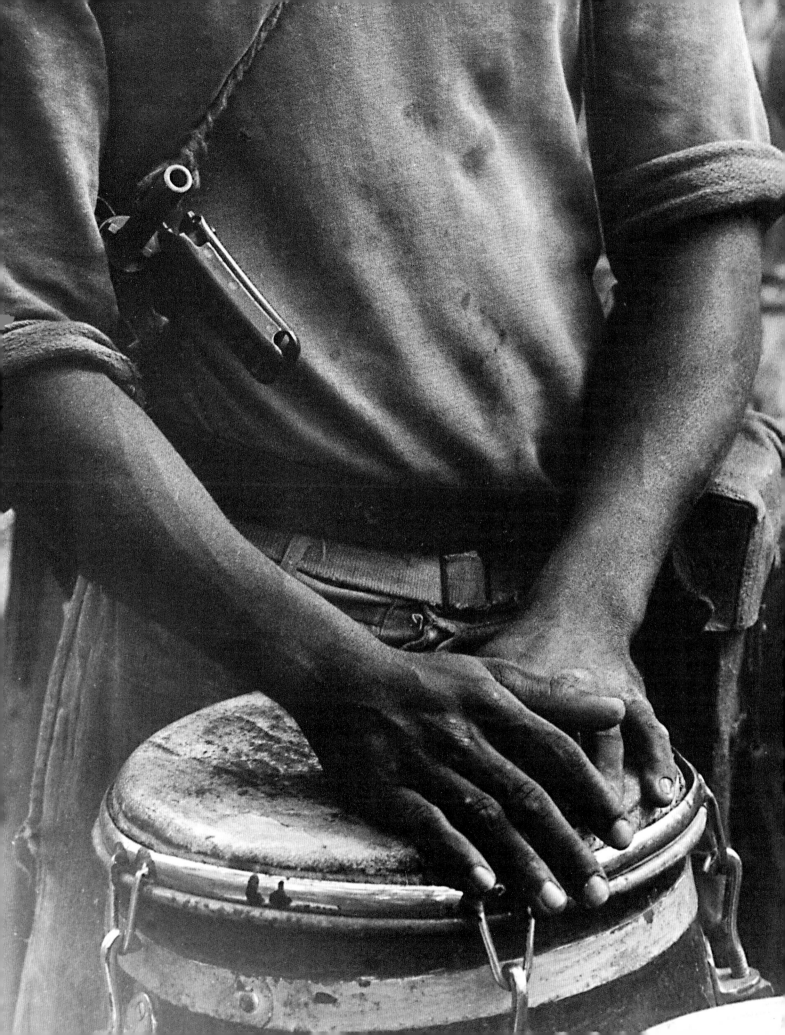

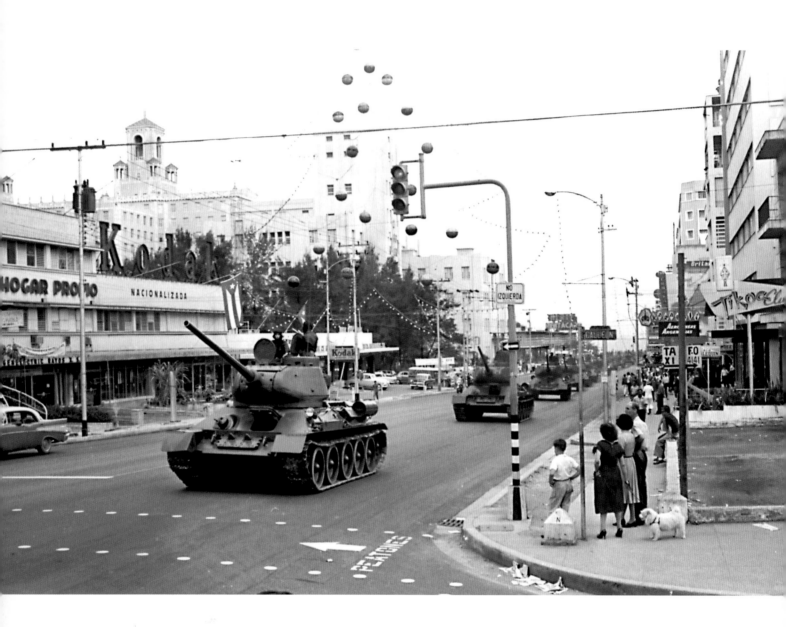

PRENSA LATINA ARCHIVE, *Tanks on Calle 23,* **1 January 1961**

Soviet-built tanks roll down Calle 23, the main commercial street in the Vedado district of Havana, in a show of strength. It is the second anniversary of the Revolution. To the left a sign announces that the Kodak photographic store has been nationalized. Behind, the Hotel Nacional, which by this time would have been mostly empty. Students from the university used to take rooms for a few pesos a night and party through the weekend.

The Soviet presence was so important for 30 years that it is remarkable that it has left so few traces. A decade after the collapse of the Soviet bloc, the Russians have melted away like ice in the tropics. There are still Lada cars on the streets, and Kamaz trucks, and the monstrosity of the Soviet Embassy continues to loom over the Miramar district like a huge bottle provoking jokes, but otherwise very little remains visible from those years.

next page left: **OSVALDO SALAS,** *Fidel Castro pitching baseball,* **1960**

next page right: **PERFECTO ROMERO,** *the "Los Barbudos" team,* **1959**

Fidel Castro has always been fanatical about sports, and creating a world-level Cuban Olympics team must have been one of his great satisfactions. It is said that when the Baltimore Orioles visited Havana in 1999 for the first baseball match between a U.S. professional team and Cuba in 40 years, Castro personally coached the national team. The U.S. team won, but only narrowly, and Cuba won the return match in the United States.

In his last year at the elite Jesuit college of Belén in Havana, Castro was proclaimed Cuba's outstanding high school athlete. His main sports were baseball, basketball, track, table tennis, and mountaineering.

After the Revolution, Castro put together his own baseball team with his colleagues, which they named *Los Barbudos*—the bearded ones. They used to play against the top Cuban teams. These matches would often go on into the early hours of the morning, until *Los Barbudos* could hit a home run or otherwise acquit themselves honorably.

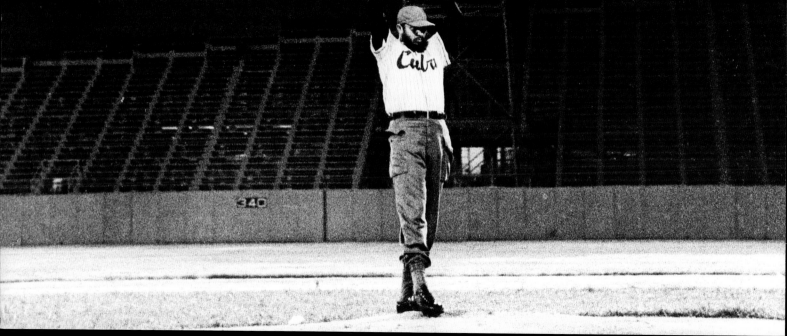

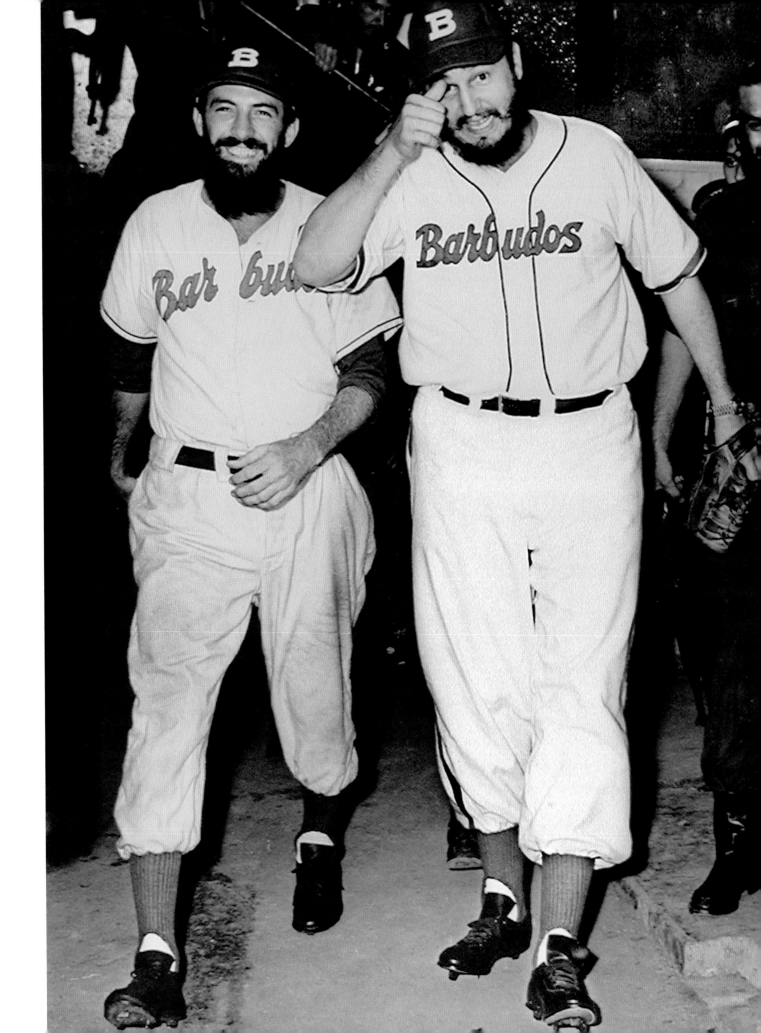

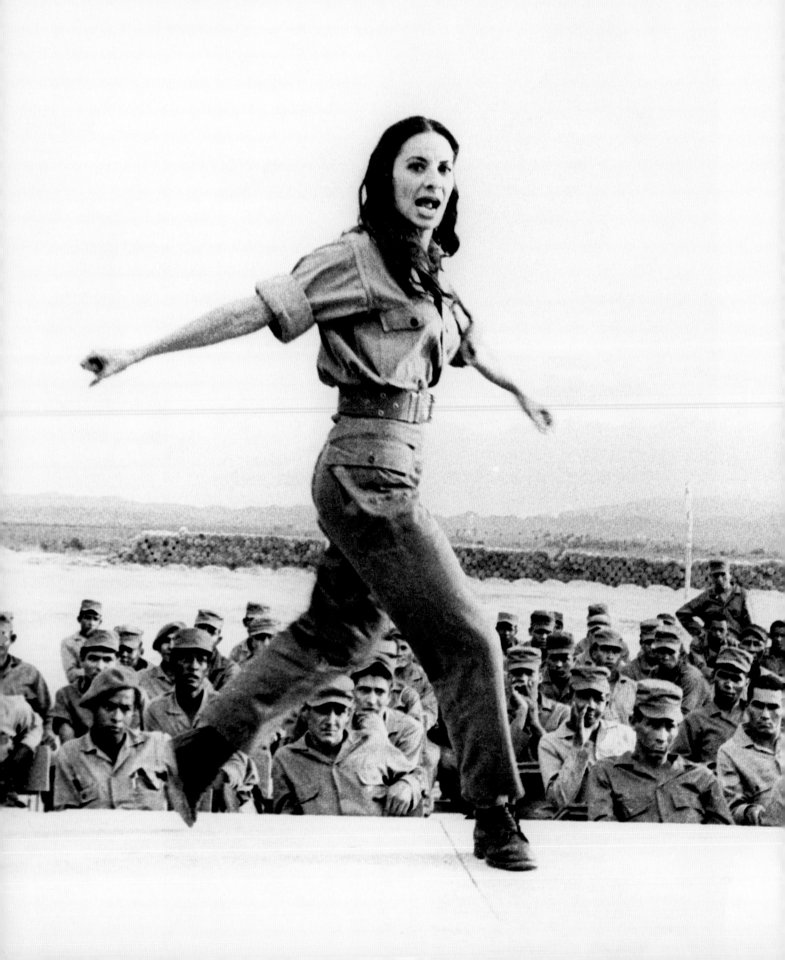

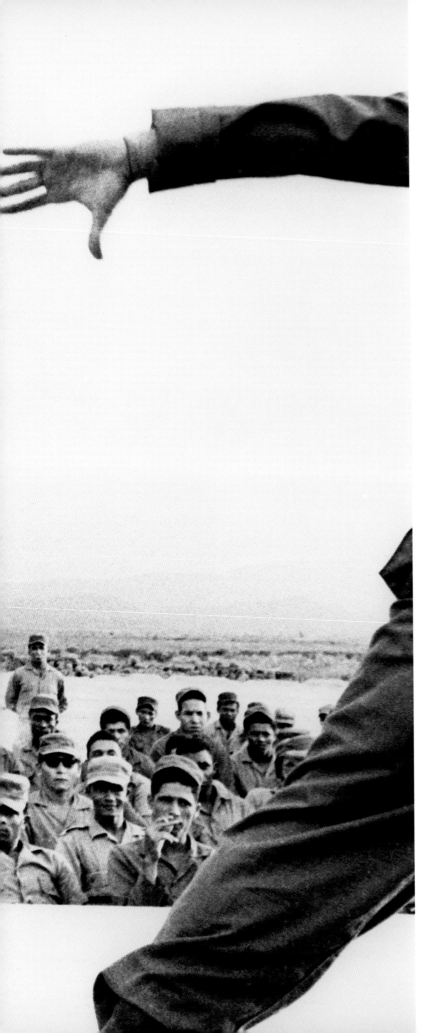

Alicia Alonso was already an international ballet star before the Revolution, better known in New York than in her own country. In Cuba everyone dances, but ballet was not popular with boys and the local ballet was in its infancy.

After 1959 Alicia Alonso returned to join the Revolution and set about creating a ballet company, which today is internationally renowned. She sought out athletic boys in the gyms of Havana and persuaded them that ballet was a noble art.

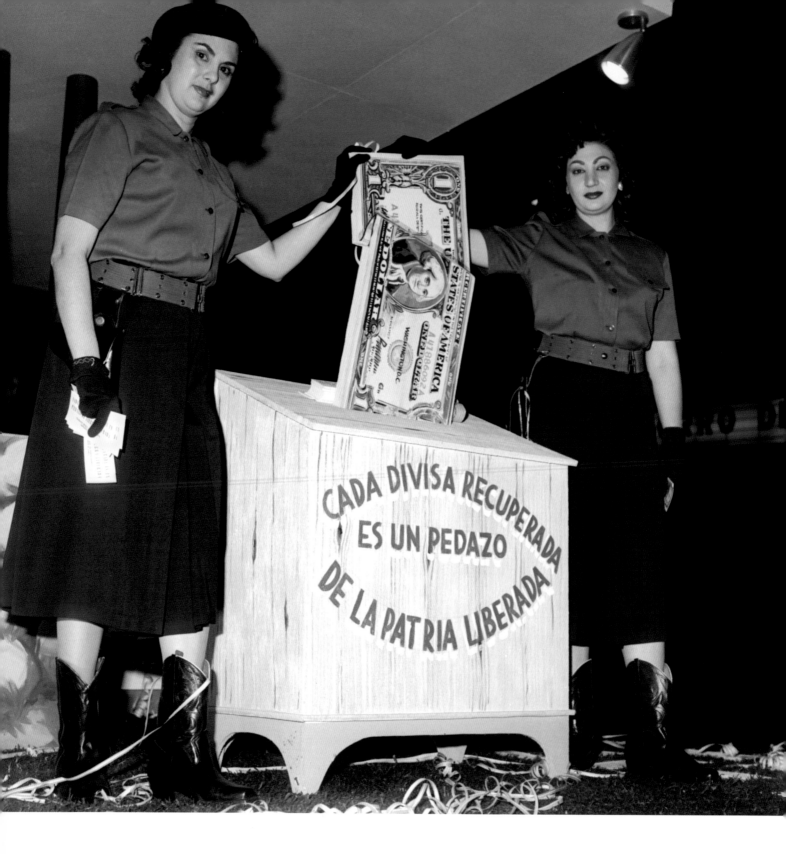

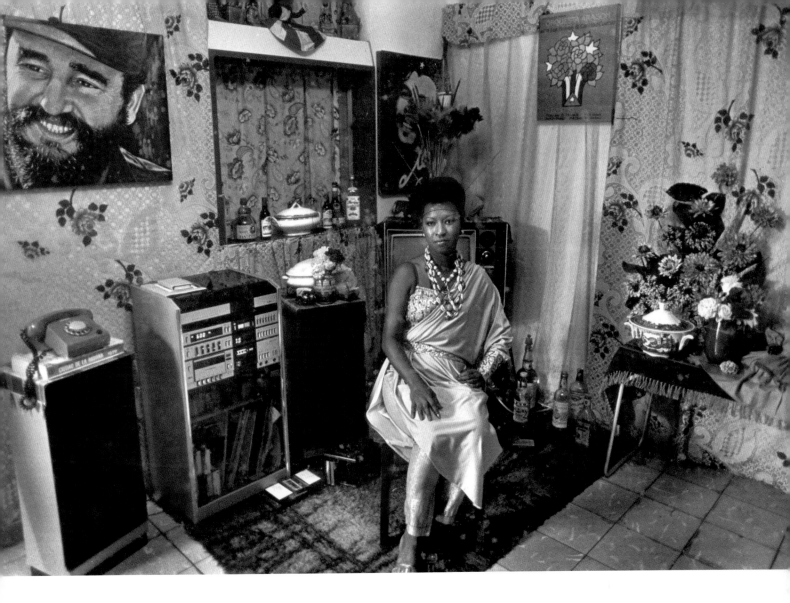

left: **PRENSA LATINA ARCHIVE,** *Militia Women during the Carnival,* 1964

The band played on, but dollars were in short supply. Ironically for a country struggling with all its might to escape from being a semi-colony of the United States, dollars were critical to secure essential imports that could not be obtained for Cuban pesos. And so the militia made publicity during the Carnival to encourage people to hand in dollars stashed away at home. "Each dollar recovered represents a piece of the liberated fatherland," reads the slogan on the mock treasure chest.

above: **MARIA EUGENIA HAYA (MARUCHA),** *Caridad Cuervo,* 1984

The baroque in its elemental form, eclecticism with a tropical flavor—Cuban culture is a culture of mixtures that throws out startling images. Among the plastic flowers and ceramics, images of political figures transformed into myths look out, a living part of daily life.

revolution

right: OSVALDO SALAS, *Fidel Castro and Yuri Gagarin,* **26 July 1961**

By 1961 Cuba was moving firmly into the Soviet camp. At the mass rally to mark the 26 July national holiday that year, the guest of honour was Yuri Gagarin, the Soviet astronaut who made history as the first person launched into outer space. One can imagine the psychological impact of this symbolism on a struggling nation. In the course of barely two years, Cuba had moved from being a semi-colony of the United States to being cast as its enemy. Here was proof that it had powerful new friends, who had beaten the United States in the great technological rivalry of the age.

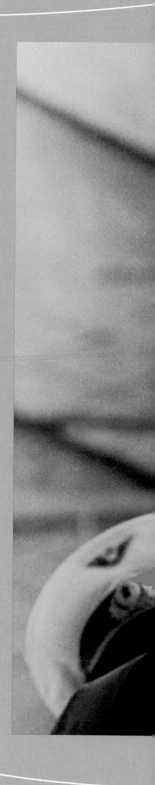

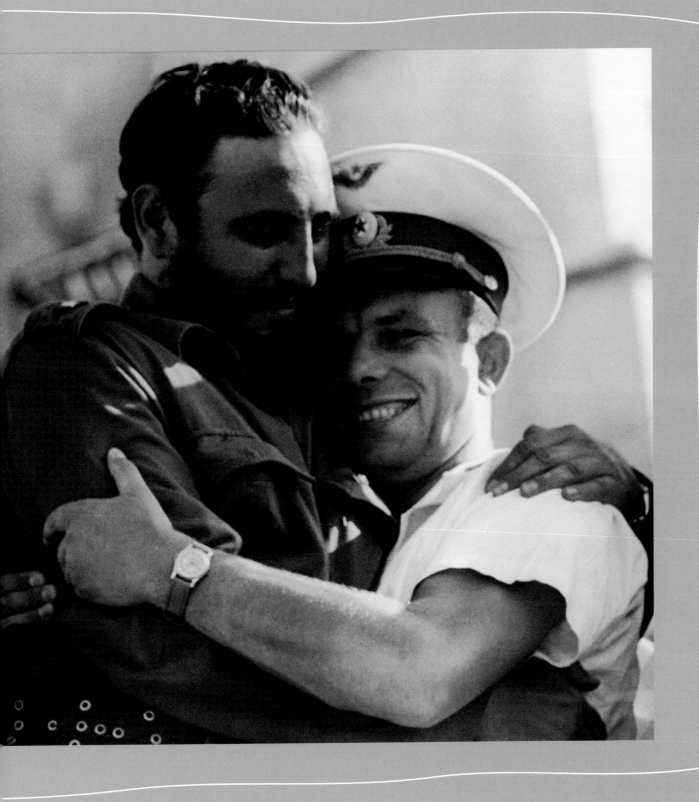

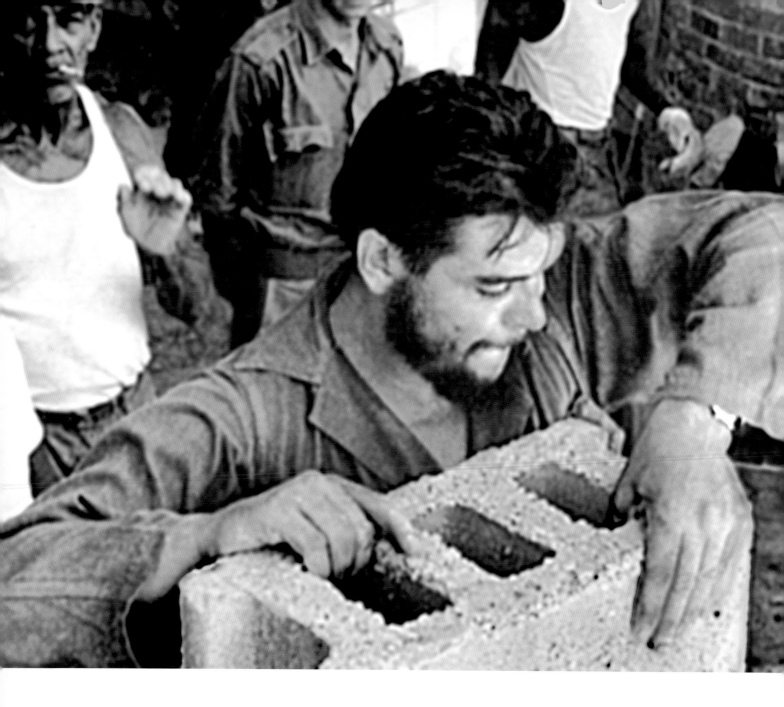

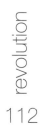
above: **PERFECTO ROMERO,** *Che Guevara doing volunteer work in construction,* 1962

right: **OSVALDO SALAS,** *Che Guevara as Minister of Industry,* 1961

Che Guevara got his hands dirty as Minister for Industry. There was probably little choice since Guevara, like the other young leaders, had little experience of organizing anything other than a revolution. As U.S.-made machinery broke down for lack of spare parts, the government turned increasingly to Soviet imports to keep the economy going. Enthusiasm and ingenuity had to substitute for the skills that left Cuba as the middle classes packed their bags for a new life in Miami.

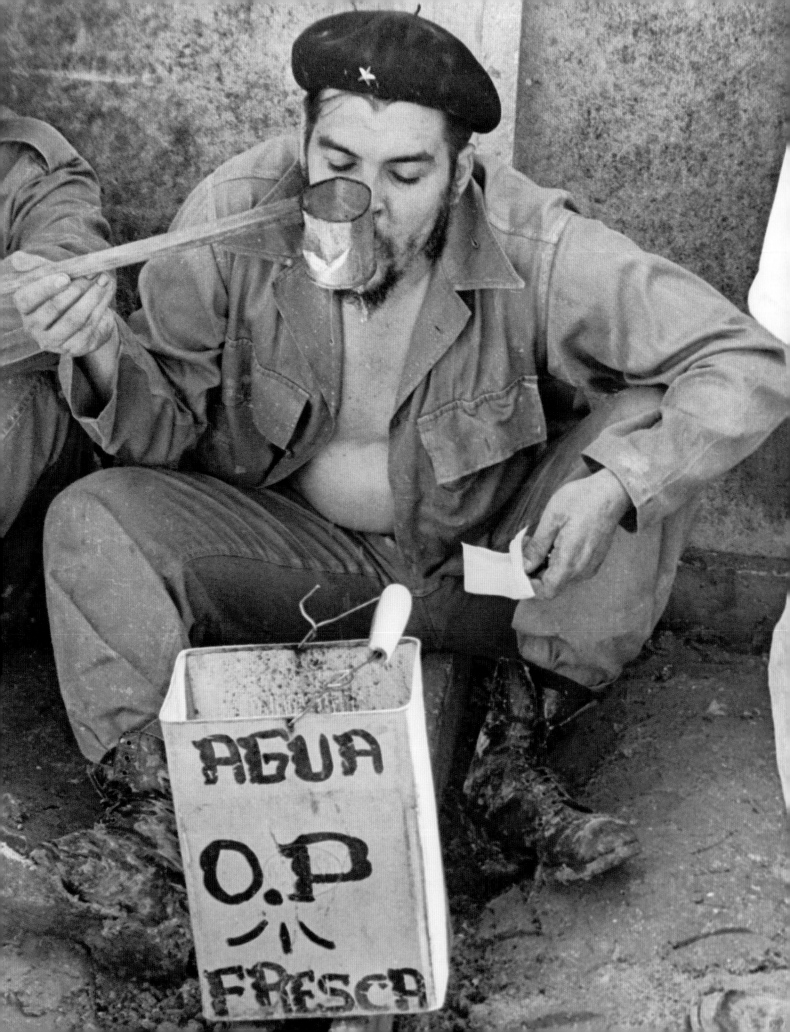

AGUA

O.P

FRESCA

Let me say, at the risk of appearing ridiculous, that the true revolutionary is guided by great feelings of love. . . . One of the great dramas of a revolutionary leader arises from his need to combine a passionate spirit with a cold mind and to take sad decisions without flinching.

CHE GUEVARA, from *SOCIALISM AND MAN IN CUBA*

right: OSVALDO SALAS, *Che Guevara poster behind Cuban flag,* **1968**

After his death trying to launch another revolution in Bolivia in 1967, Che Guevara's image was displayed frequently in public places, as it has been ever since.

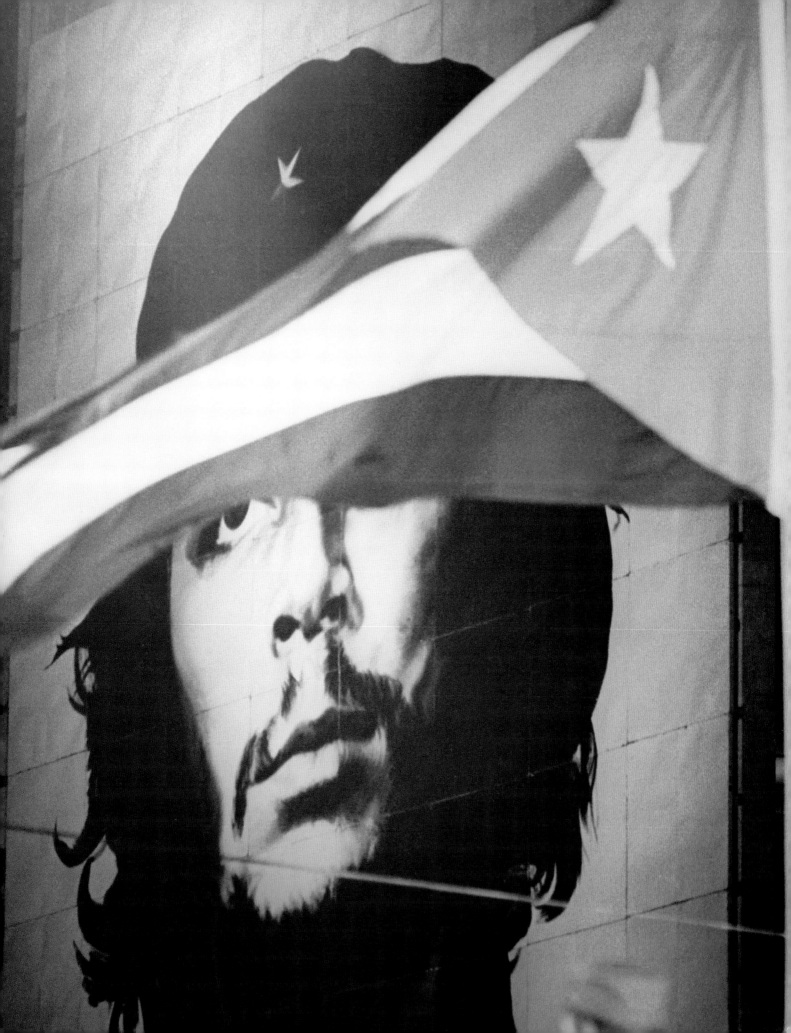

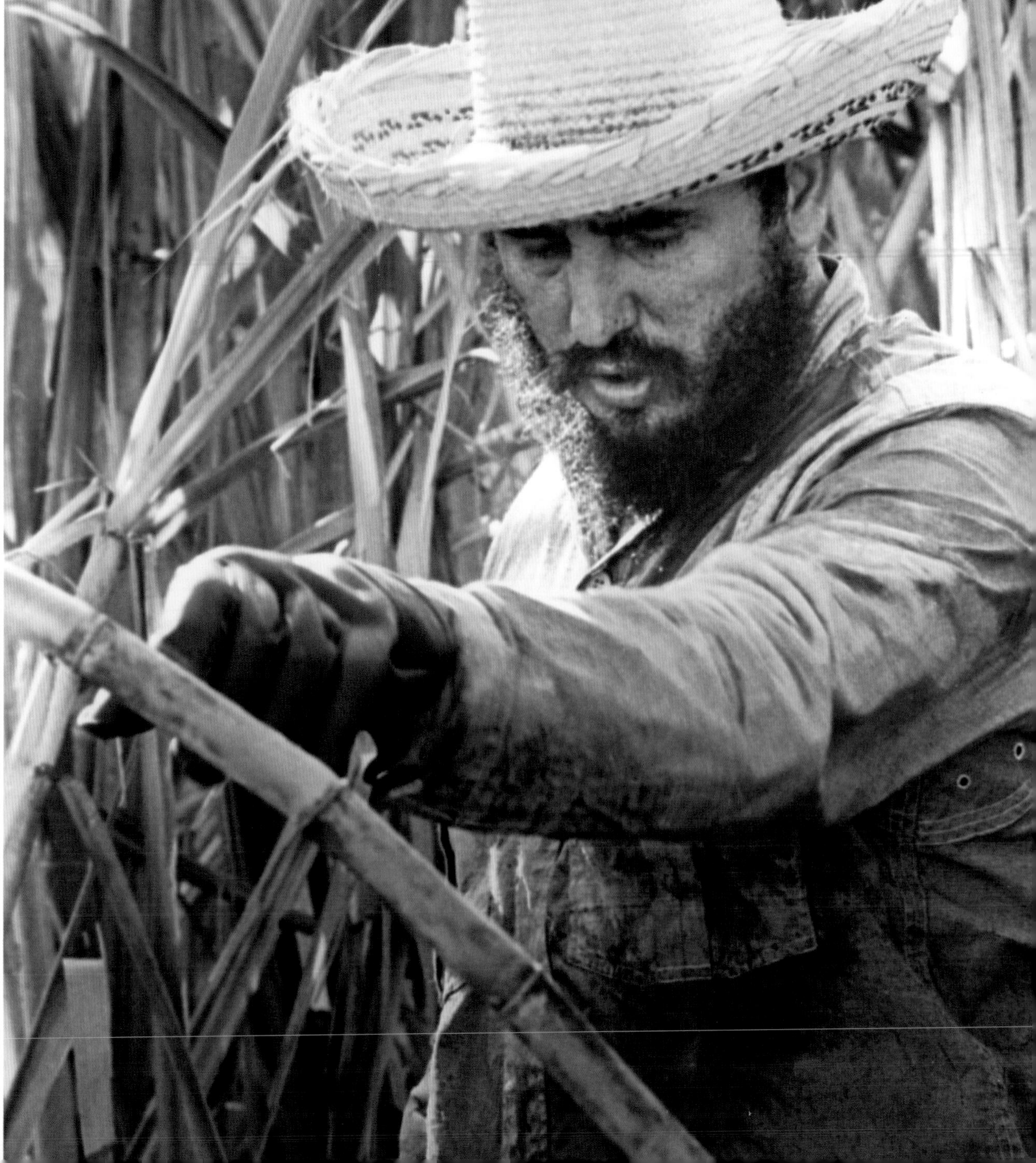

left: **OSVALDO SALAS**, *Fidel Castro cutting sugar cane*, 1970

Fidel Castro's political style since his student days has been to stay close to his supporters, listening to them and leading by example. On different occasions he spent hours at a time in the fields cutting sugar cane. In 1970, at a very difficult time for the country economically, he announced the goal of achieving a national sugar harvest of 10 million tons, an unheard-of target in Cuba. In order to achieve it, people and resources were diverted from other tasks and large parts of the economy virtually ground to a halt. Fidel Castro later took the blame personally for what he admitted had been a disastrous policy.

below: **ALBERTO KORDA**, *Fidel Castro in a jeep with parasol,* 1960

The popularity of the Revolution from the early years had much to do with the high level of direct contact between the leaders and the ordinary people. Fidel Castro, hated and demonized by his enemies, established a strong personal bond with his supporters.

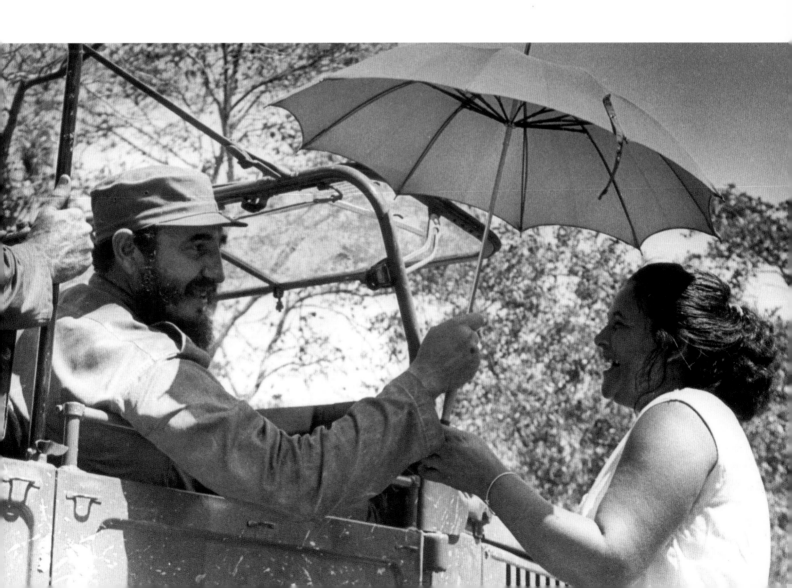

left: OSVALDO SALAS, *Celia Sánchez*, 1979

There has been just one woman who has worked at the highest levels of the Cuban government since the Revolution—Celia Sánchez Manduley. She held the position of executive secretary of the Council of Ministers and was a member of the Central Committee of the Communist Party.

In addition to this formal responsibility she was for 23 years, until her death from lung cancer in 1980, Fidel Castro's devoted friend and aide. Five years older than Castro, she never married, and she informally occupied the role of the "first lady" of the Revolution. She was much loved by ordinary people for making herself available to them and for giving social problems her personal attention. She developed many social and cultural projects, including the Coppelia Ice Cream Park, the art schools (now the Higher Institute for the Arts), Lenin Park, and the Guamá tourism center.

Celia Sánchez was one of five daughters of a doctor in the southeast of the island, in what is today the province of Granma. Because of her knowledge of the region and the people who lived in the mountains of the Sierra Maestra, she was one of the main organizers of the network of peasants that provided logistical support to the guerrilla movement led by Castro. Castro met her when she was 36 years old, three months after his revolutionary band landed in the east of the island from Mexico in December 1956. Since her death in 1980, no woman has appeared at his side on the podium at political rallies.

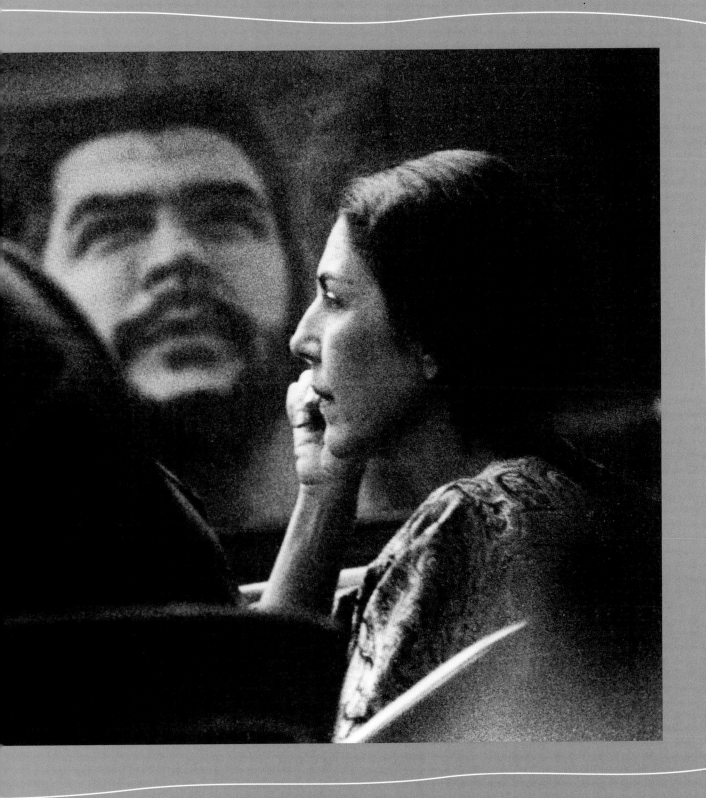

I shall bring back a great many Havana cigars, some of which can be laid down in the cellars of 35 Cumberland Place.

SIR WINSTON CHURCHILL in a letter to his mother, October 1895

right: OSVALDO SALAS, *Fidel Castro with cigar,* **1976**

The fingers, the nose, the beard. . . . Nothing more is necessary to identify the subject. But the cigar? Fidel Castro, like most of the early revolutionary leaders, was famous for smoking Cuban cigars. A new cigar was even created for him, the Cohiba. However, in 1980, after the death of his close friend and confidante Celia Sánchez from lung cancer, he gave up smoking and launched a national anti-smoking campaign. Sir Winston Churchill, who first visited Havana in 1895 as a war correspondent, was perhaps the most famous smoker of Havanas. The largest size of Havana cigar is known as a Churchill.

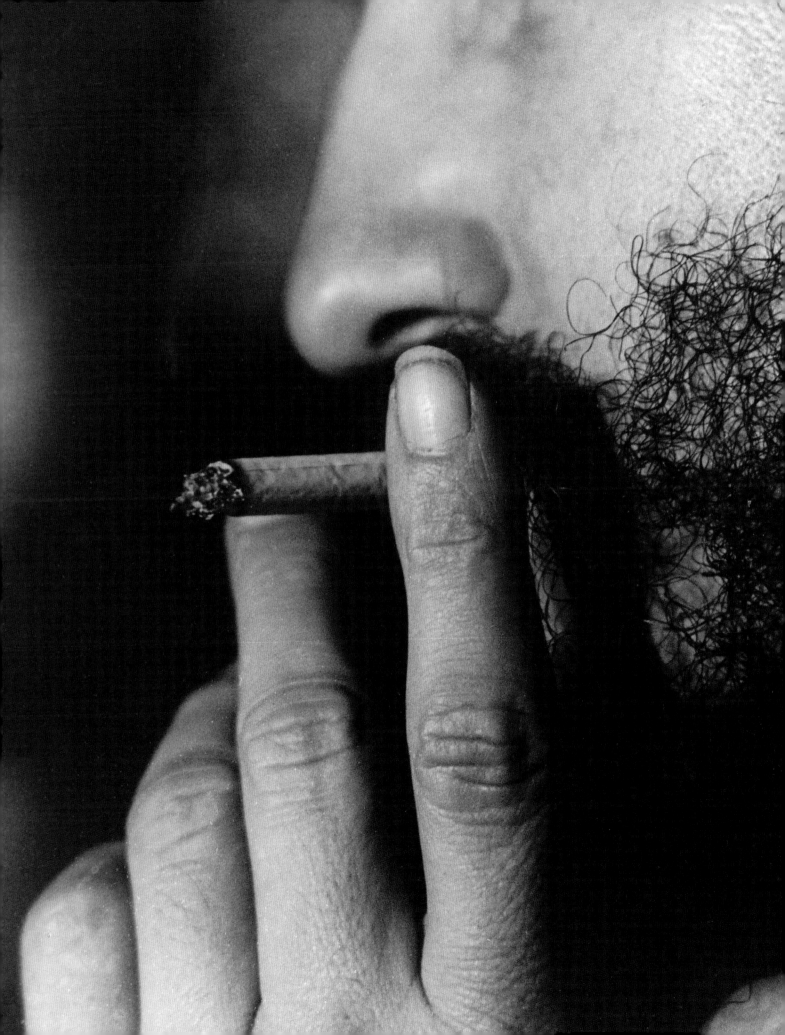

The sign reads: VIVA FIDEL, ABUELOS de MARIANAO

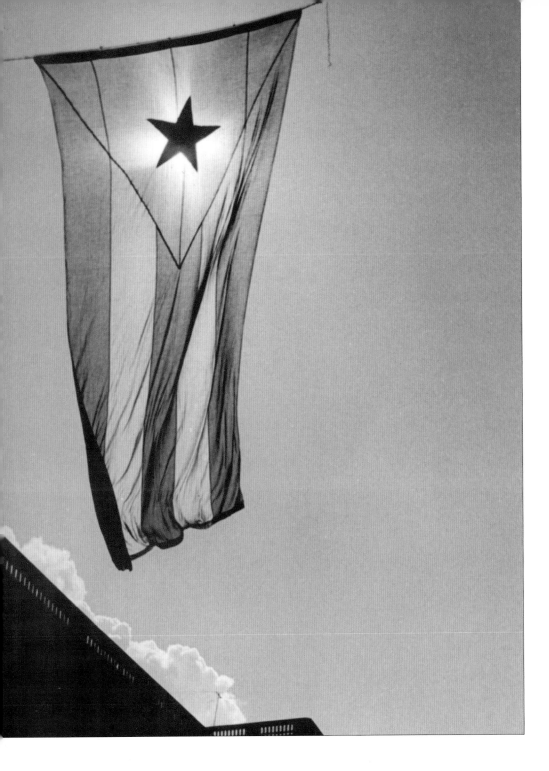

left: FRANCISCO BOU, *Grandparents of Marianao support Fidel Castro,* **1986**

The generation that made the Revolution with Fidel Castro are now grandparents.

above: MARIO DIAZ, *My flag, my Havana,* **1980**

The national flag, simple and elegant, is seen all over Havana. One of the undoubted legacies of the Revolution is a sense of nationhood fulfilled.

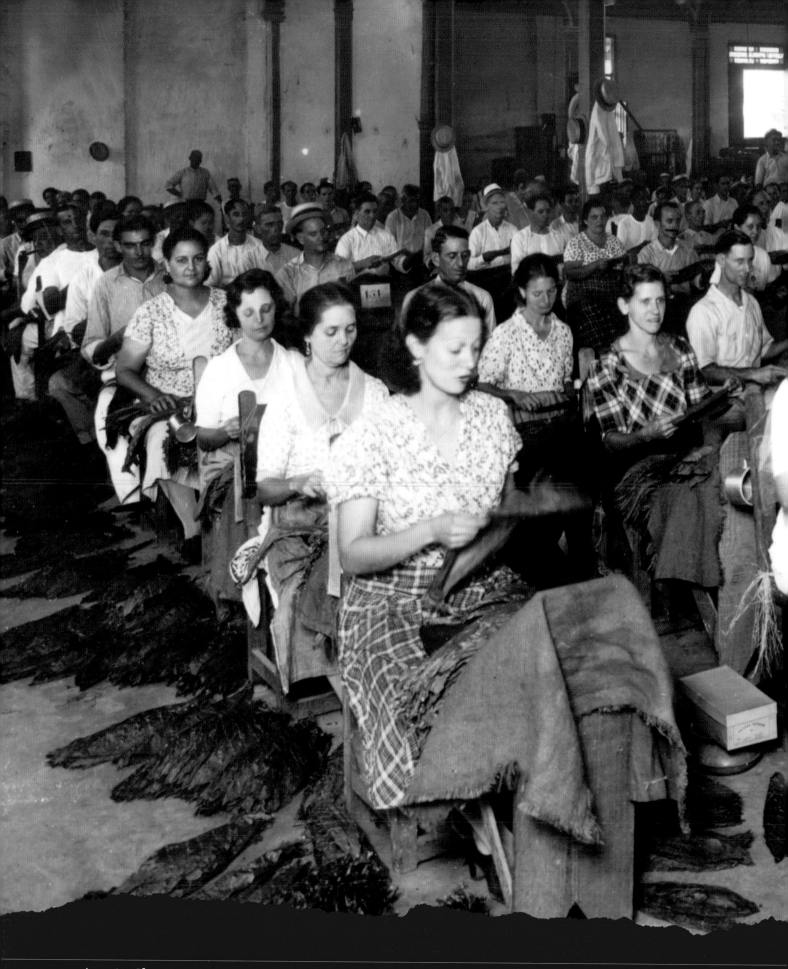

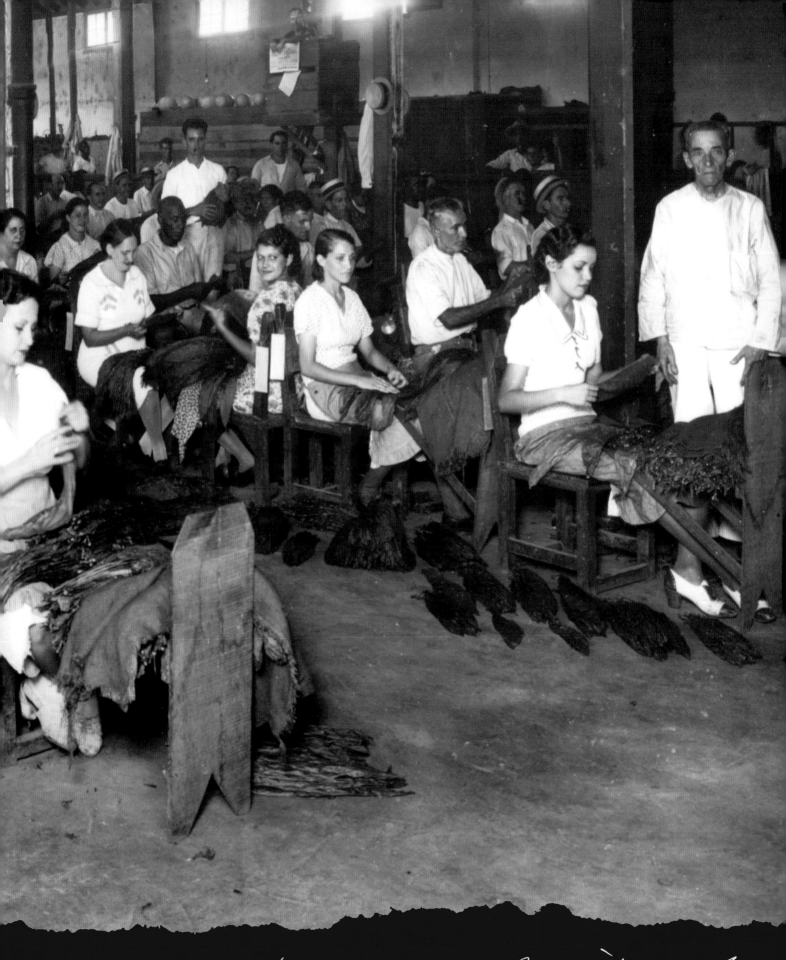

everyday and ritual

everyday and ritual

As the Cuban ethnologist Fernando Ortiz once remarked, Cuba is an *ajiaco criollo*, a Creole garlic stew in which everything is mixed together. People of different races, cultures, and religions have been thrown together on this beautiful island, with its wonderful climate, and have created a new society of mixtures. Not a melting pot, but a pot in which all the various ingredients retain their own identities, yet all intermingle.

This intermingling was greatly speeded up by the wars of independence of the 19th century and by the profound social and political revolution that gathered momentum in the 1950s and burst the dam of U.S. domination in 1959.

Its effect may be seen in the changed fortunes of the rumba, a popular national dance. The rumba has its roots in the drum traditions of western Africa and the guitar traditions of southern Spain and is a powerful, expressive dance. It existed for many years on the margins of society, largely confined to poorer districts where people danced in the streets. It only entered the mainstream of Cuban popular dances after the Revolution.

Religious beliefs and rituals retain a great force in Cuban society, and in this area too there is a great mingling of cultural traditions. Throughout centuries, slaves imported from western Africa helped to maintain their cultural identity by creating a kind of mirror image religion, in which their traditional gods shadowed the saints of the Catholic religion. The followers of this hybrid religion, known as Regla de Ocha or Santería, are quite at home attending a service in a Catholic church.

It is remarkable to see how the cult that grew up around the tomb of the Lady of Miracles in the Columbus Cemetery rapidly assimilated her into the beliefs of the Regla de Ocha. This is the tomb of a young woman from a white Catholic family who died in childbirth a century ago, which became a place of pilgrimage for women who are pregnant or have problems conceiving. The Yoruba religion of Africa recognizes a miraculous quality in a child who dies at birth, and people who visit the tomb believe that the mother and child can help them with their problems.

The African gods enter into the everyday at many levels. Santería used to be looked down on by the white middle classes, but in recent years its influence has spread much more widely. At a trivial level, it is quite common when a bottle of rum is opened for a few drops to be poured onto the floor in the corner of the room as an offering to the gods. But there are many people who live their lives in strict observance of the complex rituals of the religion, and who undertake severe penances to win the support of the gods. Each year on the day of the Catholic Saint Lazarus, thousands of people make their way, crawling, to a church dedicated to Saint Lazarus to call on Babalú Ayé—Saint Lazarus in the Catholic religion—for help and protection.

This culture of mixtures can be seen in the way people decorate their houses. A living room may contain, alongside ceramics and plastic flowers, a shrine to the gods and photographs of Che Guevara and other political leaders.

One can speculate that the great energy within Cuban society—its exuberant dances, its prowess in sports, the ingenuity of its people— derives from this intermingling of cultural elements, within which national aspirations, moral codes, and the spiritual life are inseparable. This may also help to explain how this island people, so friendly and welcoming to visitors and outside influences, are also so clannish and protective of their culture.

previous page: **BOHEMIA ARCHIVE,** *Cigar workers,* **1947**

Cigar-making was traditionally one of the most skilled trades, and cigar workers the most cultured and literate of all. During the working day one worker would read to the others from the daily press, poetry, novels, and even works by Marx and Engels. The Monte Cristo cigar was named after Alexandre Dumas' novel *The Count of Monte Cristo*, because this was a big favorite.

The cigar workers who emigrated to Tampa, Florida, during the economic crisis of the 1890s, and set up a tobacco industry there, helped to finance the independence war of 1895–98. The message that the war was about to begin was sent to Havana wrapped inside a cigar from Tampa by the independence leader José Martí.

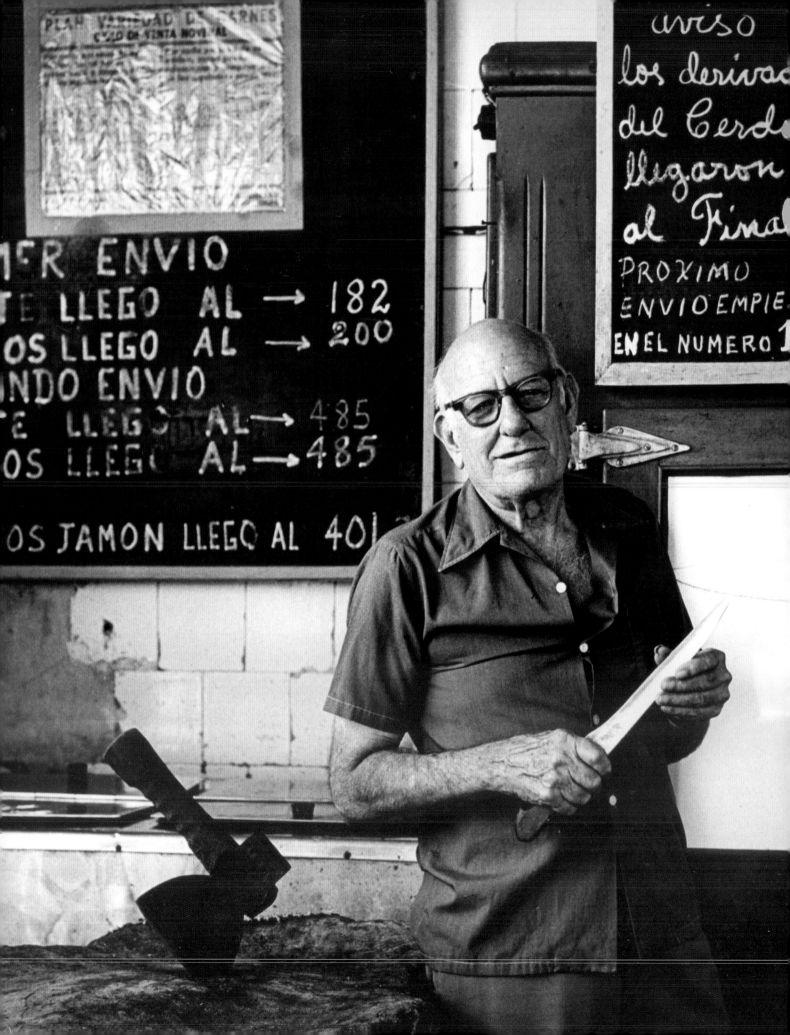

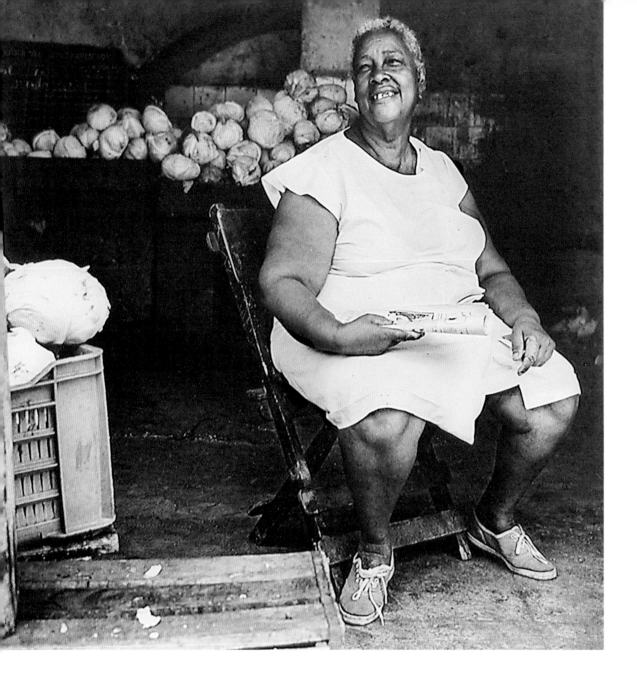

above: **TITO ALVAREZ,** *Black Cubans,* 1983

left: **TITO ALVAREZ,** *Butcher,* 1983

In times of scarcity, cattle became sacred, though in a different way from in India. When a calf is born, the peasant to whom it belongs must inscribe it in a register. If it should die, he has a tremendous responsibility to prove that it was not slaughtered, for anyone who kills a cow or bull without authorization faces, if caught, the prospect of a prison sentence almost as severe as if he had killed a person. So to be a butcher, to have direct contact with beef every day, became a great privilege, a source of social status.

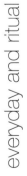

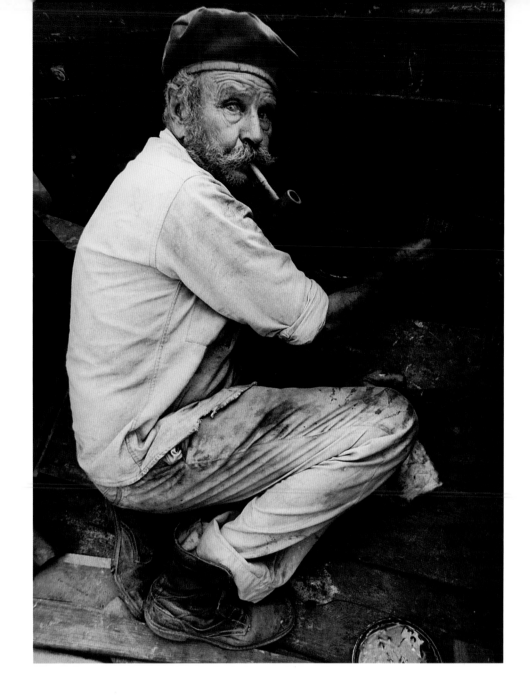

above: FRANCISCO BOU, *Ship's engineer,* **1994**

Old ship's engineers, initiates into the mysteries of mechanical engineering more by experience than formal training, have kept afloat the crumbling Cuban fishing fleet for years.

right: TITO ALVAREZ, *Iced drinks vendor,* **1975**

The traditional iced drink of Havana, made from crushed ice and fruit, is the forerunner of the smoothie. The "granizadero," or iced drinks vendor, almost disappeared from Havana's streets, but is now making a comeback, particularly outside schools at the end of the day.

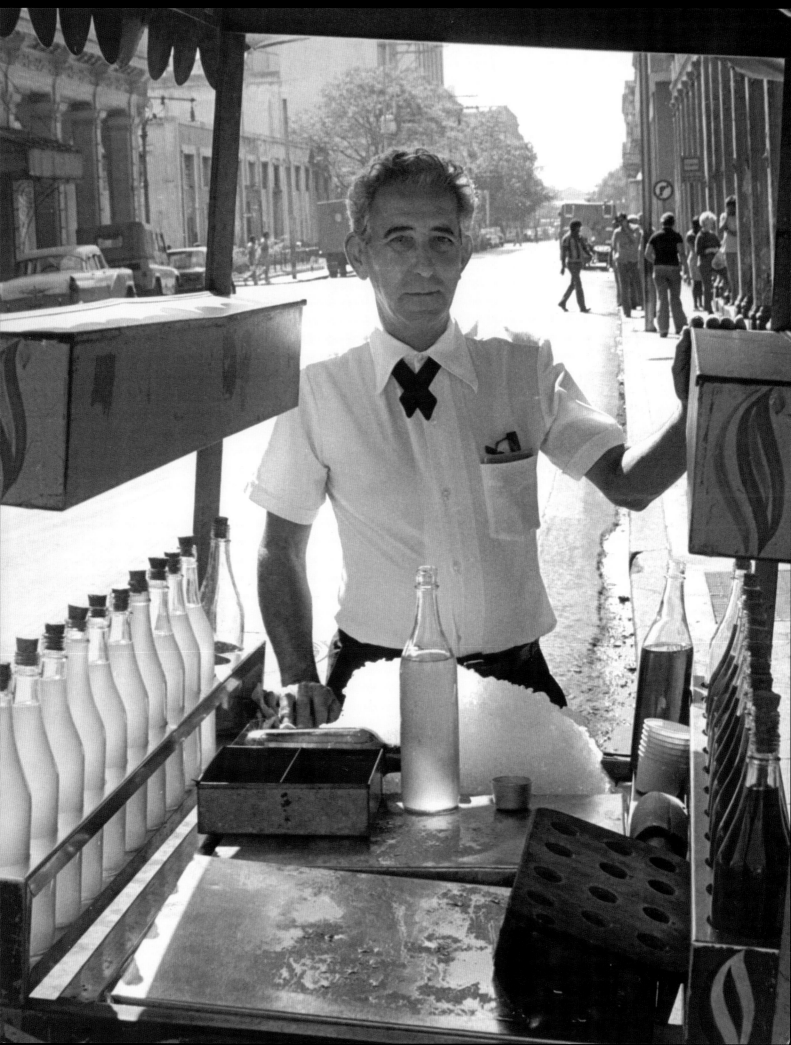

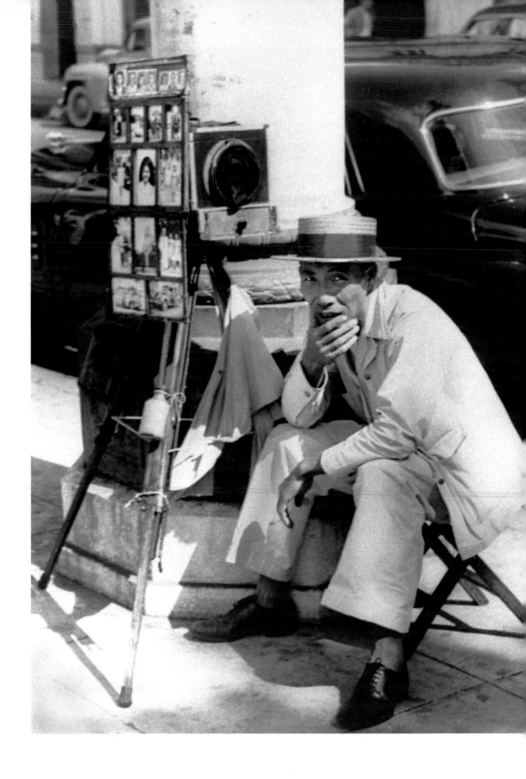

above: **PRENSA LATINA ARCHIVE,** *Chinaman,* **1952**

For Chinese emigrants the journey to Cuba was "the longest journey." On the other side of the world they became part of a completely different society, and yet preserved the essence of their own culture. Some years ago a cultural project to preserve this heritage was officially inaugurated. It was named *Ultramar*—"from the other side of the sea."

This Cuban Chinese street photographer had, rather unusually, adopted the dress and gestures of the Cuban middle class of the day.

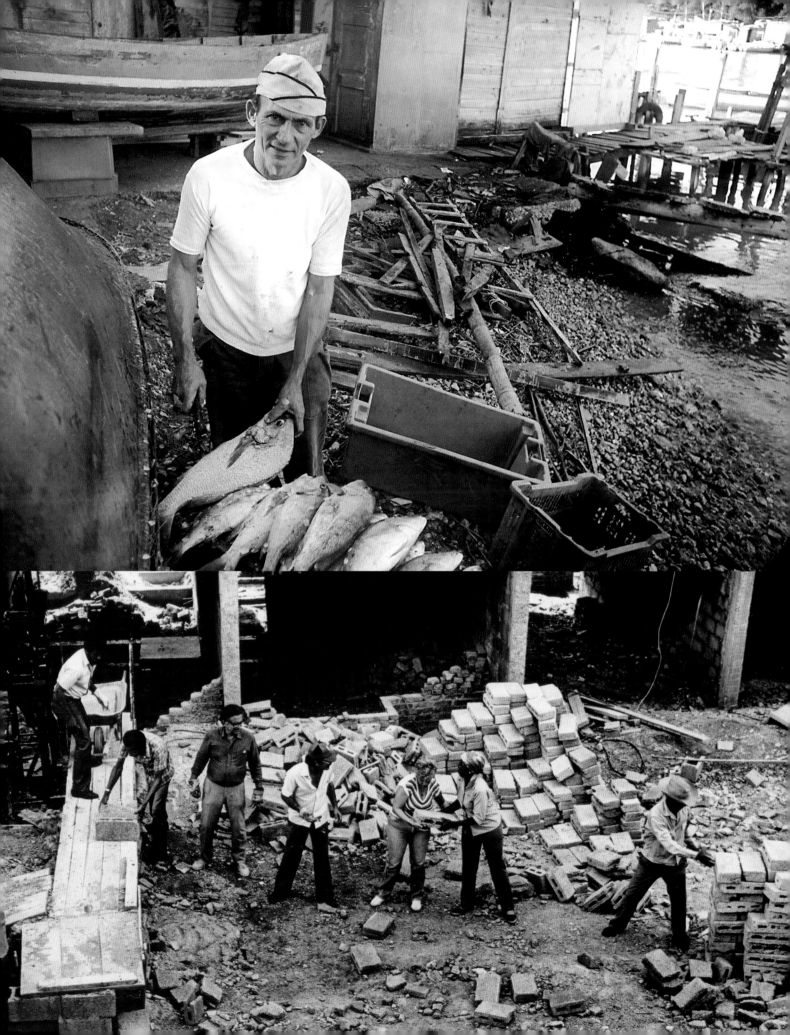

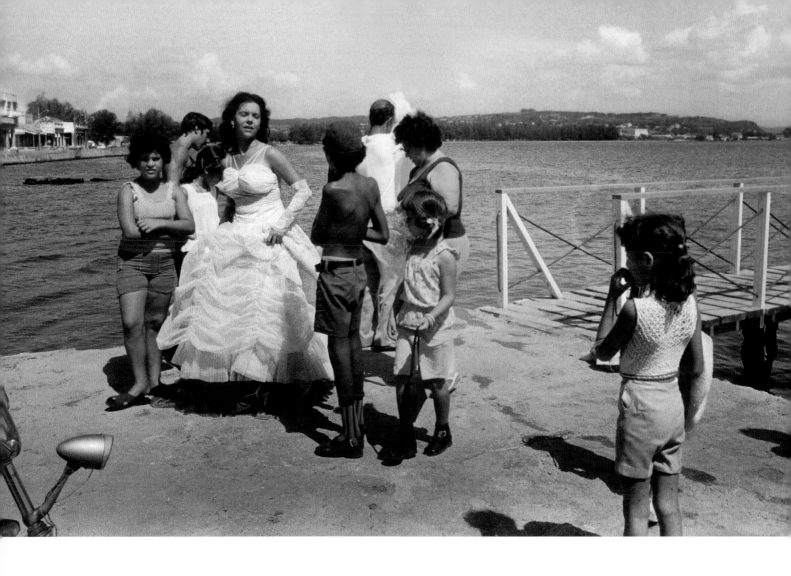

everyday and ritual

previous page top: MIGUEL FLEITAS, *Fisherman*, 1984

For many *habaneros*, and especially those living in the districts of Santa Fe and Cojímar and near the Malecón, fishing is a way of life and a means of supporting the family. Since ownership of boats is restricted, fishermen float in the sea along the Havana shoreline on truck inner tubes and rafts made from planks and oil drums. In the season when *pargo*—a Caribbean snapper—swarm, it is common at night to see hundreds of little lights in the sea of fishermen awaiting their luck.

previous page bottom: SERGIO ROMERO, *Microbrigade construction*, 1988

In an attempt to remedy the housing shortage, "microbrigades" of workers were created in the 1970s. Groups of workers would be given leave from their normal jobs to build their own homes with prefabricated materials. Since they were not skilled, quality often suffered.

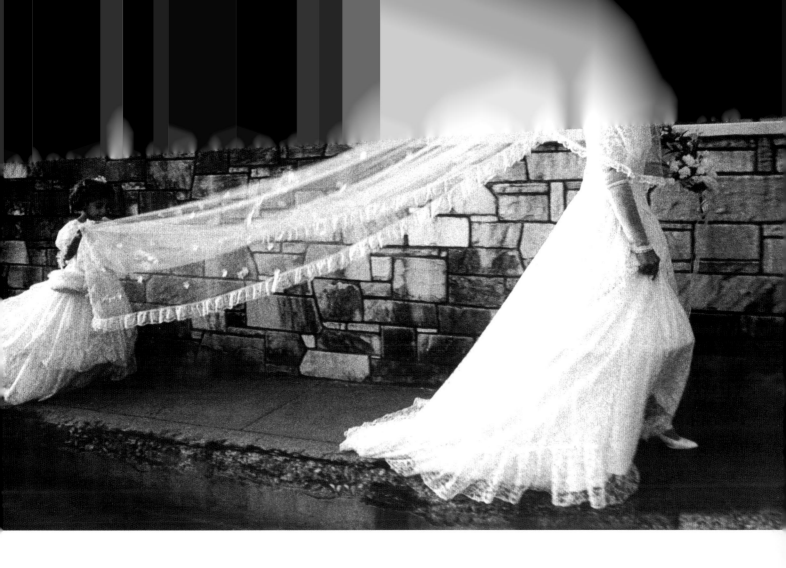

above left: MARIA EUGENIA HAYA (MARUCHA), *Fifteenth Birthday,* 1980

For young Cuban women, their 15th birthday marks their coming of age. Their parents traditionally hire, make, or borrow an array of costumes for them to be photographed in at elegant locations.

above: ALFREDO SARABIA, *The Bride,* 1984

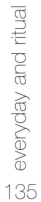

everyday and ritual

135

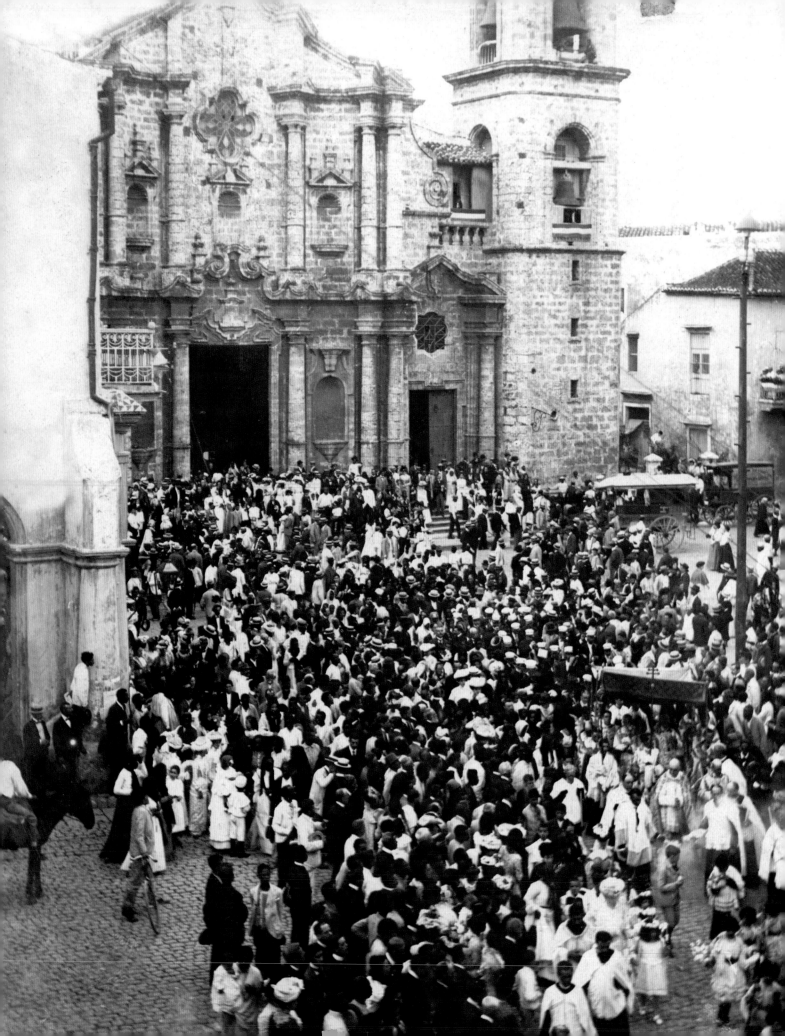

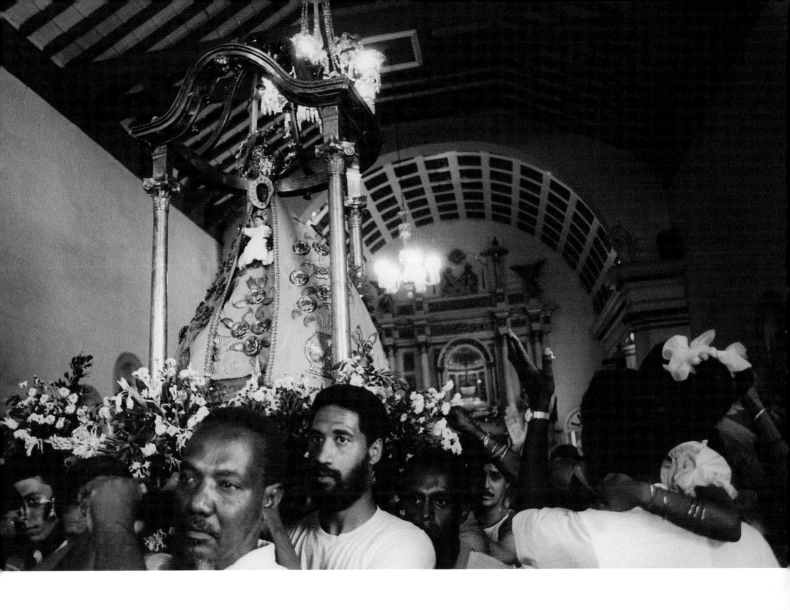

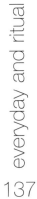

left: **NATIONAL LIBRARY ARCHIVE**, *Religious procession,
Cathedral Square*, 1956

At midnight on Christmas Eve the Cathedral of Havana opens its doors for
its famous "Cockerel Mass," at the hour when the cockerel ushers in the
commemoration of the Nativity. The procession is led by priests carrying the
infant Jesus in a crib. Not only Catholics, but also followers of the Afro-
Cuban religions, enter the cathedral and join in the singing and prayers.

The cathedral is one of the oldest religious buildings in Cuba, dating from
the second half of the 18th century. Its architectural style is baroque, but
more austere than many other famous cathedrals of Latin America.

above: **FRANCISCO BOU**, *Procession in a church*, 1994

We've been together since long ago,
   young, old,
   white and black, all mixed

NICOLAS GUILLEN, from "SON NUMBER 6"

right: FRANCISCO BOU, *Church service with Donald Duck,* **1995**

There are few social or cultural practices more essentially Cuban than Santería, the religion that developed during the long years of slavery by fusing the saints of the Catholic religion with the Yoruba traditions of West Africa. Through Santería the slaves were able to preserve their cultural identity, despite the appalling conditions in which they lived.

Devotees of Santería involve themselves with passion in its rites, which include animal sacrifice and the preparation of special foods for the gods, which they place in front of shrines in their houses. In public ceremonies they may fall into a trance.

The white middle classes traditionally looked down on Santería, and the Pope refused to acknowledge it as a religion during his 1998 visit to the island. Nevertheless, it has steadily gained ground and is by far the most widely practiced religion in Cuba. It is not unusual, for example, to see internationally famous musicians wearing the white headdress and costume of a "santo," an initiate into the inner mysteries of the religion.

Santería embodies a benign, embracing, and peaceful approach to the world, a world in which even Donald Duck is welcome.

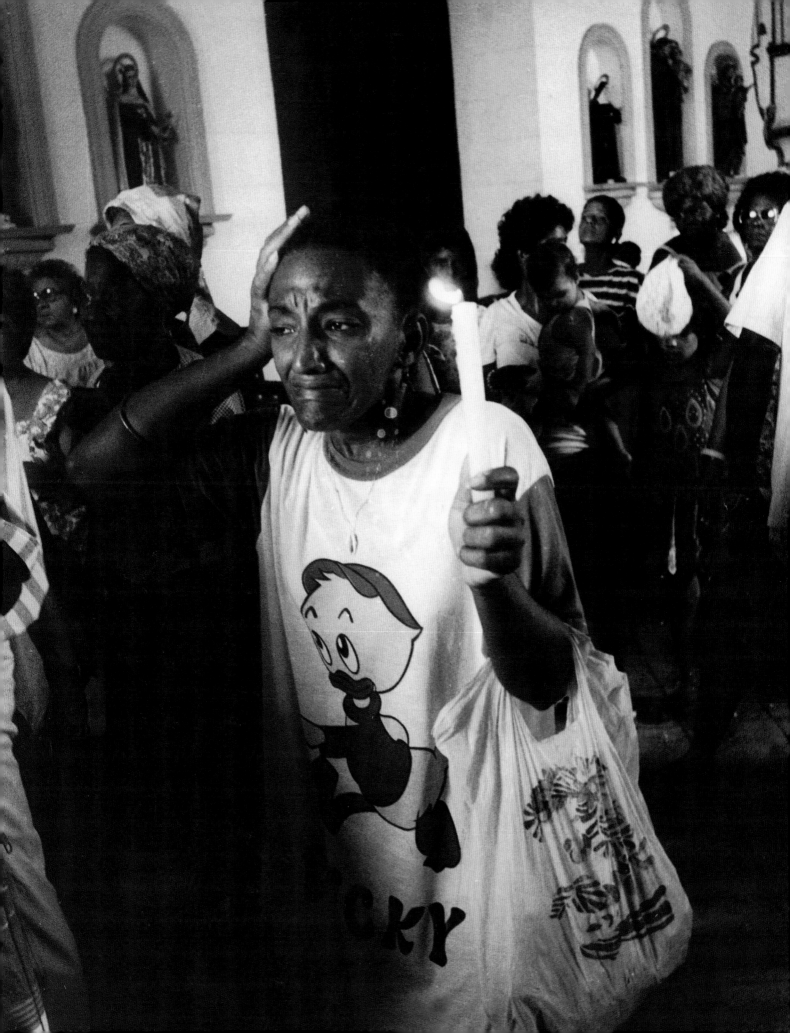

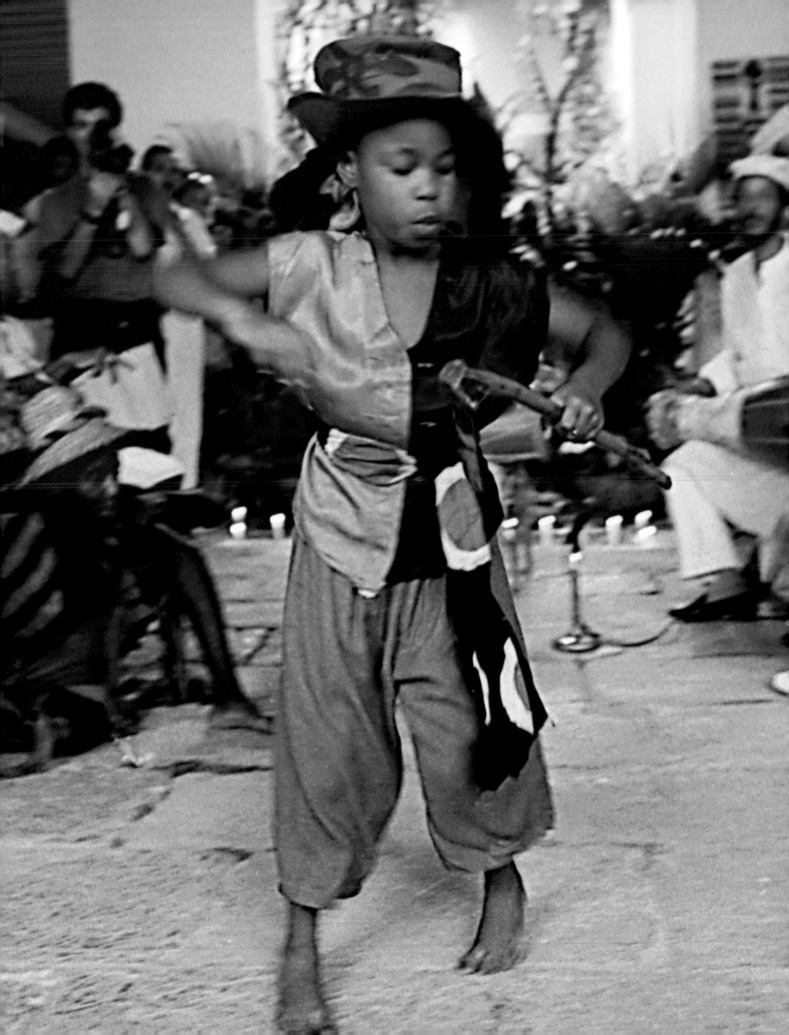

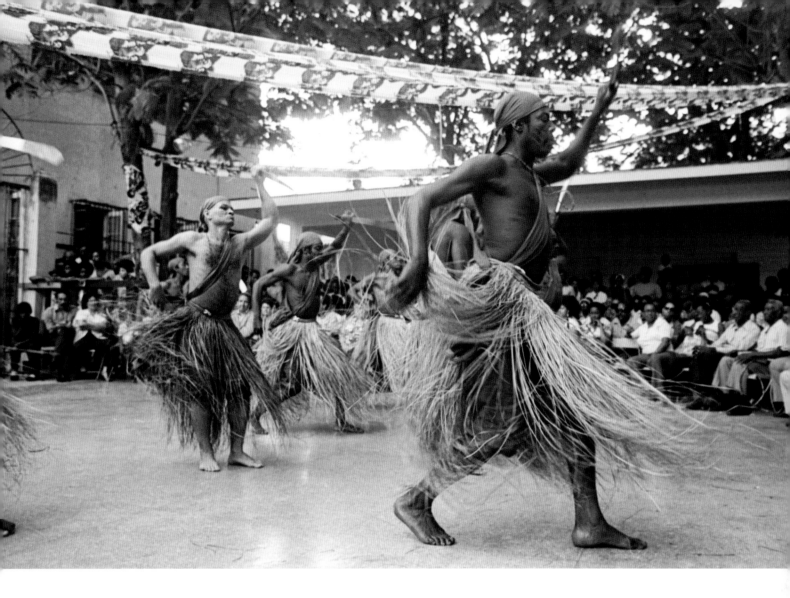

left: PRENSA LATINA ARCHIVE, *Elegguá*, 1992

The mischievous child Elegguá, dressed in red and black, is the god who opens and closes the path. In Cuba, as in Africa, his devotees place his image behind the door of the house so that, when they enter or leave, he frees them from evil.

In Africa Elegguá's dance is erotic, but in Cuba it seems to have lost this character—perhaps because the ritual of fertilization disappeared in a slave society, perhaps also because it was repressed by the slave owners as being obscene.

above: PRENSA LATINA ARCHIVE, *Afro-Cuban dance*, 1985

The ritual dances of the Yoruba culture, with their complex rhythms, color, and movements, are an essential part of Cuban dance. Each deity has its own special costume in a particular color, its own rhythm and gestures, and a special beat of the batá drum. This dance is dedicated to Babalú Ayé—Saint Lazarus in the Catholic religion—who heals the sick.

everyday and ritual

141

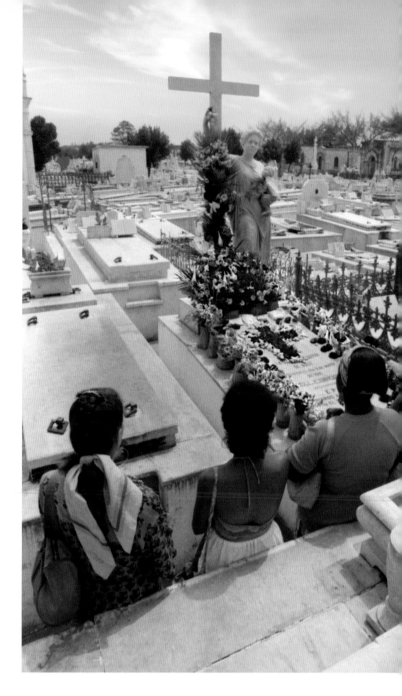

right: MIGUEL VINAS, *The Lady of Miracles,*
Columbus Cemetery, **1993**

This is a favorite place of pilgrimage for women who
are pregnant or have problems conceiving, or whose
children are sick. It is the tomb of Amelia Goiry Adot,
who died in 1902 during childbirth. Her husband,
devastated at the loss of his wife, went every day for 40
years to the cemetery to weep for her, and placed on
the grave a life-sized statue of her in Carrara marble. A
myth grew up around Amelia, assimilating her into the
beliefs of Santería, which recognizes a miraculous
quality in a child who dies at childbirth. When people
visit the cemetery, both men and women, they knock on
the tomb, calling her and talking with her, asking her to
work miracles. When they leave they walk backward,
without turning their back. According to legend, Amelia
was buried pregnant, about to give birth, and when,
according to Catholic custom, her body was exhumed
for reburial, she was holding her baby in her arms.

right: PRENSA LATINA ARCHIVE, *Callejón de*
Hamel, **1993**

Famous for its rumbas, its walls and houses covered
with paintings and graffiti, often of mythological scenes
and secret codes, the Callejón de Hamel in the Cayo
Hueso district of Havana has become a celebration of
Spanish, African, and other cultures in Cuba. It is an
incredible living monument to the beliefs and passions
that infuse so much of Cuban culture.

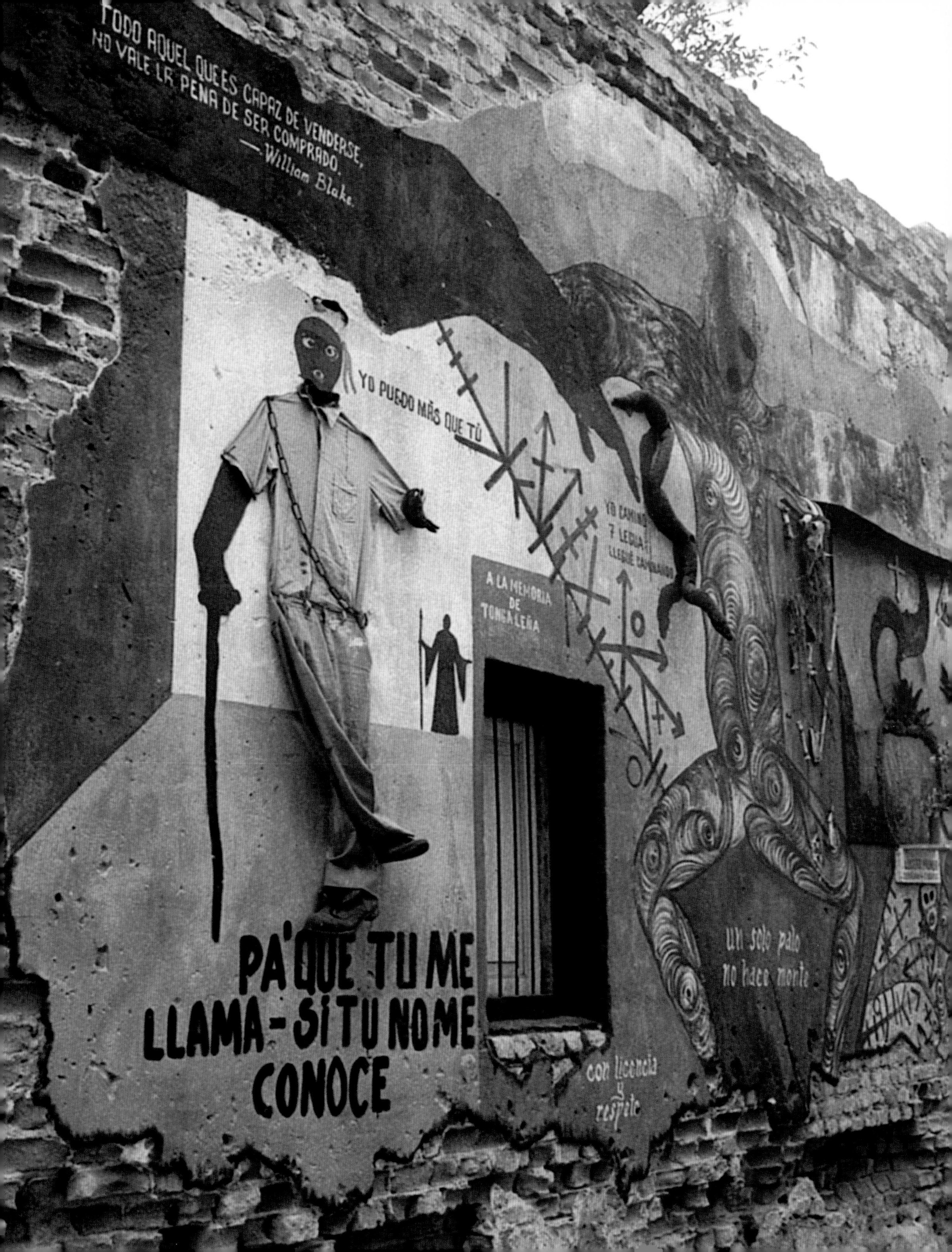
TODO AQUEL QUE ES CAPAZ DE VENDERSE,
NO VALE LA PENA DE SER COMPRADO.
—William Blake.
YO PUEDO MÁS QUE TÚ
A LA MEMORIA DE TONGA LEÑA
PA'QUE TU ME LLAMA - SI TU NO ME CONOCE
un solo palo no hace monte
con licencia y respeto

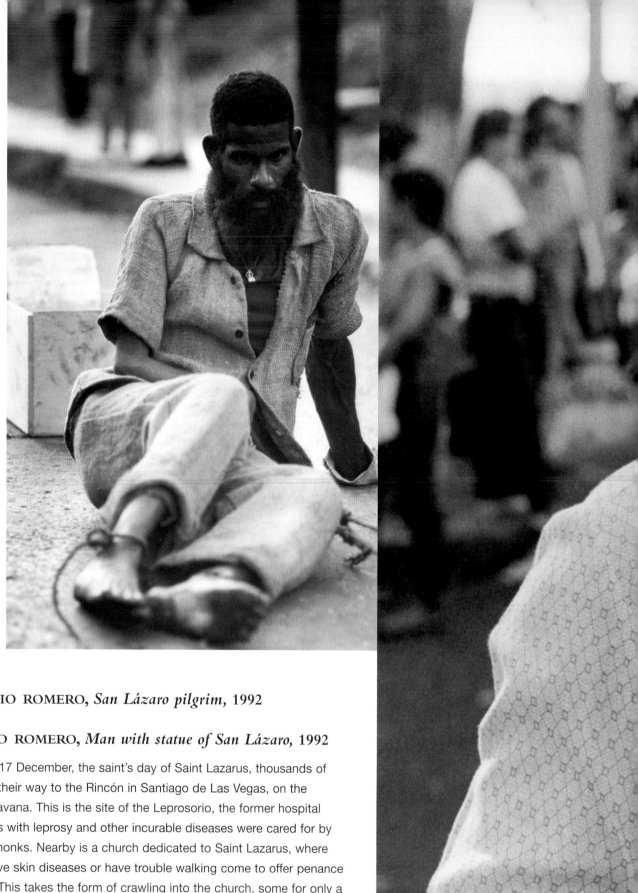

above: **SERGIO ROMERO,** *San Lázaro pilgrim,* 1992

right: **SERGIO ROMERO,** *Man with statue of San Lázaro,* 1992

Each year on 17 December, the saint's day of Saint Lazarus, thousands of people make their way to the Rincón in Santiago de Las Vegas, on the outskirts of Havana. This is the site of the Leprosorio, the former hospital where patients with leprosy and other incurable diseases were cared for by doctors and monks. Nearby is a church dedicated to Saint Lazarus, where those who have skin diseases or have trouble walking come to offer penance for their sins. This takes the form of crawling into the church, some for only a short distance, others even for miles, dragging weights to make their journey still harder. The god Babalú Ayé—Saint Lazarus in the Catholic religion—helps and protects the poor and heals the sick.

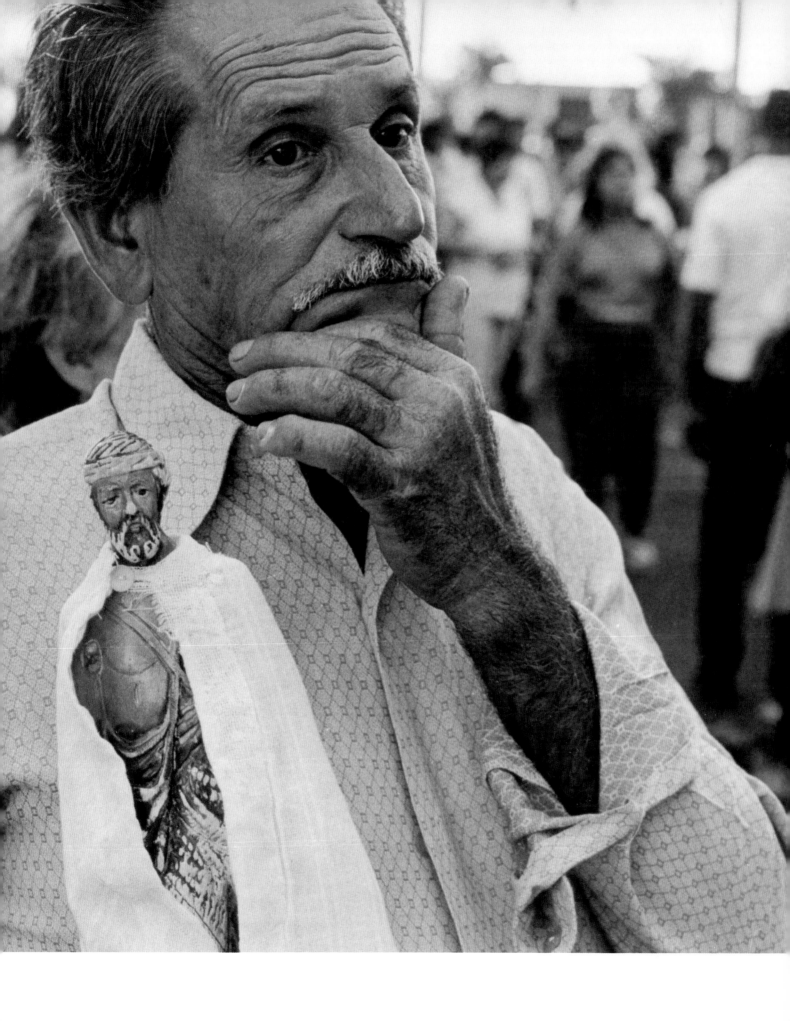

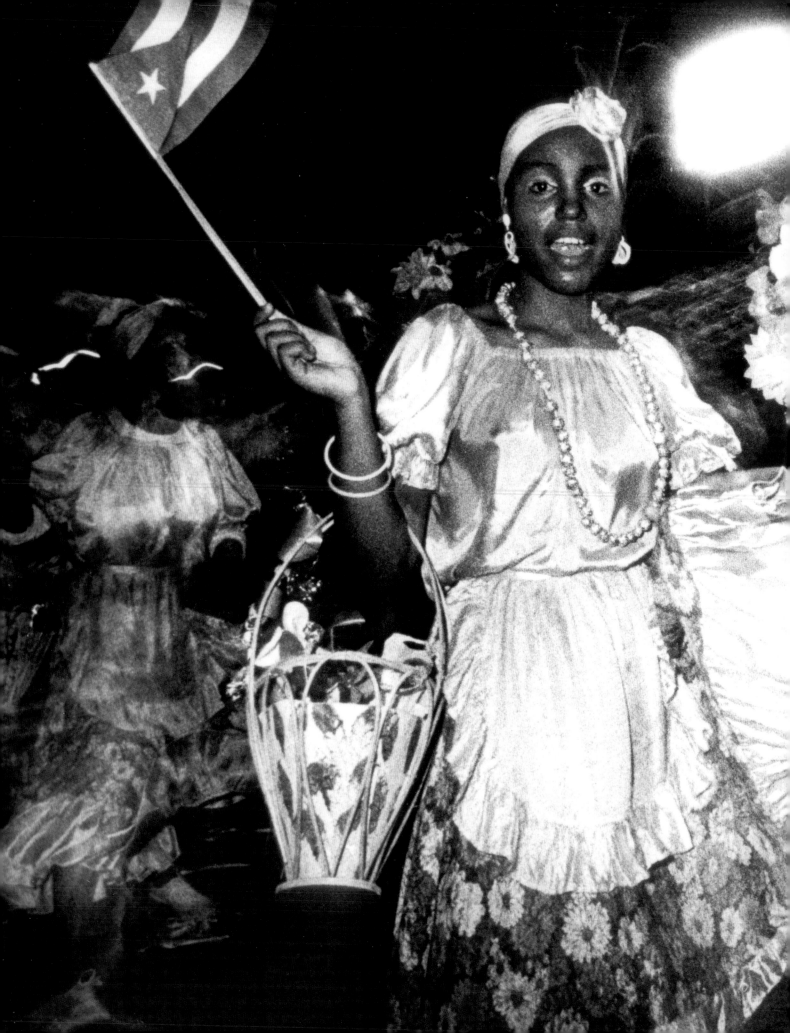

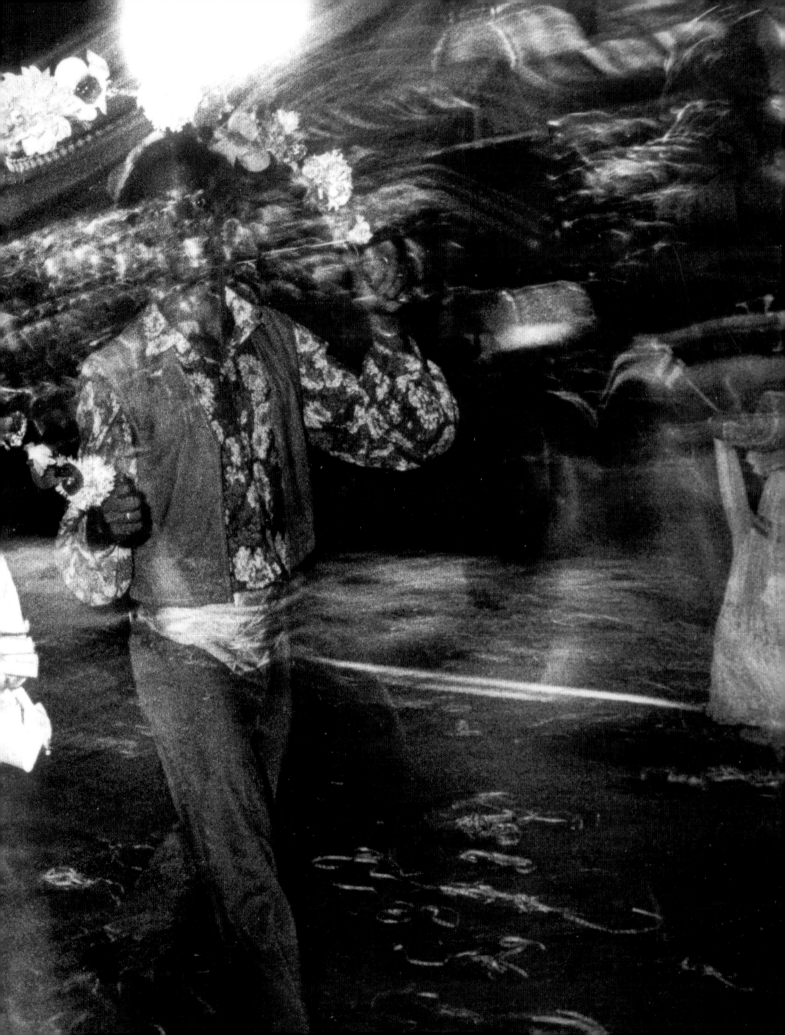

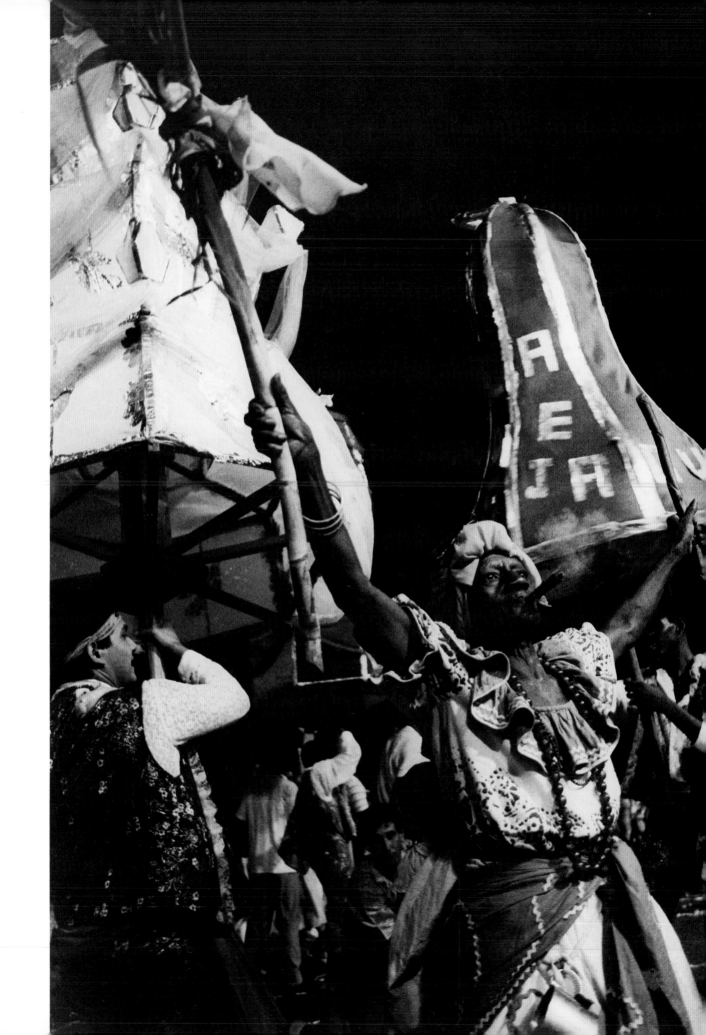

Havana emerges among cane fields and the sound of maracas, Chinese horns, bells, and marimbas. And who should come welcome me at the port but the dusky Trinidad of my childhood, the one who "went walking one morning along the quayside in Havana, down the quayside in Havana one morning went walking."

And here come the blacks, with rhythms I realize derive from our great Andalusia—friendly Blacks, with no anguish, who show the whites of their eyes and say "We are Latins."

FEDERICO GARCIA LORCA, from his lecture *A POET IN NEW YORK*

previous page: **SERGIO ROMERO,** *Flying a flag in the Carnival,* **1987**

The Carnival is an occasion for people to let out all their passions and frustrations in the street, a euphoric catharsis.

left: **FRANCISCO BOU,** *Woman with cigar in the Carnival,* **1989**

The carnivals of Havana are part of a long tradition that began as a dispensation given to slaves to enjoy themselves. Together with Río de Janeiro, the Havana and Santiago de Cuba carnivals are considered the most exuberant in the Americas for their fantastic floats, their street processions, and their high spirits. Even during periods of economic crisis, the Havana carnival has continued to be an authentic expression of popular culture.

everyday and ritual

top right: SERGIO ROMERO, *Carnival*, 1995

Many *habaneros* are fanatical about the Carnival, and spend the better part of the year preparing their costumes and choreographing their processions. Local pride takes on a highly competitive hue.

bottom right: ABIGAIL GARCIA, *The Buendía family*, 1986

A family in the Juanelo district of Havana dedicated themselves full time to teaching their neighbors to make papier-mâché figures. Soon the neighborhood came alive with papier-mâché butterflies, exotic birds, exuberant masks, and, of course, a special museum to show off these enchanting works of art.

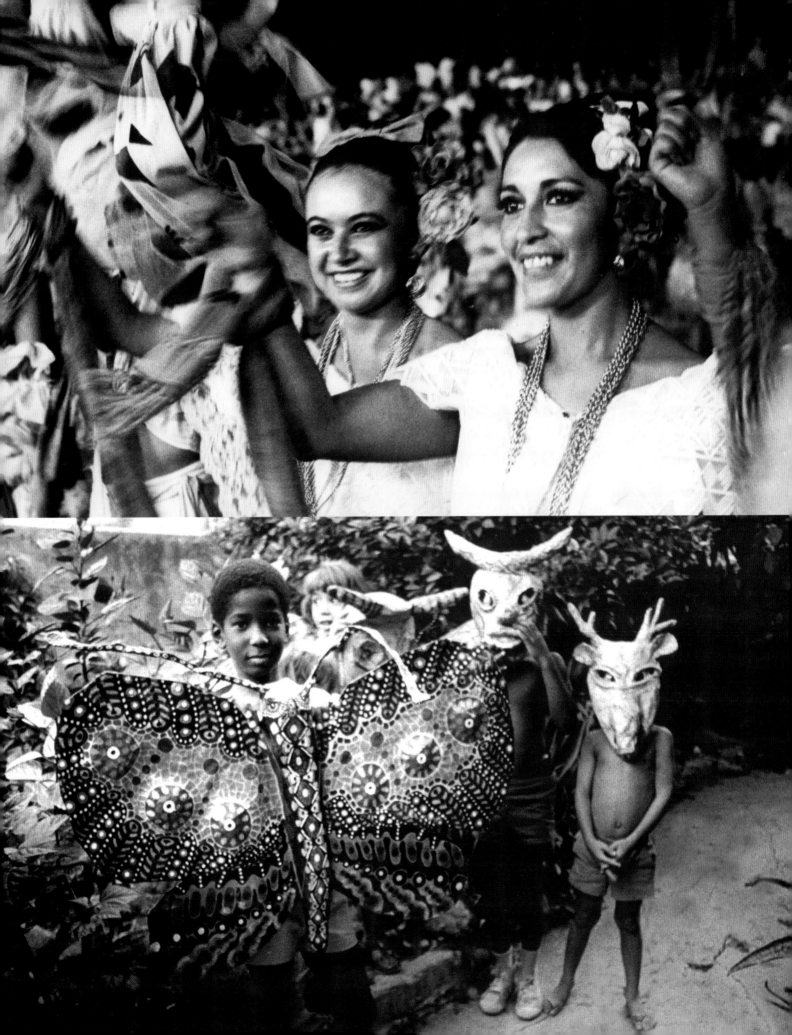

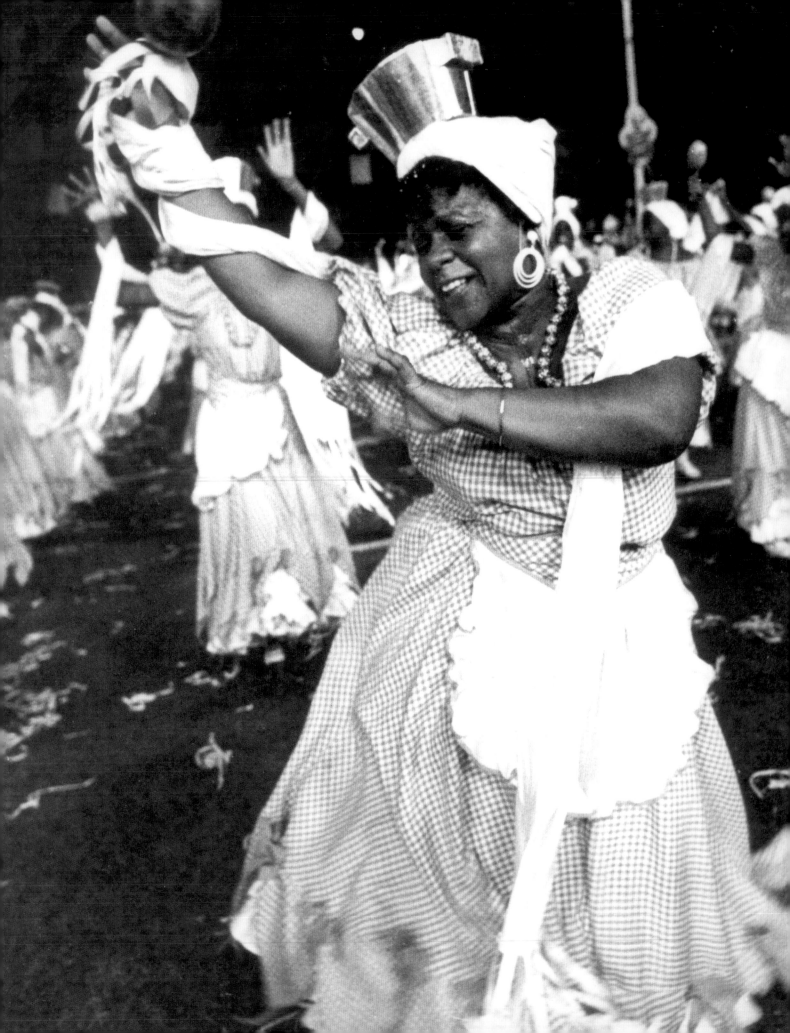

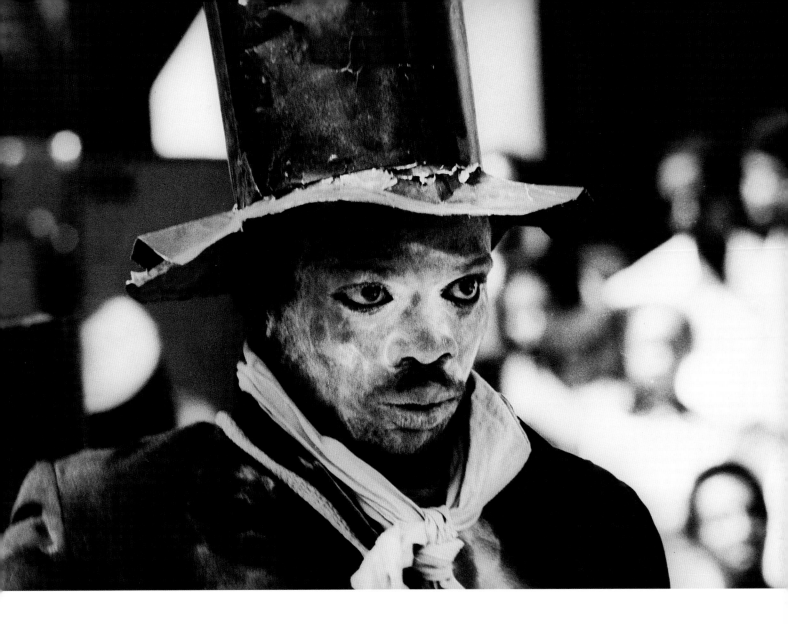

left: **SERGIO ROMERO,** *Carnival,* **1995**

Every district has its procession, the most exuberant of which are from the old districts of Regla and Guanabacoa on the other side of the harbor, and Ataré in Old Havana.

above: **FRANCISCO BOU,** *Man with whitened face in the Carnival,* **1989**

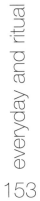

right: SERGIO ROMERO, *Carnival*, 1985

next page: OSVALDO SALAS, *Carnival*, 1980

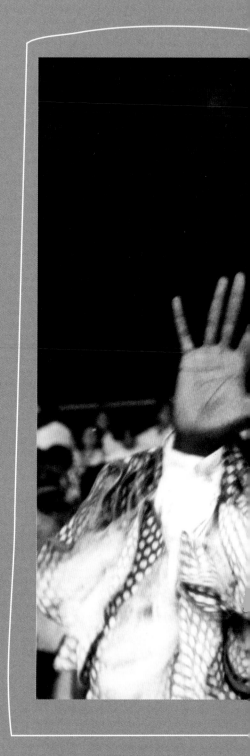

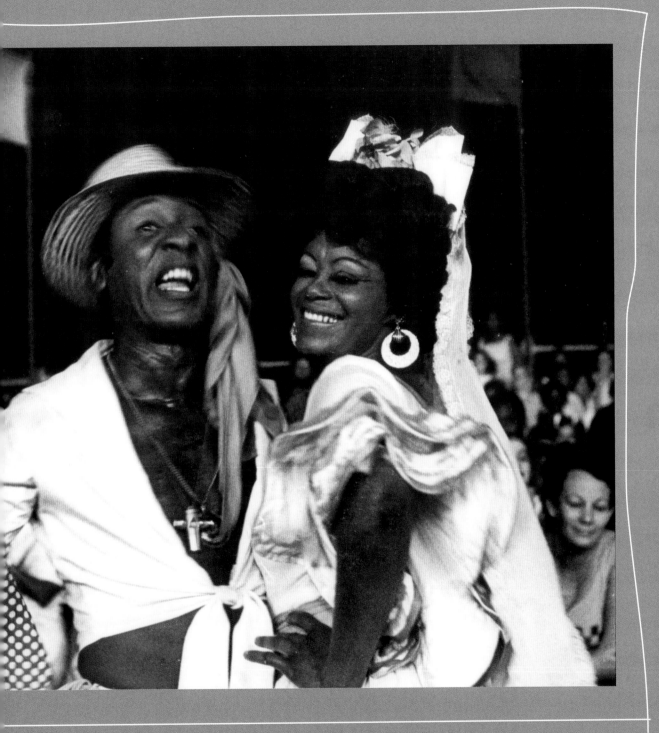

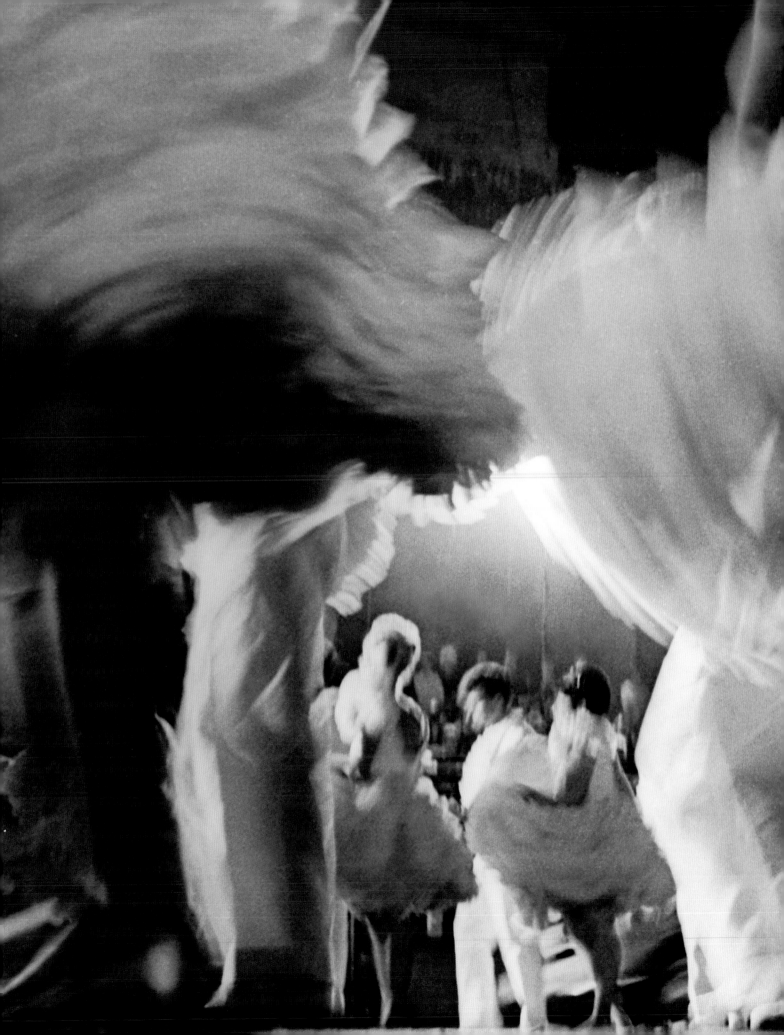

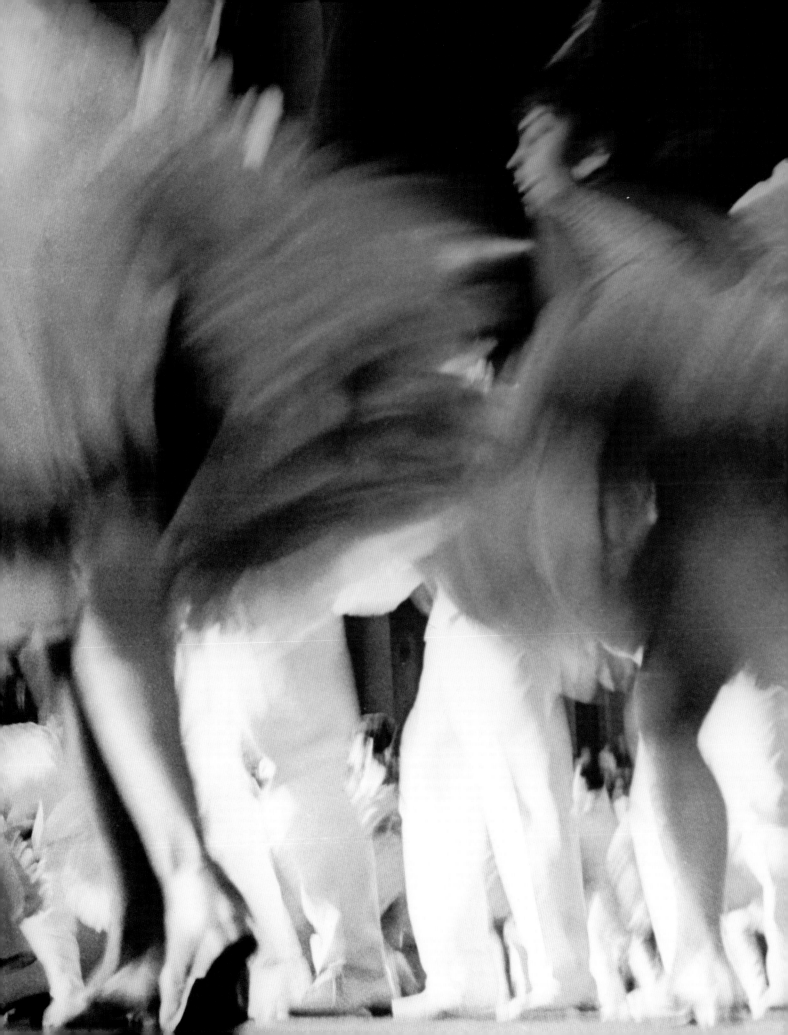

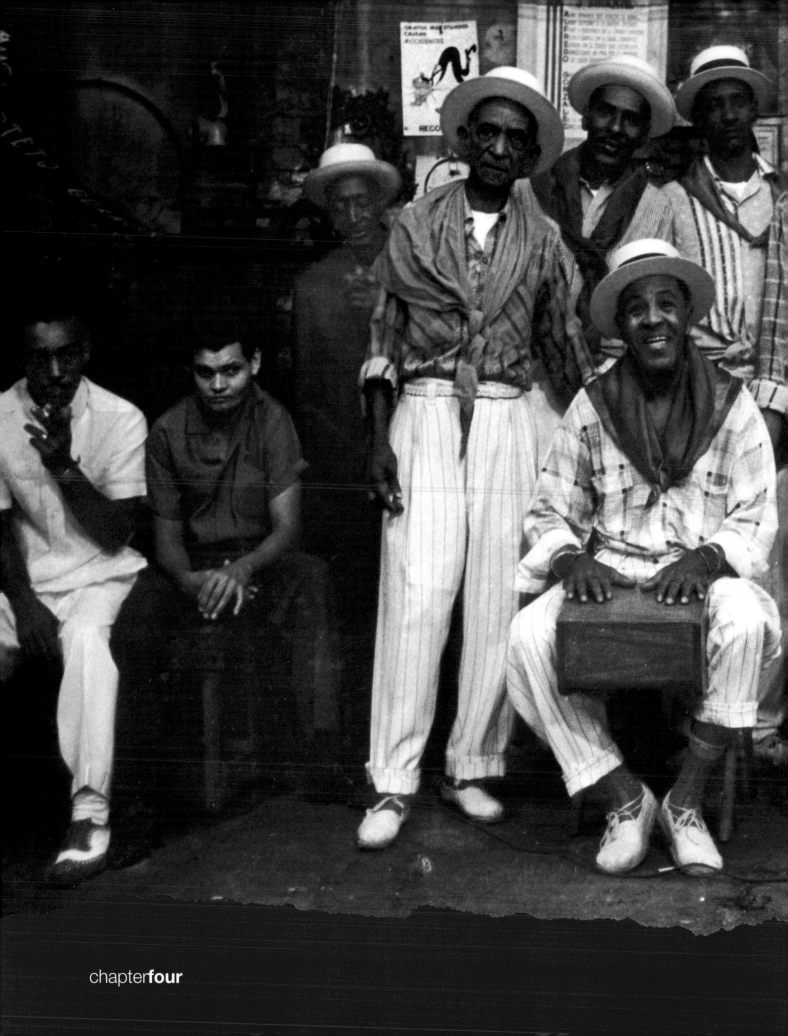

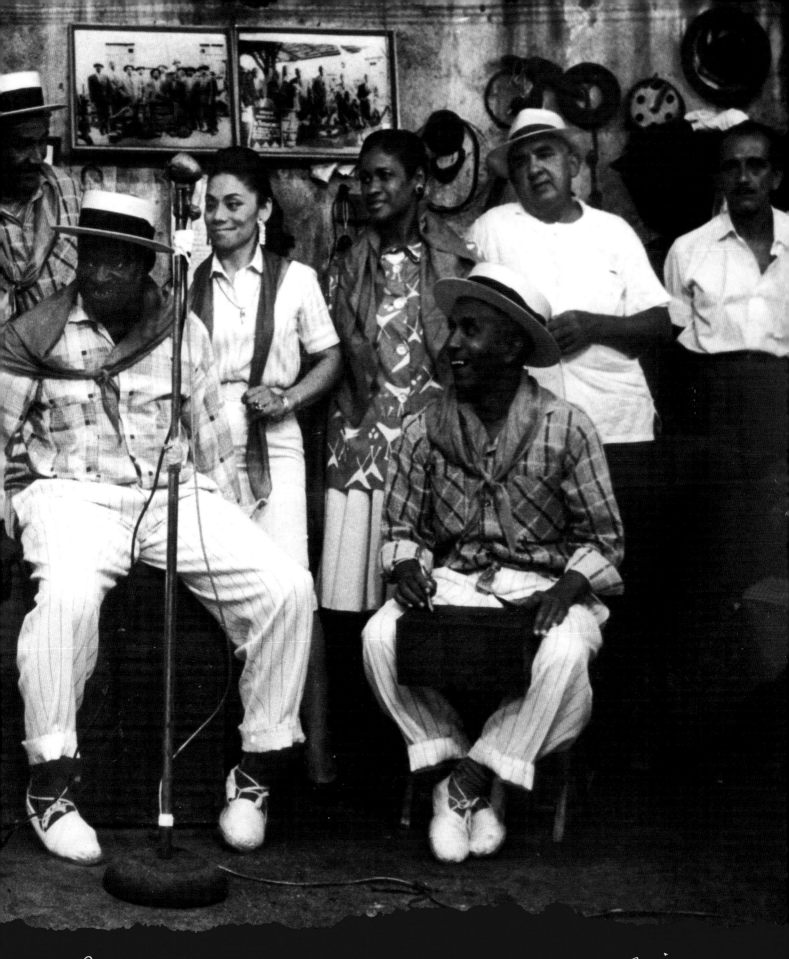

performers and artists

performers and artists

Everyone who visits Havana is surprised by the variety and richness of Cuban culture, the dances, the plastic arts, literature, cinema, and music. Music especially is an essential part of being Cuban, a sensibility toward life that permeates the everyday. It is impossible to imagine Cuba without its music, its rhythms, which are constantly sought out by foreign musicians to enrich their own compositions.

The trios who perform traditional country music in bars and restaurants, energetic young salsa musicians in nightclubs, solitary piano players with more reflective offerings . . . it seems that half the city is engaged in presenting one kind of music or another. Stay a few days and you can also hear the most subtle Latin jazz, string orchestras playing the works of Ernesto Lecuona, or the national symphony orchestra playing mainstream European classical music. It soon becomes obvious that all this creative activity does not flourish merely by chance. The majority of these musicians are classically trained and have sophisticated technique.

Music strongly influences Cuban poetry too. Musical rhythms and cadences infuse the poems of Nicolás Guillén, Dulce María Loynaz, Cintio Vitier, Eliseo Diego, and many others, perhaps most of all the poems of Guillén, who was fascinated by the rhythms of the traditional Cuban music known as *son*.

With ingenuity and determination, musicians overcome tremendous obstacles. Violinists have been known successfully to substitute telephone cable for catgut when new strings were unavailable. Getting to rehearsals and transporting large instruments from one side of the city to the other on Havana's decaying buses requires tenacity, and yet people manage, for the love of their art.

Even arts that rely on expensive equipment manage to maintain impressive programs. The national ballet earns its living by touring overseas for much of the year, and it has a world-class reputation.

The film industry has a tougher time. Very few films have been made in the last 10 years. Nevertheless, even at the height of the economic crisis in 1993, Tomás Gutierrez Alea (Titón) was able to make his beautiful film *Strawberry and Chocolate*, a celebration of friendship amid all the problems of daily life in Havana.

Cuban painters and sculptors have established strong traditions of their own, particularly since the 1930s. René Portocarero and Wifredo Lam are by now part of a classical tradition and have been followed by painters such as Amelia Peláez, Antonia Eiriz, Servando Cabrera, Manuel Mendive, Nelson Domínguez, and a whole new generation of young artists such as Raúl Cordero and Belkis Ayón. Many sell their work successfully in the international market. Whereas many Cuban painters left to work abroad in the 1990s, now Havana is beginning to attract artists from all over Latin America.

The arts cannot prosper without leisure time, the opportunity to be exposed to varied influences, and an audience. Much of what has been achieved in recent years has been made possible by the creation of new schools and institutes in the 1960s. The Instituto Superior de Arte, promoted by Celia Sánchez, the Casa de las Américas, promoted by Haydée Santamaría, and the film institute ICAIC are important examples. But so too is the support that was given to painting and music throughout the school system.

When the Spanish poet and playwright Federico García Lorca visited Havana in 1930, he caused a sensation. Reading about the visit one has the impression that in those days it was quite rare for a famous foreign artist to visit.

Havana is once again fashionable. Artists such as Graham Greene, Gabriel García Márquez, Anna Pavlova, Rachmaninov, Wole Soyinka, and Julio Cortázar traveled quietly to Cuba for years. Now Hollywood directors, fashion models, rock bands, art collectors, and the like are making their way there in growing numbers.

previous page: **MARIA EUGENIA HAYA (MARUCHA)**, *La Peña de Sirique,* 1975

This was a traditional country-style group, similar to the Buena Vista Social Club and equally well known.

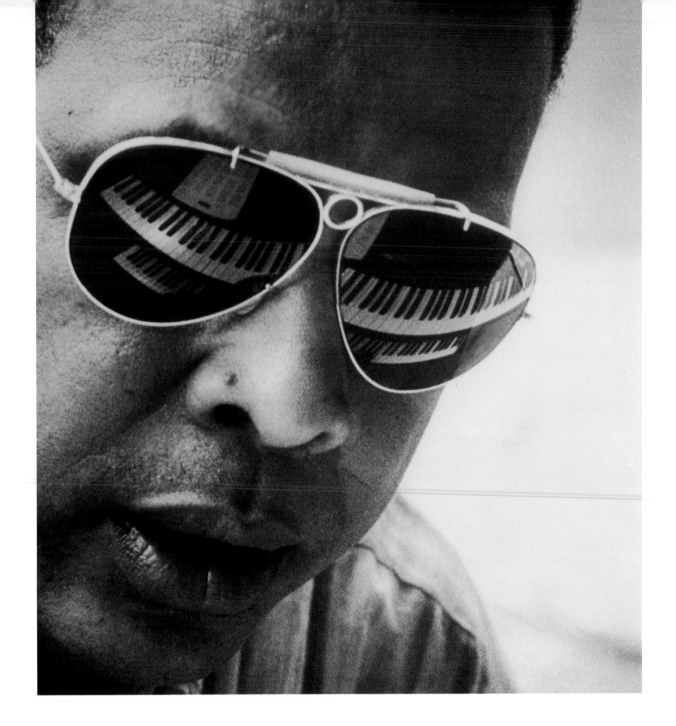

above: **ORLANDO MARTINEZ MAQUEIRA,** *Chucho close-up,* 1991

Chucho Valdés is one of the all-time greats of Cuban music and has brought Latin jazz to new heights. He came to fame as the leader of the group Irakere.

top right: **LUIS TOCA,** *Leo Brouwer,* 1985

Leo Brouwer is a composer and conductor who works in a variety of musical genres. Here he conducts the Latin jazz group Irakere.

bottom right: **LUIS TOCA,** *Enrique Pla,* 1993

Enrique Pla is one of Cuba's leading percussionists. Here he is performing during the Havana Jazz Festival.

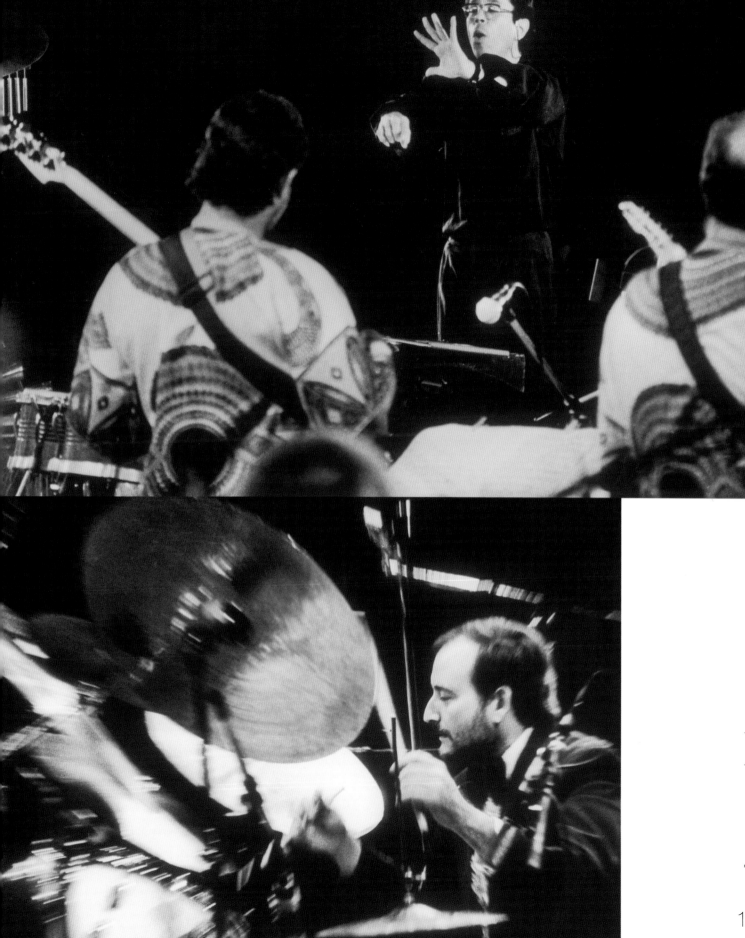

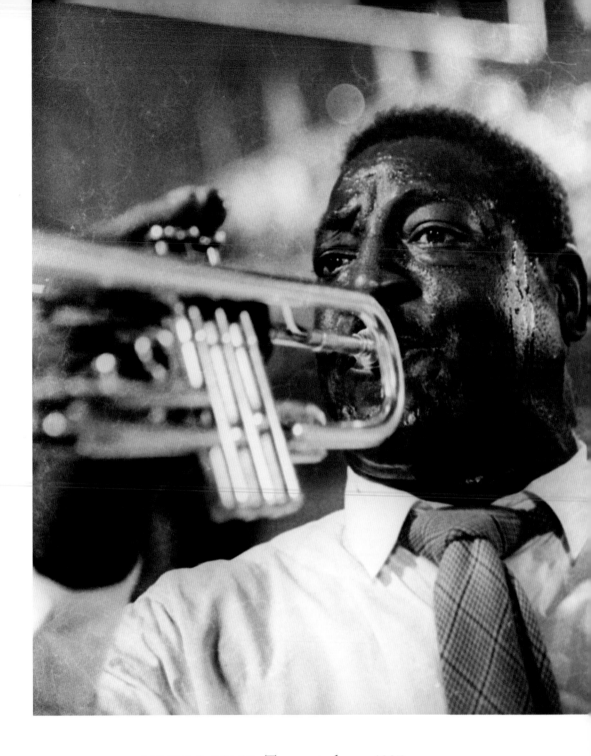

above: OSVALDO SALAS, *Trumpet player,* 1987

The trumpet, which dominates the rhythms of much traditional Cuban music, is the perfect instrument for the improvisations of Latin jazz.

right: BOHEMIA ARCHIVE, *Chano Pozo,* 1951

Chano Pozo, the percussion maestro of all time, was the King of the Rumba, drawing his strength from the most varied roots of Cuban percussion. He left Cuba for the United States in the 1950s and worked successfully with leading American musicians of the day.

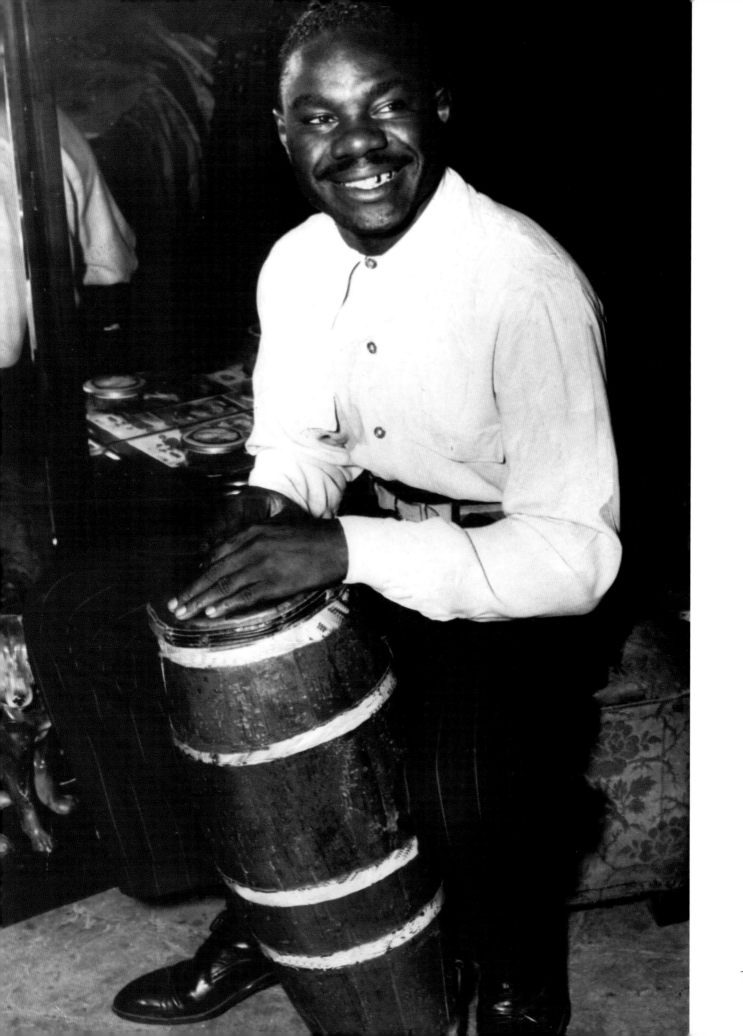

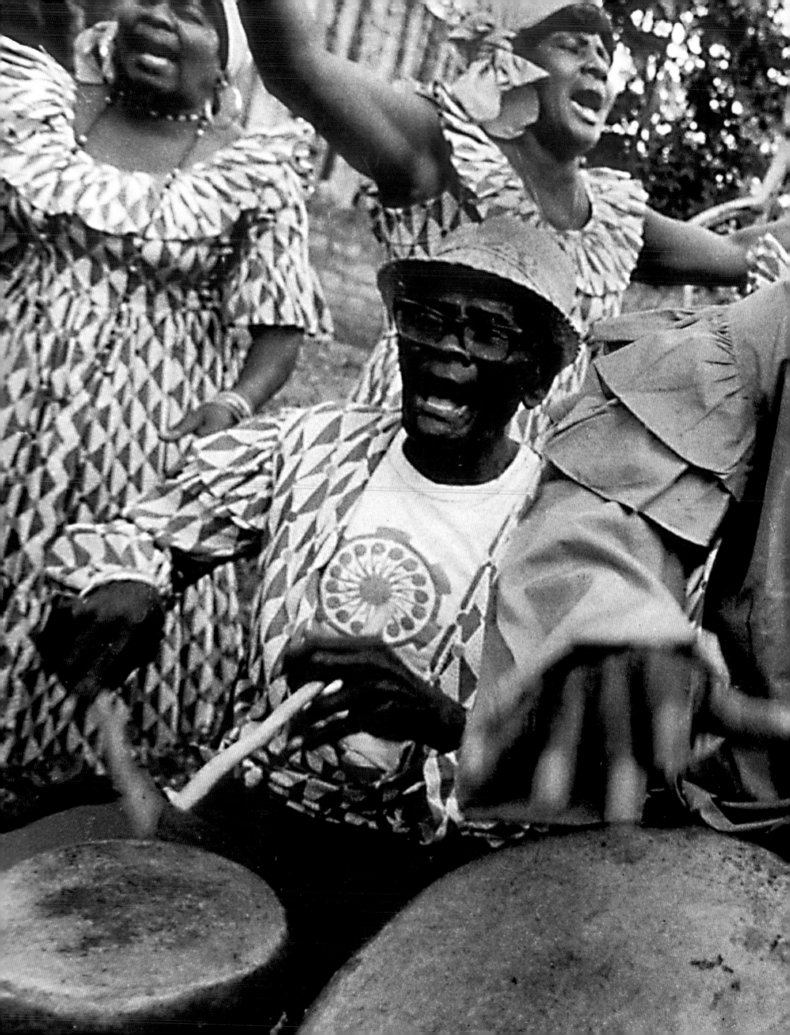

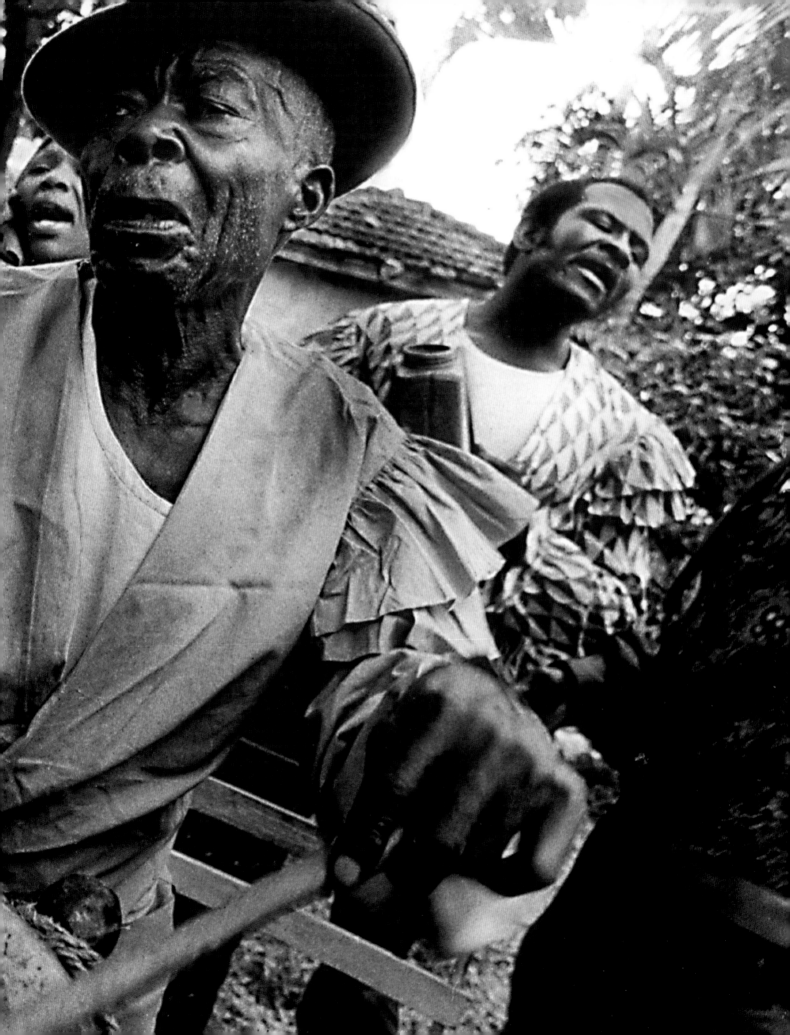

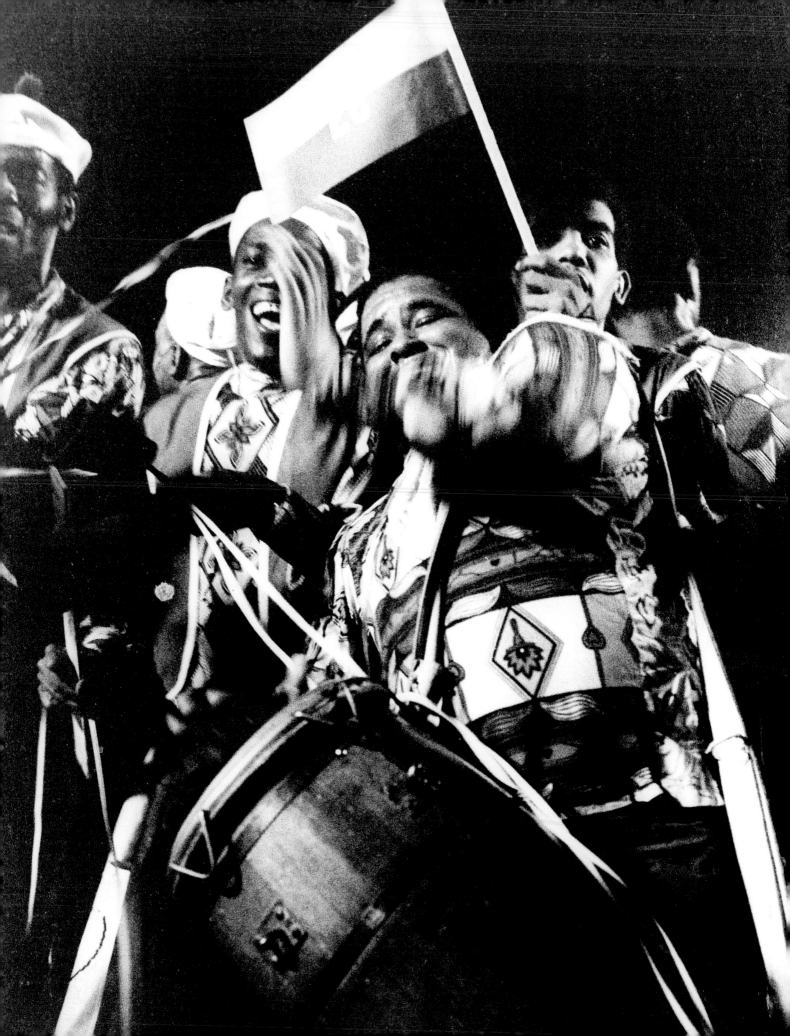

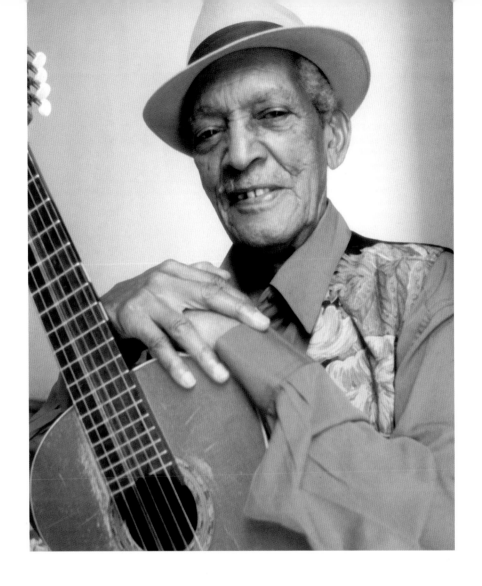

previous page: **RAMON GRANDAL,** *The Rumba,* 1974

The rumba has its roots deep in the traditions of western Africa and southern
Spain. For many years, it existed on the margins of society and was only
danced in poorer districts. Rumba drummers would extract the most
incredible sounds and rhythms by beating wooden boxes. After 1959 the
rumba entered the mainstream of popular dances.

left: **OSVALDO SALAS,** *Drummer,* 1975

The Cuban drum, apparently so simple, requires dexterity, rhythm, and magic
to produce its impressive range of sounds. Made of special woods and
tanned goatskin, it has made Cuban rhythms famous throughout the world.

above: **LUIS TOCA,** *Compay Segundo,* 1998

Compay Segundo became an international superstar in his 90s when the
Buena Vista Social Club was rediscovered.

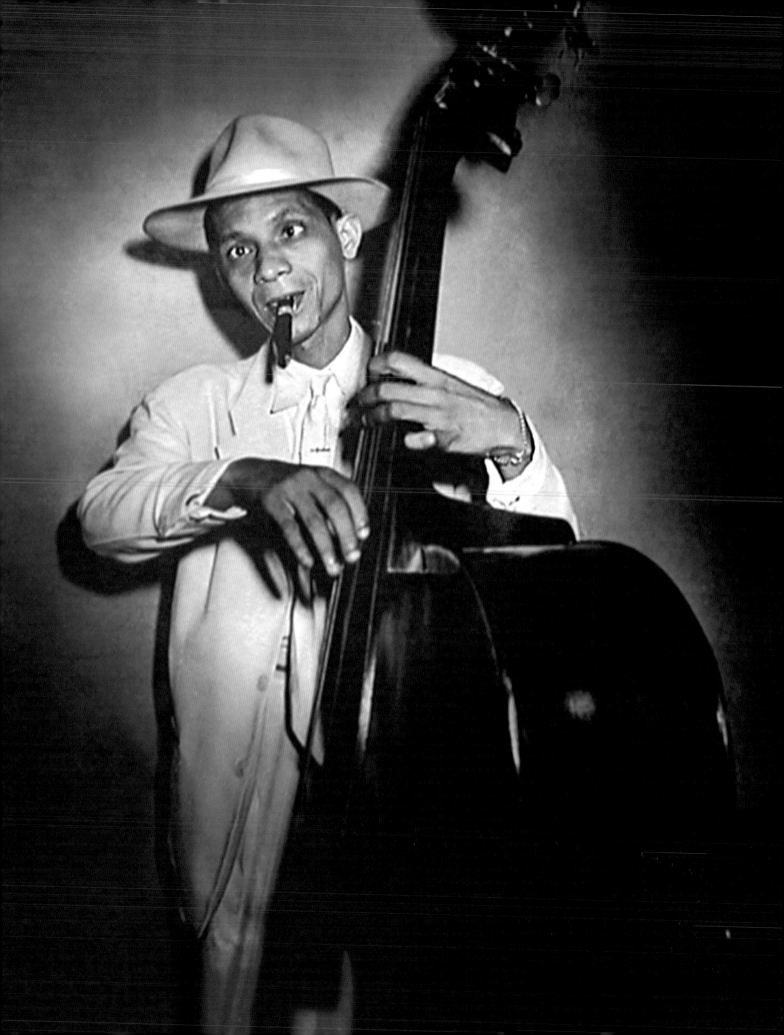

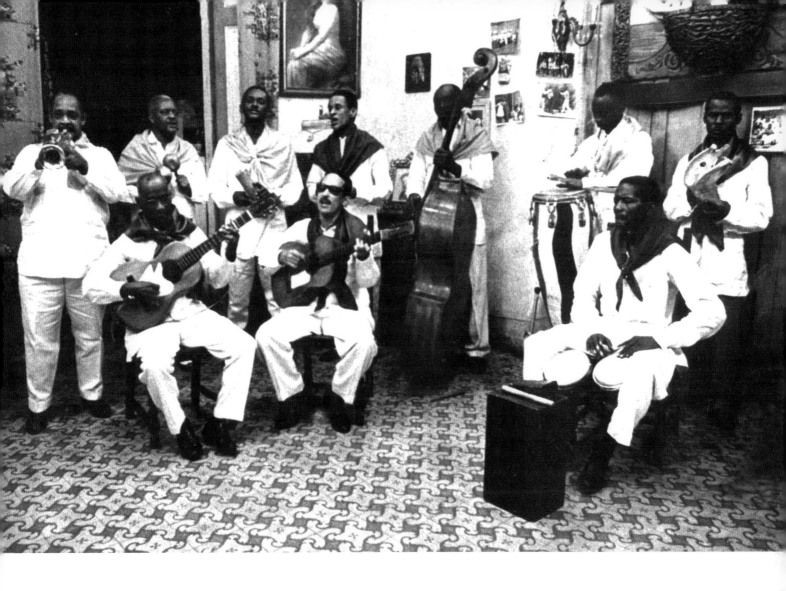

left: CONSTANTINO ARIAS, *The cross-eyed man,* 1950

This photograph is an homage by Constantino Arias to all those musicians who play in the shadows of an orchestra, who play their heart out night after night to earn their daily bread. The double bass player particularly, who has to find a way of moving his heavy instrument from place to place, and whose strong bass music is always the backing for more extrovert instruments, never takes center stage.

above: MARIA EUGENIA HAYA (MARUCHA), *Musicians,* 1983

Cuban musicians go on and on, as the cult Buena Vista Social Club has reminded a new international audience. The eldest of the group's musicians was over 90 years old at the time they were rediscovered. Since the Buena Vista Social Club came to fame in 1998, young Cuban musicians have been seeking out venerable "viejitos" (little old men) to give their groups credibility.

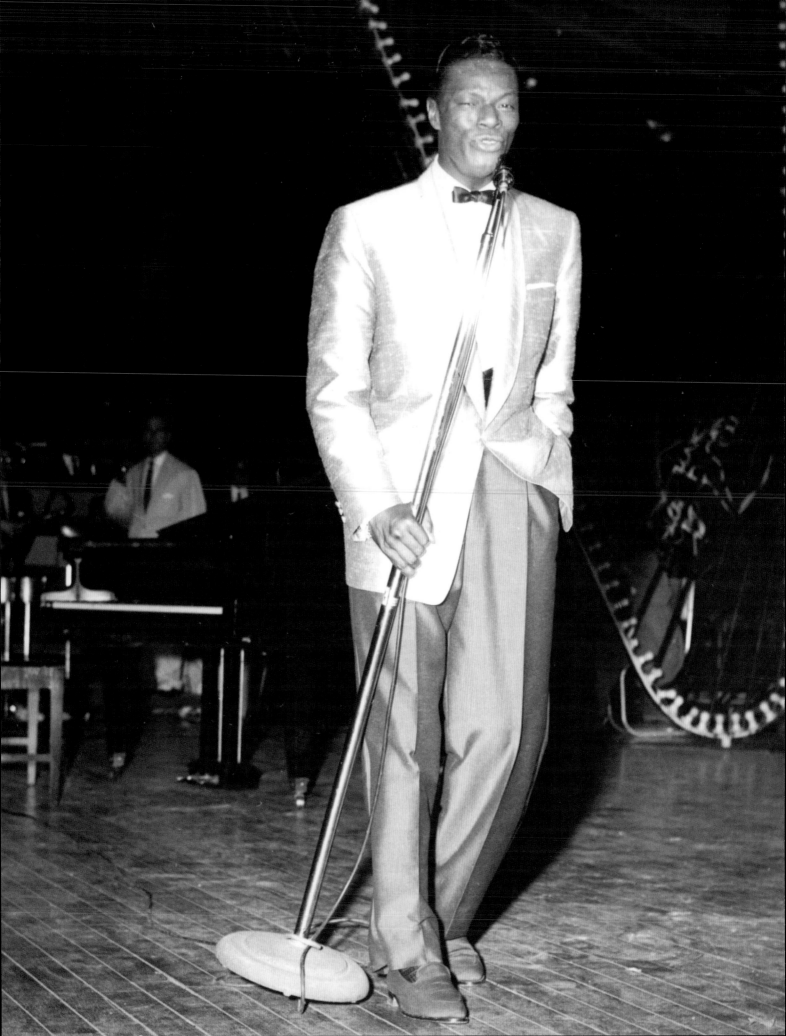

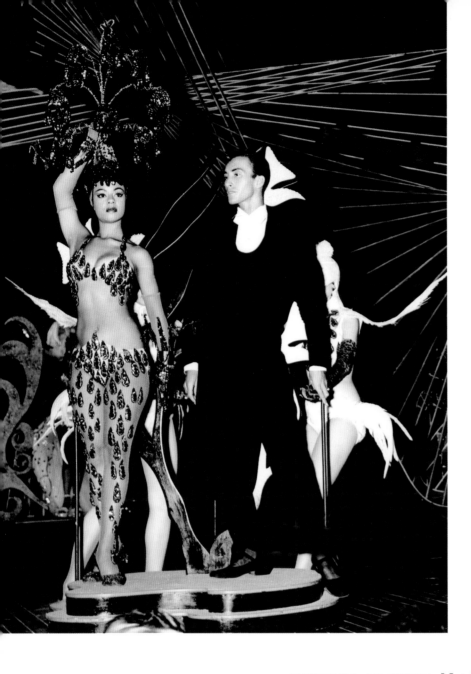

left: BOHEMIA ARCHIVE, *Nat King Cole at the Tropicana nightclub,* **1957**

In the 1950s many big-name American stars such as Nat King Cole performed at the Tropicana. But while blacks could be celebrities, Cuba ran a color bar that, for example, prevented blacks from staying at the Hotel Nacional. Even President Batista, an ally of U.S. business, was barred from the exclusive white country clubs because he was of mixed race.

above: NATIONAL LIBRARY ARCHIVE, *Tropicana,* **1955**

Promoted as "Paradise under the Stars," the Tropicana cabaret and its casinos were frequented by mafia bosses in the 1950s. Its combination of glamour and kitsch may have fallen out of fashion, but the Tropicana remains a place of pilgrimage for those nostalgic for that other age.

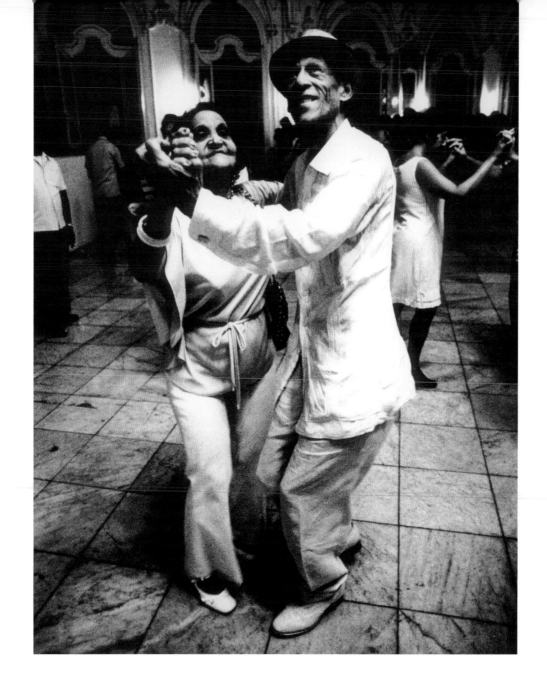

above: **MARIA EUGENIA HAYA (MARUCHA),** *Esperanza and Chevaro,* **1980**

A couple dance to the music of the danzón in the dance hall El Liceo.

right: **BOHEMIA ARCHIVE,** *Rita Montaner and Bola de Nieve,* **1951**

Ignacio Villa, affectionately known as Bola de Nieve (Snowball), was the leading "piano man"—a Cuban term signifying much more than just a pianist—from the 1950s up to the 1970s. He had the gift of being able to improvise and rework old songs in a very original manner. Rita Montaner, who often sang with him, was known as La Unica for her marvellous voice and her special way of singing *El Manicero* (The Peanut Seller).

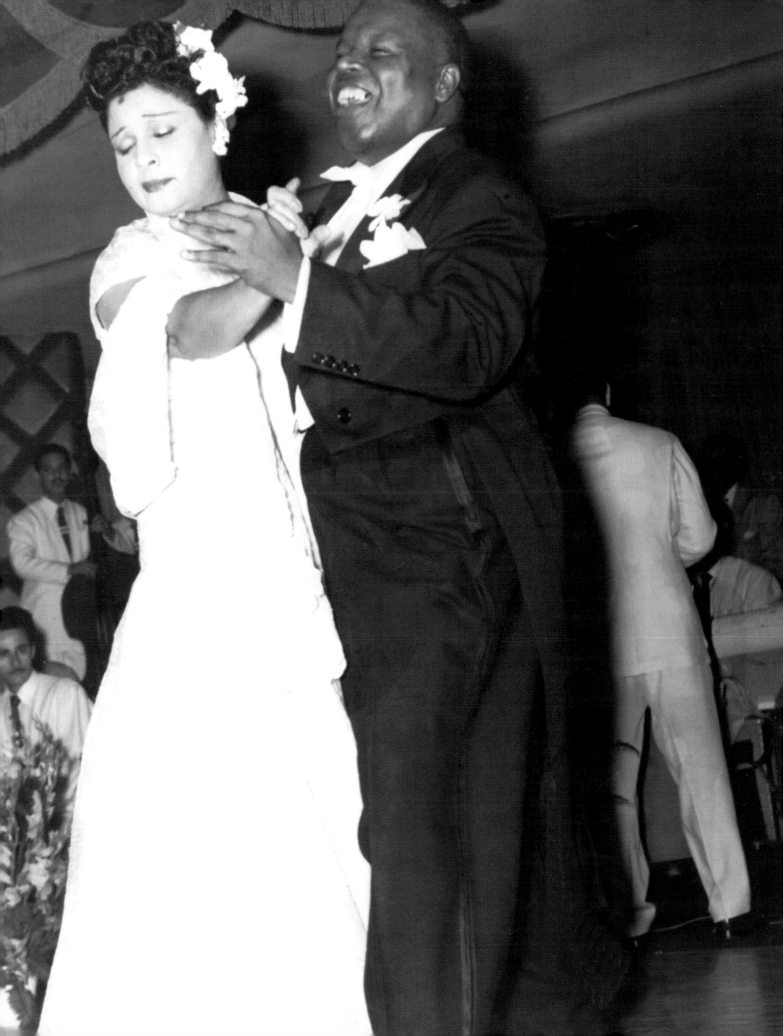

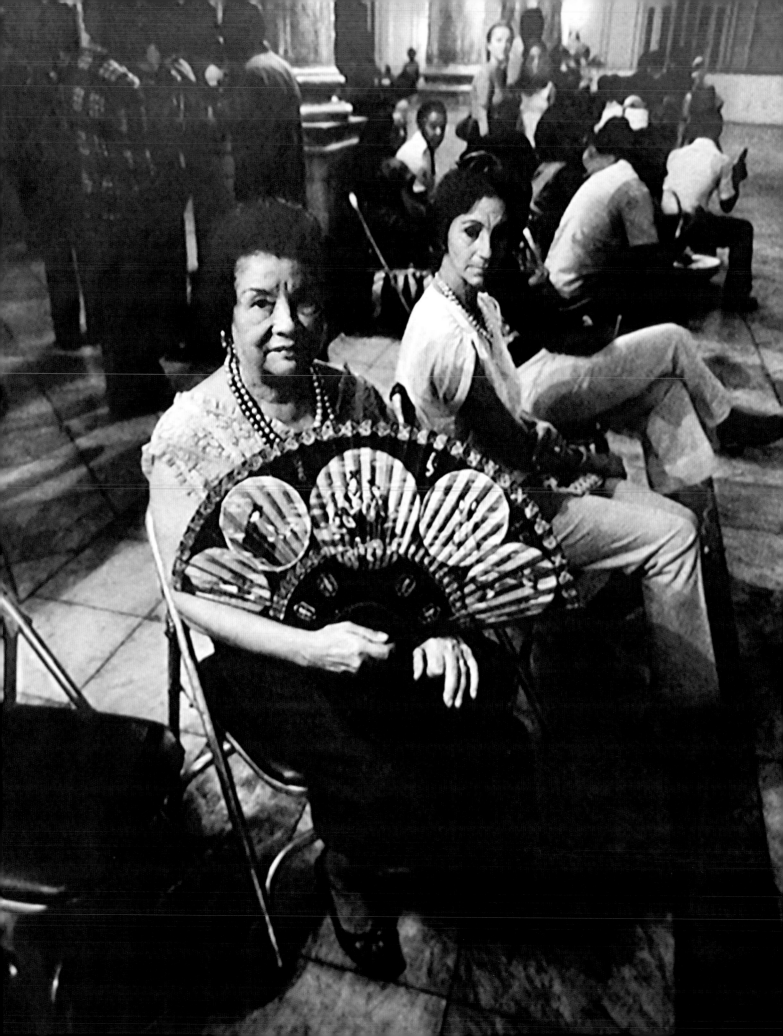

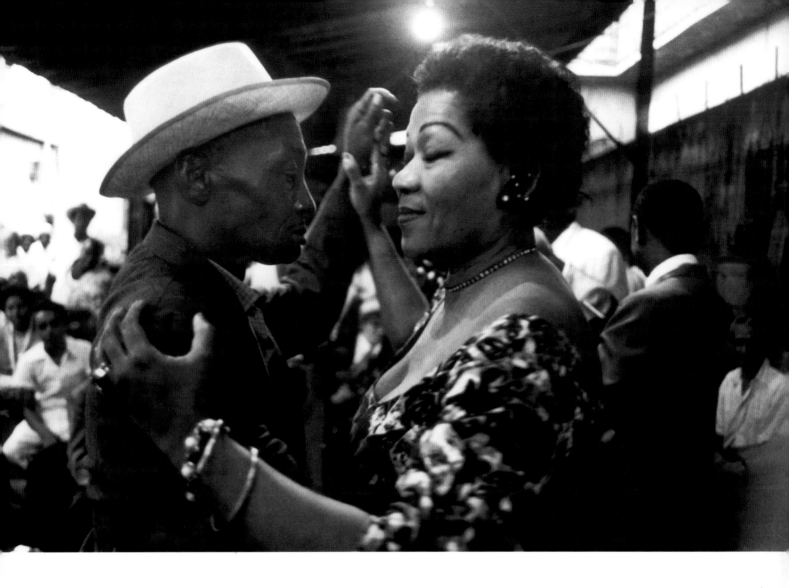

left: MARIA EUGENIA HAYA (MARUCHA), *The Judge,* 1983

The danzón has claims to be Cuba's national dance. It emerged more than two centuries ago from an earlier dance known as the Contradanza. This in turn has its origins in German, English, and French country dances, especially the minuet.

The danzón today continues to evolve. It played a role in the repertoires of the Cuban big bands of the 1950s, and now inspires rock and heavy metal musicians. It is played with strings and flute, percussion, double or electric bass, piano, and vocalists.

The judge at this danzón contest holds a Havana fan—an *abanico*. Fans were traditionally used by Cuban women to send coded social signals.

above: MARIA EUGENIA HAYA (MARUCHA), *La Peña de Sirique,* 1980

Dancing to the country music of La Peña de Sirique.

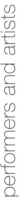

performers and artists

177

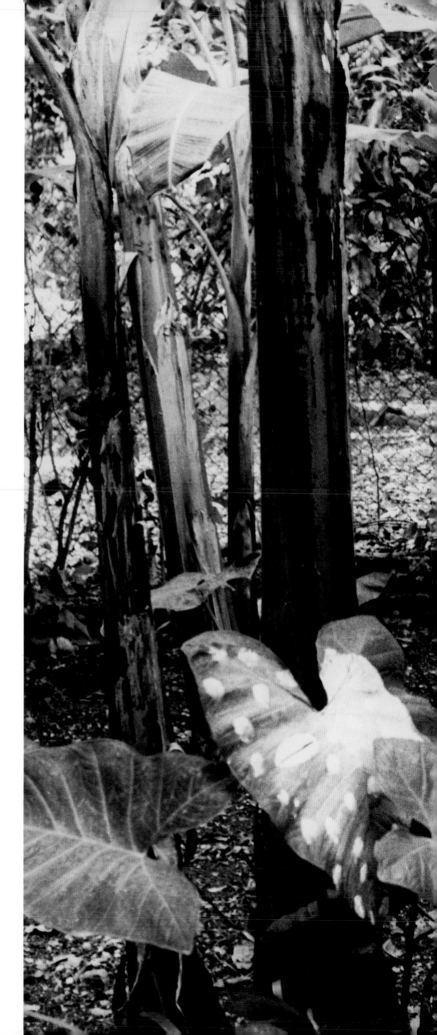

right: OSVALDO SALAS, *Manuel Mendive, 1986*

Manuel Mendive is a key figure in Cuban painting, between the generation of Amelia Peláez and Wifredo Lam and the group that emerged in the 1970s. He integrates themes from African art into his paintings, and presents performances in which he paints naked dancers. Here the leaves of his garden have been asked to perform for him.

Mendive now lives and works surrounded by animals, birds, and flowers on a lush estate he and his friends have hacked out of woodland at Tapaste, south of Havana.

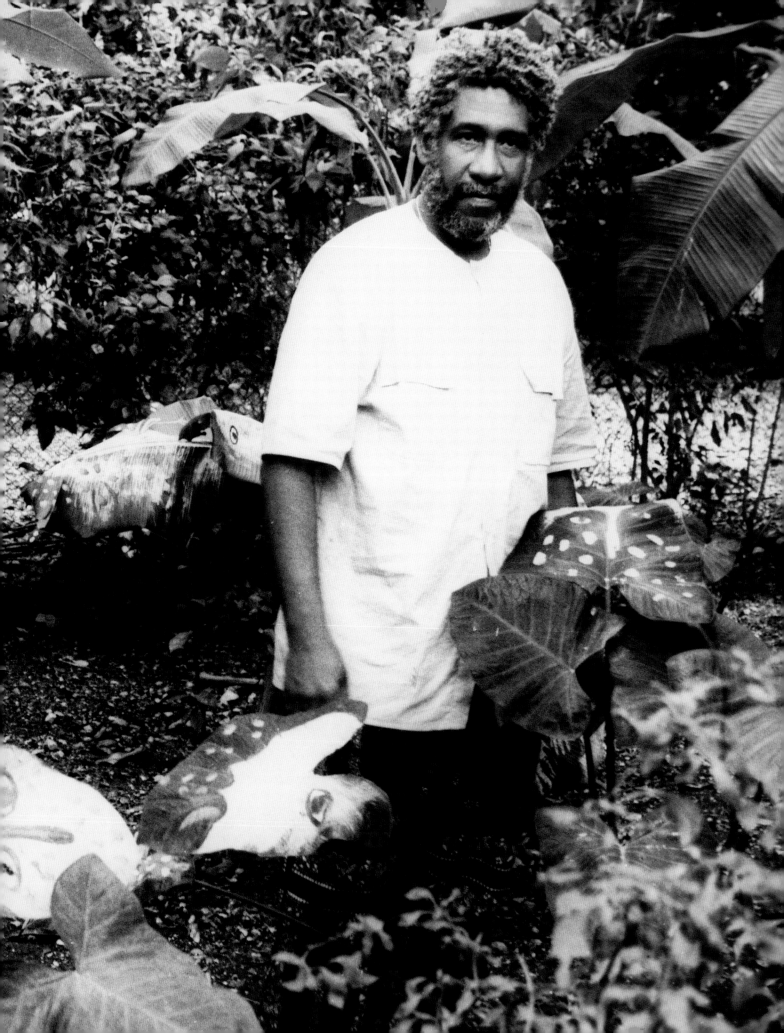

Wifredo Lam, a painter of Chinese, African, and Spanish ancestry, was the outstanding figure of Cuban painting in the middle of the 20th century. As a young man he lived for some time in Paris, where he mixed with the group of artists around the French surrealist André Breton. When Breton visited Lam in Cuba he reportedly remarked, "This country is truly too surreal to live in." Of Lam, Breton commented that "he has discovered the secret of unifying physical perception with mental representation."

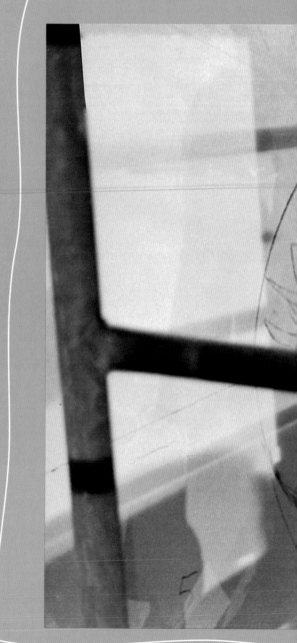

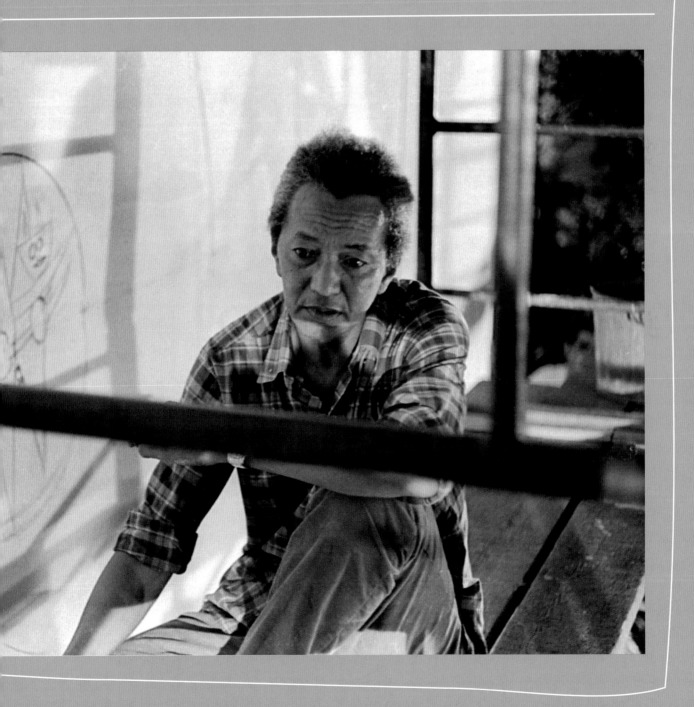

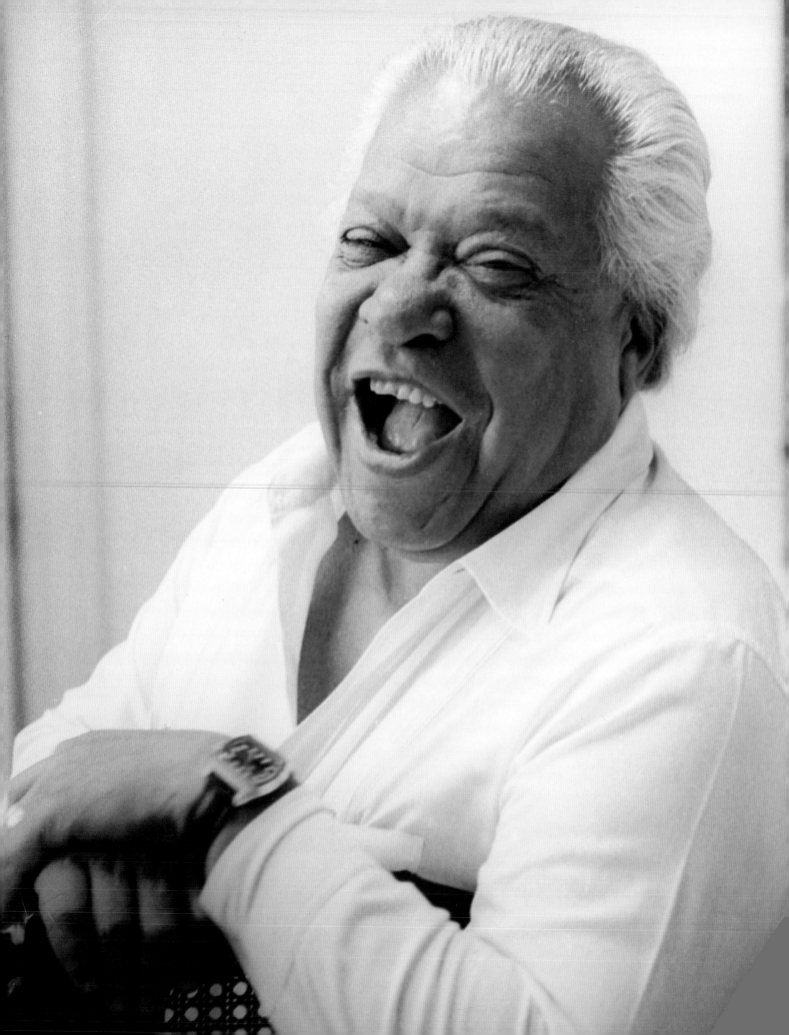

I love the bars and taverns
beside the sea,
where people chat and drink
for the sake of drinking and chatting.
where John Nobody enters and asks
for his simple drink,
and where sit John Rough and John Jack-knife
and John Nostrils and even John
Simple, the only, the simply
John.

There the white wave
beats with friendship;
a friendship of ordinary people, without affectation,
a wave of Hi! and How're you doing?
There it smells of fish,
of mangrove, of rum, of salt
and of sweaty shirts hung out to dry in the sun.

Look for me, brother, and you will find me
(in Havana, in Oporto, in Jacmel, in Shanghai)
with the simple people
who just for a drink and a chat
hang out in the bars and taverns
beside the sea.

NICOLAS GUILLEN, "BARS"

left: **OSVALDO SALAS,** *Nicolás Guillén,* **1979**

Nicolás Guillén, Cuba's poet laureate, died in 1990 at age 87.

Island of mine, how beautiful you are and how sweet!…
Your sky is a living sky, yet with an angelic warmth, whose
other side is of the stars…

You are refreshing as the fruit of your trees, as the word of
your Apostle.
You smell of rose–apple and of jasmine; you smell of clean
earth, of sea, of sky.

DULCE MARÍA LOYNAZ, from *POEMS WITHOUT NAME*

top right: LIBORIO NOVAL, *Gabriel García Márquez and Haydée Santamaría*, **1976**

The Colombian Nobel Prize-winning novelist Gabriel García Márquez has for many years been a visitor to Havana, where he has a house. The author of *One Hundred Years of Solitude*, *Love in the Time of Cholera*, and many other novels, he developed the style of Latin American magical realism. He is a close confidant of Fidel Castro.

Here he is in conversation with Haydée Santamaría in the cultural center Casa de Las Américas, of which she was president. She was an early member of the revolutionary movement. She participated with Fidel Castro in the 1953 attack on the Moncada barracks in Santiago de Cuba.

bottom right: PRENSA LATINA ARCHIVE, *Dulce María Loynaz and Alicia Alonso*, **1993**

Dulce María Loynaz is greeted by Cuba's prima ballerina Alicia Alonso on her return from Madrid in 1993, where she had received the Cervantes Prize for Literature in recognition for her poetry. She was born in 1902 as the first child of Enrique Loynaz del Castillo, a general in the Liberation Army which fought against the Spanish in the War of Independence of 1895–98. She died in 1997. When the Spanish poet and playwright Federico García Lorca visited Cuba in 1930 he was a frequent visitor at the Loynaz house.

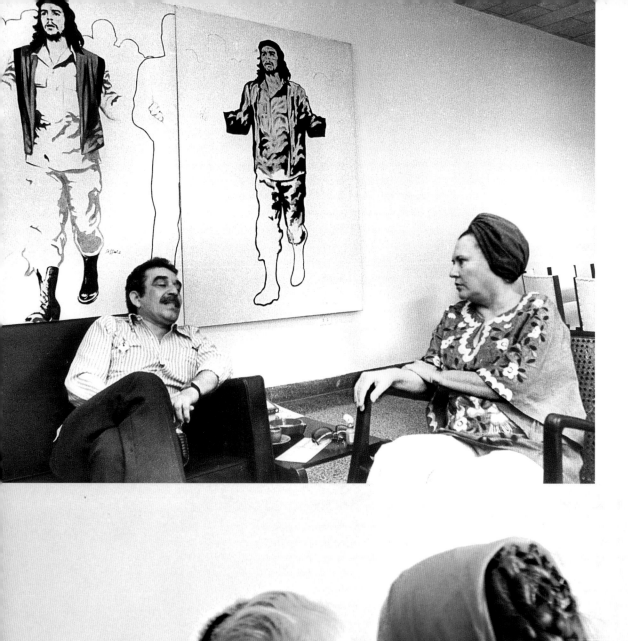

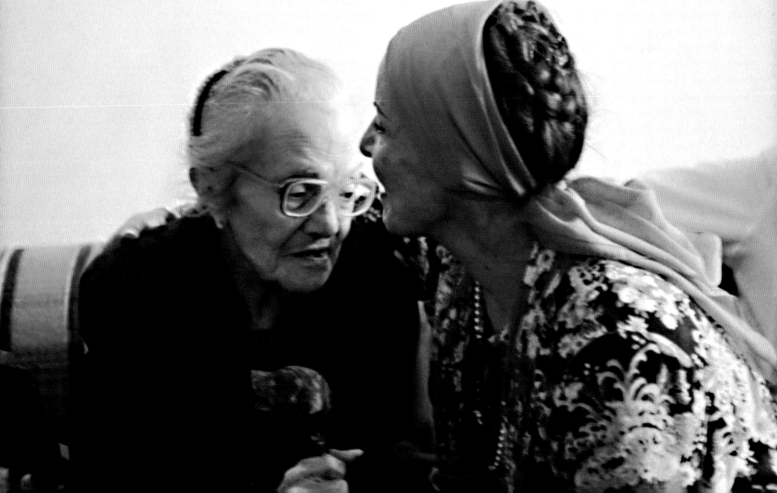

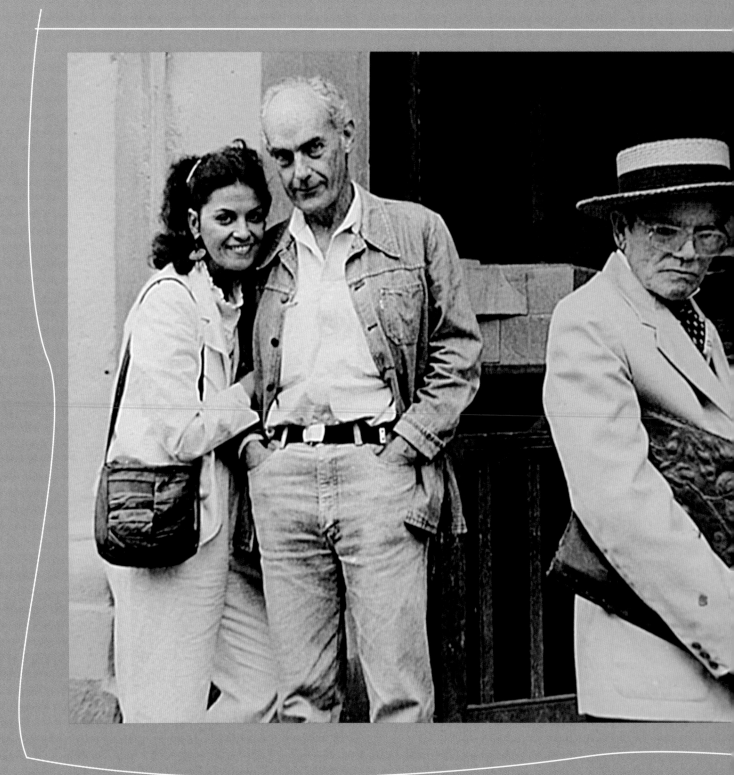

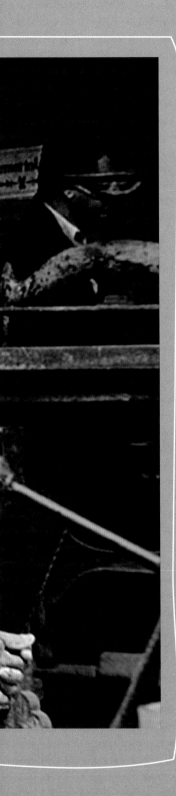

above: RAMON PACHECO, *Tomás Gutiérrez Alea (Titón) with Mirtha Ibarra on the set of Cartas del Parque,* **1988**

Tomás Guttiérez Alea (Titón) was Cuba's most gifted and successful film-maker. He learned his craft in Italy in the 1950s, and the subtlety of mood in his film remind one of postwar Italian cinema. He was a leading influence on the new Latin American cinema.

Titón's career spanned three decades. His *Memories of Underdevelopment* (1968) dealt with the angst of a young middle-class Cuban man living in Havana in the early years of the Revolution. His second-to-last film, *Strawberry and Chocolate* (1993), broke new ground with its delicate portrayal of the friendship between a gay aesthete and a young hardline party member who meet in the Coppelia Ice Cream Park opposite the Habana Libre Hotel. These and other films Titón made present a loving, ironic, but often critical picture of life in Havana. Titón, who died in 1996, was married to the actress Mirtha Ibarra, who played the female lead in *Strawberry and Chocolate*. This photograph was taken on the set of *Letters from the Park,* based on a script inspired by the story by Gabriel García Márquez.

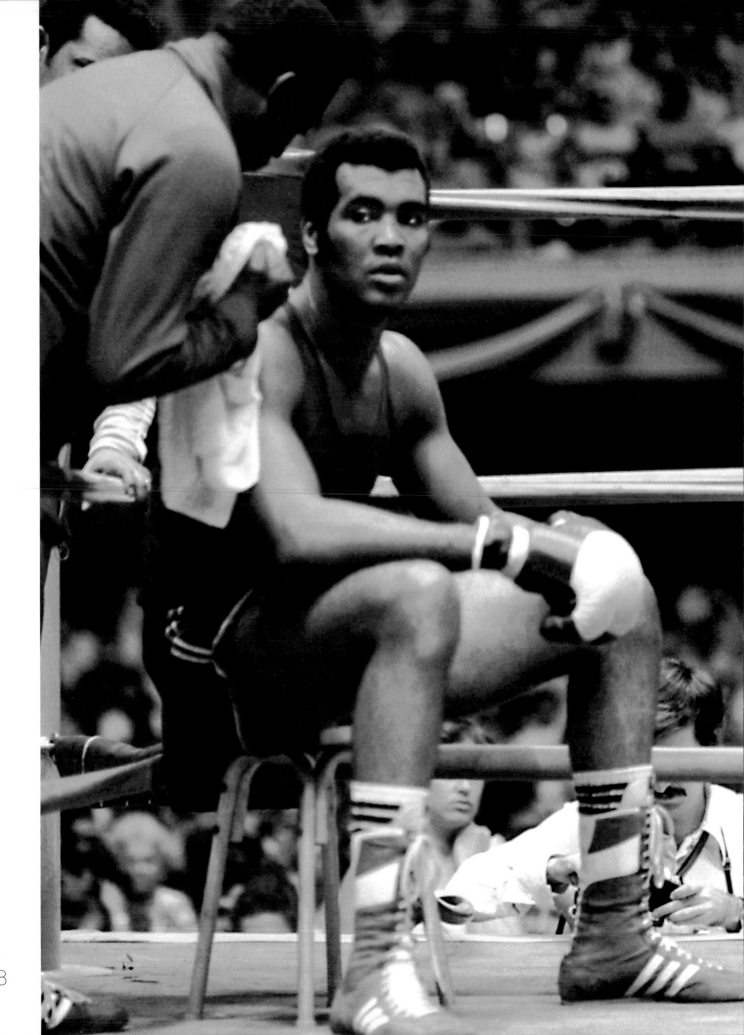

performers and artists

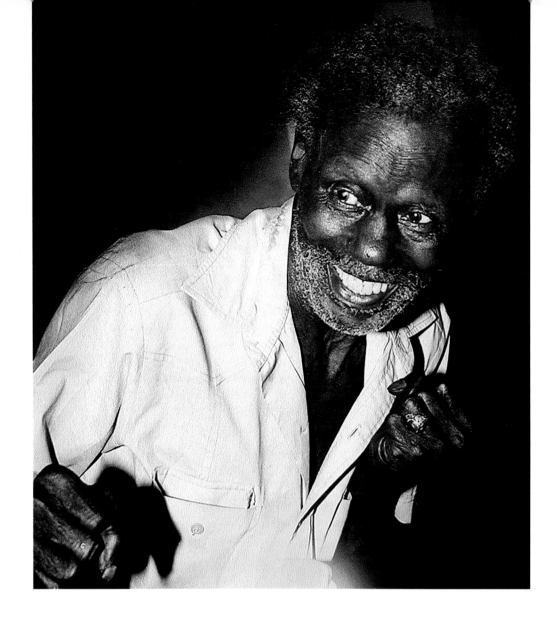

left: **MIGUEL VINAS,** *Teófilo Stevenson,* **1979**

Teófilo Stevenson is the man who could have beaten the great Muhammad
Ali, as Ali acknowledged on one of his visits to Cuba. In 1972, at the age
of 20, he won the heavyweight title in the Munich Olympics, repeating his
success in 1976 and 1980.

  Stevenson came from a poor immigrant family in eastern Cuba. He was
an early beneficiary of the special training given to talented young athletes
by the Castro government, and was sent to Havana to train when he was 13.
He went on to become the Revolution's first great sports hero, turning down
many offers by American fight promoters to leave Cuba.

above: **PERFECTO ROMERO,** *Kid Chocolate as an old man,* **1989**

Kid Chocolate, the featherweight champion Eligio Sardinas, was Cuba's first
great boxer, dominating the sport in the 1930s.

José González Alvarez (Tito Alvarez) b. Havana, 1916. His initial training was with the Club Fotográfico de Cuba. He has had many individual exhibitions in Cuba, Latin America, and Europe.

Constantino Arias Miranda Havana, 1920–91. Worked as a photojournalist for the Agencia Gráfica 1939–40 and for the magazine *Bohemia* 1941–81. During this time he was also official photographer for the Hotel Nacional in Havana (1941–67) and worked for the magazines *Alma Mater* and *La Calle* and for a U.S. advertising agency. During the years before 1959 much of his work documented disparities in living conditions. From 1960 he worked for various magazines, including *Bohemia*. He had individual exhibitions in Cuba.

Francisco Bou b. Havana, 1940. Has specialized in photography for publicity and the arts, including work for foreign companies and magazines such as *Marie Claire* and *Dunia*. Since 1986 he has worked as a photojournalist for the magazine *Cine Cubano* of the Cuban Film Institute (ICAIC). He was director of the Fototeca del Gran Teatro de La Habana (1989–91). He has had individual exhibitions in Cuba and Spain.

Iván Darío Cañas Boix b. Havana, 1946. Trained in photography and design and studied journalism at the University of Havana (1979–83). Worked as a photographer for the magazine *Cuba* (1968–80), as head of publicity and public relations for the Complejo Cultural Mella in Havana (1980–1991) and as a photographer for Editorial América, Miami (1993–96). He has had individual exhibitions in Cuba, Latin America, Europe, Japan, Canada and the United States.

Raúl Corral Fornos (Corrales) b. Ciego de Avila, 1925. From 1944 to 1959 worked in Havana as a photographer for *Cuba-Sono-Films, Noticias de Hoy, Prensa Obrera de Cuba, América Deportiva, Ultima Hora, Bohemia,* and *Carteles,* and as director of photography for *Publicitaria Siboney*. In 1959 he was appointed director of the Department of Photography of the National Institute of Agrarian Reform (INRA) and accompanying photographer of Fidel Castro. From 1959 to 1962 he worked as a photographer for *Revolución* and photographic editor of *Cuba*. From 1962 to 1991 he was head of the Department of Photography of the Cuban Academy of Sciences, and head of the microfilms and photography department of the historical issues office of the Council of State. He has had individual exhibitions in Cuba.

Mario Díaz b. Holguín province, 1950. Worked in the Ministry of Culture 1979–85. Has held teaching posts in Mexico and Brazil, and has had individual exhibitions in Cuba, Brazil, and Mexico. From 1994 to 2000 he was Director of the Fototeca Nacional de Cuba.

Luis Fernández (Pirole) Havana, 1947–93. Trained in journalism, and worked as a photographer for the magazines *Revolución y Cultura* and *Cuba Internacional*.

Alberto Díaz Gutiérrez (Korda) Havana, 1928–2001. Trained in journalism and commerce, and established his own photographic studio "Estudios Korda" in 1956. He adopted the pseudonym Korda from the Hungarian film-makers Alexander and Zoltan Korda, anticipating that it would remind customers of "Kodak." He specialized in fashion photography until 1959, after which he began actively collaborating with the magazine *Revolución*. In that same year he accompanied Fidel Castro to Venezuela and the United States, and continued to accompany him on his journeys around Cuba and his trips abroad until 1968. He developed an epic style to capture images of the revolution as it unfolded, in 1961 taking the famous photograph of Che Guevara that was sold as a poster all over the world, and which is arguably the most reproduced photograph in history. He exhibited widely in Cuba, Latin America, Europe, and the United States.

José Alberto Figueroa Daniel b. Havana, 1946. Began his career as an assistant to Alberto Korda 1964–68. He worked as a photojournalist for the magazine *Cuba Internacional* 1969–76, and then as a cameraman in the cinematography department of the Ministry of Education while he studied journalism at the University of Havana. He served as a war correspondent in Angola in 1982. His work has been exhibited in group and solo exhibitions throughout Europe, the Americas, Australia, and Japan.

Miguel Fleitas Suares b. Havana, 1956. Trained as a film cameraman before specializing in still photography. His series of photographs on the Almendares river and the lives of the fishermen who sail from its estuary has won several prizes.

Abigail García Fayat b. Havana, 1964. Started work in 1984 in the film studios of the Cuban armed forces, moving to the Cuban Film Institute (ICAIC) as a photographer in 1985. She has had individual exhibitions in Cuba.

Leovigildo González b. Havana, 1943. Began work as a self-taught photographer at the age of 16. Between 1961 and 1971 he worked for the Cartographic Institute, and 1971–75 on the editorial staff of the Cuban Book Institute. He studied color photography in Germany in 1975, and worked as a photojournalist in the Angolan war in 1977. His photographs have appeared in many Cuban publications and on music covers.

Ramón Grandal b. Havana, 1950. Studied in the Free School of the Plastic Arts 1963–65, and at the Museum of Fine Arts in 1970. He worked as a photographer for the magazine Revolución y Cultura 1972–86, before specializing in fashion and publicity photography. He has had individual exhibitions in Cuba and Switzerland.

Orlando Martínez Maqueira b. Havana, 1942. Began working as a photojournalist and designer in 1965. He currently works for the magazine *Bohemia*. He has worked frequently outside Cuba, and has had 10 individual exhibitions.

Maria Eugenia Haya Jiménez (Marucha) Havana, 1944–91. Studied animation and the history of photography at the Cuban Film Institute (ICAIC) 1961–63. She obtained a degree in Philology from the University of Havana in 1978. She worked as researcher and joint scriptwriter for three Cuban films, and as curator of photographic and painting exhibitions. From 1986 to 1991 she was Director of the Fototeca de Cuba, and in 1988 she edited *Cuba: Photography from the 1960s*. She has had individual exhibitions in Cuba.

Liborio Noval b. Havana 1934. Began work as a market researcher in 1953, then worked as a publicity photographer 1957–60. He joined the staff of *Revolución* in January 1959. He founded the national newspaper *Granma* in 1965, where he still works. He has had individual exhibitions in Cuba, Europe, and Latin America. He has had three books of his photographs published, and his photographs have appeared in nine other books.

Ramón Pacheco Salazar b. Las Villas, 1954. Worked as a photojournalist for the armed forces 1975–80 and subsequently for the magazine *Girón* in Matanzas. He has had personal exhibitions in Cuba and Europe.

Celso Rodríguez Rodríguez b. Havana, 1951. Began work as a photojournalist for the agency Prensa Latina in 1967. He has worked for many Cuban and foreign publications, including those of the United Nations, and his photographs have appeared in various books including *Hemingway in Cuba* and *Chano Pozo*. He worked as a war photographer in Angola and Ethiopia.

Perfecto Romero b. Cabaiguán, Sancti Spíritus, 1936. Began work as a photographer in 1955, the same year he joined the 26th of July Movement. He went with other young people into the Escambray mountains to meet Che Guevara, hoping to join his guerrilla group. Although he had no weapon, he had a camera, and Guevara accepted him as his official war photographer. After the 1959 revolution he worked for the armed forces' magazine *Verde Olivo*, continuing to work closely with Che Guevara when he was Industry Minister. He also became an expert submarine photographer. He has had individual exhibitions in Cuba, Europe, and Latin America. His photographs have appeared in nine other books.

Rigoberto Romero Havana, 1947–95. Worked from 1970 as a photographer for the Cuban Book Institute, and subsequently for various cultural publications.

Sergio Romero b. Cienfuegos, 1955. Has worked for many Cuban publications, including *Cine Cubano*, *Prisma*, and *Revolución y Cultura*, and covered many cultural events. Since 1992 he has specialized in design and publicity work for *Modas*, *Turismo*, and for various companies, including music companies. He has had many individual exhibitions in Cuba.

Osvaldo Salas Merino Havana, 1914–91. Worked as a photographer in New York 1947–58 for various Spanish-language publications. He returned to Cuba in 1959 and worked for the magazine *Revolución*, running its photographic department 1962–65. He then moved to the new national newspaper *Granma*. He published 10 books of photography. He has had individual exhibitions in Cuba, Europe, the Soviet Union, Vietnam, and Latin America.

Roberto Salas Merino b. Bronx, N.Y., 1940. Began work in the New York studio of his father Osvaldo in 1956. They moved back to Cuba in 1959 to work for Revolución. Between 1960 and 1967 he worked for various magazines, including the magazine of the National Institute of Agrarian Reform, *Cuba*, and *Granma*. He was a war photographer in Vietnam in 1966–67 and again in 1972–73. He has had individual exhibitions in Cuba, Africa, Vietnam, Europe, Latin America, Cambodia, Mongolia, the United States, and Jamaica.

Alfredo Sarabia Domínguez Havana, 1951–92. Worked as a photographer for the Steel Machinery Industry Ministry 1975–84. Has had individual exhibitions in Cuba and Mexico.

Isabel Sierra b. Havana, 1958. Graduated in French language and literature. President of the photographic section of the Casa de Cultura of Old Havana. She has had three individual exhibitions, including her photo-essay on Havana's Chinatown.

Luis Toca Camejo b. Havana, 1941. Worked as a sports and news photographer 1963–75 and as a war correspondent in Angola, Nicaragua, the Western Sahara, and Afghanistan.

Miguel Viñas Fuentes b. Havana, 1936. Worked as a laboratory technician and architectural photographer 1952–59, when he joined the newly formed agency Prensa Latina. He has traveled widely as a photographer accompanying President Fidel Castro, and published his photographs in many Cuban magazines and newspapers.

Agencia Prensa Latina Created in 1959 by Ernesto "Che" Guevara and the Argentinian Jorge Ricardo Massetti. Prensa Latina is a news agency with the aim of spreading information about the Cuban Revolution internationally. It had a special aim of coordinating the exchange of information among the countries of Latin America and the developing world, in an effort to combat the monopolization of news by the international media corporations. It has an excellent photographic archive created from the work of its correspondents in Cuba and throughout the world.

Fototeca Nacional de Cuba The National Photographic Library was created under the auspices of the Ministry of Culture in 1986, with the aim of organizing the archives of Cuban photographers since the end of the 19th century. It also contains important collections of photographs by photographers from Latin America, the United States, and Europe who have mounted exhibitions in its gallery. Each year the Fototeca organizes exhibitions, workshops, and competitions. Its first director was Constantino Arias.

Revista *Bohemia* Founded in 1908 by Miguel Angel Quevedo, the magazine *Bohemia* began life as a cultural magazine. It developed to include national and international political, economic, cultural, and sports news, and its famous social pages. It was nationalized in 1960. It has an excellent photographic archive, which is particularly strong on the social, political, and cultural life of Cuba, especially Havana. Photographers such as Osvaldo Salas, Constantino Arías, Raúl Corrales, and Alberto Korda are all represented.

Biblioteca Nacional de Cuba The Cuban National Library was founded in 1901 under the direction of Domingo Figarola Caneda. It was originally situated in the Castillo de la Real Fuerza. In 1958 it moved to the newly completed Plaza Cívica, now the Plaza de la Revolución. Among its directors have been the historian Dr Julio Le Riverand and Dra María Teresa Freire. The sociologist Don Fernando Ortiz was for many years closely associated with the library. It has an important photographic archive.